From Script to Book

From Script to Book

A Symposium

ODENSE UNIVERSITY PRESS · 1986

The publication of this volume was made possible
by the generous support of the Carlsberg Foundation and by a
grant from Odense University on the recommendation of
Dr Aage Trommer, Mrs Else Varnild and Dr Anne Riising

Proceedings of the Seventh International Symposium
organized by the
Centre for the Study of Vernacular Literature
in the Middle Ages
Held at Odense University
on 15-16 November, 1982

Edited by
Hans Bekker-Nielsen
Marianne Børch
Bengt Algot Sørensen

© 1986 Odense University Press
Photoset in Baskerville and printed in Denmark
by OAB-Tryk a/s, Odense
Cover by Ulla Poulsen
Illustrations from p. 62 and p. 76
ISBN 87 7492 568 7

Contents

Preface.	7
The first printed book in Danish and the first library in Denmark.	
By TORBEN NIELSEN	9
From script to print.	
By JOSEPH W. SCOTT.	19
Johann Snell.	
Von URSULA ALTMANN	35
The Breviarium and the Missale Nidrosiense (1519).	
By LILLI GJERLØW	50
Studien zum Wachstum und zur Entwicklung von Bibliotheken in Südostniedersachsen am Ende des 15. und zu Beginn des 16. Jahrhunderts.	
Von HELMAR HÄRTEL	78
William Caxton: a review.	
By N.F. BLAKE	107
Typologie du livre et de la lecture dans l'Italie de la renaissance: De Petrarque à Politien.	
Par ARMANDO PETRUCCI	127
The copying of printed books for humanistic bibliophiles in the fifteenth century.	
By ALBERT DEROLEZ.	140
Discussion	161
The Missale Nidrosiense 1519: an appendix	
By LILLI GJERLØW	168
Members and associate members of the Symposium.	170

Preface

This volume contains the papers read at the Seventh International Symposium organized by the *Centre for the Study of Vernacular Literature in the Middle Ages* at Odense University on 15-16 November 1982. The Symposium was arranged as a modest contribution to the festivities which surrounded the fivehundredth anniversary of the introduction of the art of printing into Denmark and Scandinavia in 1482, and the meeting attracted members and associate members among bookmen from many countries.

It is not easy within the bounds of a slender volume of transactions, to give proper due to the many fascinating discussions of the theme of the meeting *From Script to Book* (and the very title of the symposium, see p. 167). We remember the occasion as a most successful scholarly gathering and hope that the papers and the summary of the general discussion published here will be a welcome keepsake for the members of the symposium, perhaps also of interest to the wider circle of readers who share our joy in the subject. In editing the papers we have endeavoured to see that each is internally consistent in its form and references but we have not tried to impose one system overall. For various reasons it has taken longer to produce this volume than any of the other collections of papers issued by the Medieval Centre, and we apologize for this tardiness to the authors and to the other members of the Symposium.

It is with sadness that we record the death of Joe Scott, whose contribution to this volume reminds us of, but in no way matches, his contribution to the pleasure and scholarship of those of us who were his friends.

Without munificent subvention from the Carlsberg Foundation the proceedings might never have appeared, at least not in a format worthy of the subject of the book, and we also wish to express our gratitude to The Danish Research Council for the Humanities for the support that made it possible to arrange the Symposium. Warm thanks go to Odense University, Odense University Library, The Royal Library of Copenhagen, to friends and colleagues for help and advice, and to the printer and his staff.

November 1986 *The Editors*

The first printed book in Danish and the first library in Denmark

by TORBEN NIELSEN

The jubilee year of the printing in Denmark is not the only bookish quincentenary which can be celebrated this year; also the Copenhagen University Library was founded in that memorable year of 1482. 'Founded' is perhaps a too massive term, because we have no deed of foundation; we know with a reasonable certainty that a donation of a number of books was made to the university – or to be exact: to the faculty of arts – by the vice-chancellor Peder Albertsen in the year of 1482, and that in return a mass should be read in his memory at a certain day of the year.

To call it the first library in Denmark is certainly an exaggeration; there have been libraries attached to monasteries and cathedrals according to the general European pattern if not at a very great scale; but the Copenhagen University Library is the oldest now existing and the only one whose history goes back into the middle ages.

What do we really know about the mediaeval university library? We are, with two exceptions, reduced to the use of secondary sources, and my learned colleague, Harald Ilsøe of the Royal Library, uses in his chapter about the older history of the University Library in the great jubilee publication of the University of Copenhagen the term 'tradition': the prudence of the professional historian.[1]

The difficulty arouses from the fact that the older collections are not conserved; the whole library was destroyed in the great fire of Copenhagen in 1728. But one witness exists: a manuscript of mathematical and astronomical contents which for unknown reasons had been transferred to the Royal Library before the catastrophe. It bears the inscription "Liber datus vniuersitati per

---

[1] Harald Ilsøe, "Universitetets biblioteker til 1728," etc. *Københavns Universitet 1479-1979*, IV, 289-364.

doctorem Petrum Alberti" but no date; Professor Olaf Pedersen has recently,[2] on the basis of its contents, proved that the book must be posterior to 1482 and thus given to the library at a later moment. The role of Peder Albertsen as a donor does not cause any surprise; he was in fact the leading personality during the creation and the early life of the Copenhagen University.

The other primary source is a list in the oldest Liber statutorum[3] of the university, enumerating 24 books given by Peder Albertsen in 1497; but as the first mentioned manuscript is not to be found in this list, there must have been other gifts than those of 1482 and 1497.

Our knowledge about the 1482 donation is based on a secondary source. Rasmus Vinding reports in 1665[4] that four books in the University Library bear inscriptions telling that the book in question together with some others have been donated to the university by Peder Albertsen in 1482. I leave aside the discussion quoted by Ilsøe, whether the books which were expressly given to the faculty of arts could be looked upon as forming part of a general university library; the question seems to me to be of mere academic interest, and I agree in this point with one of my predecessors, Sophus Birket Smith in his treatise about the University Library before 1728.[5]

Birket Smith finds sufficient evidence for the assumption that the 1482 donation by Peder Albertsen is in fact identical with the foundation of the library; he also rejects the hypothesis that a library should have existed before that date; we have neither evidence nor any reason for suppositions in that respect. The university was a quite young and small institution, founded only three years before, in 1479, and books were scarce.

The Albertsen donations make out our whole knowledge of the holdings of the University Library in its pre-reformation period; in the religious struggles the university – and certainly also the modest library – fell into decay; during some years before the reconstitution in 1537 there was no activity at all.

But let us stay within the limits of the middle ages and have a look at the first book printed in Danish. It is at the same time the only incunabulum printed in

---

[2] Olaf Pedersen, "Som en brand ud af ilden," *Festskrift udgivet i anledning af Universitetsbibliotekets 500 års jubilæum 28. juni 1982*, pp. 27-68. (Bibliotek for Læger, 1982, supp. 1.).

[3] MS belonging to the University of Copenhagen. Publ. in *Scriptores rerum Danicarum*, VIII (1843), 346.

[4] Erasmus Vindingius, *Regia Academia Hauniensis*, Hauniæ 1665, pp. 55-56.

[5] S. Birket Smith, *Om Kjøbenhavns Universitetsbibliothek før 1728, især dets Håndskriftsamlinger*. København 1882 (repr. 1982), p. 7.

Denmark – and in Scandinavia as a whole – in the vernacular: The Danish Rhymed Chronicle which was issued from the press of Gotfred of Ghemen in Copenhagen in 1495, and when it is connected here with the oldest existing Danish library it is because the only complete copy in Danish possession belongs to the University Library; another complete copy is in the Royal Library of Stockholm, while the copy of the Danish Royal Library is defective, lacking the oldest woodcut carried out for a Danish printed book.

The Rhymed Chronicle remained for almost a decennium the only book printed in Danish – as far as we know, of course. With the same reservation we find it rather astonishing that the Danish printing begins with an effort of that kind: the book counts 188 pages, and we may ask whether the printing was due to some official initiative, or if the printer simply had estimated that there was a market for it. We do not know of any impulse from without – if not Peder Albertsen should have had a finger in the pie – and the latter possibility is at least likely to be true, when we consider that three further editions of the chronicle were printed during a seven-year period, and that after some years two other Danish printers brought out two further issues of the Rhymed Chronicle, Hans Vingaard in Copenhagen 1533, and Joh. Hoochstraten in Malmö 1534. Certainly, there are some political hints to Sweden but they could just as well be reflections of a common opinion as of raison d'état. However, Gustaf Vasa took it for a pasquinade against Sweden and let Peder Swart write a refutation to it, in 1558.

We must keep in mind that the union between the three Nordic states was still in force – in principle; just at the moment where the Swedish regent Sten Sture was making vigourous attempts to break the union in order to achieve the full independence for Sweden – but not yet with success – Gotfred published the chronicle, and it is certainly not a mere coincidence that the woodcut which ends the book represents the coats of arms of the three kingdoms, and in greater size the arms of the city of Copenhagen. The symbolism is unmistakable.

It should not be necessary to make a long speech about the Rhymed Chronicle in itself; it must necessarily overlap the excellent survey by Thorkil Damsgaard Olsen in *Kulturhistorisk Leksikon for nordisk Middelalder.*[6] An important paper about Gotfred of Ghemen should, however, be added to his references; that of Lotte and Wytze Hellinga[7] in which the authors give some corrections to the

---

[6] *Kulturhistorisk leksikon for nordisk middelalder,* XIV (1969) coll. 299-303.

[7] Lotte & Wytze Hellinga, "Gotfred af Ghemens færden ca. 1486-1510." *Fund og forskning,* XV (1968), 7-38.

chronology of Lauritz Nielsen,[8] and also reject the theory of Helge Toldberg[9] who is inclined to date the so-called Ålborg fragment (in the Copenhagen University Library) considerably earlier – he proposes 1489 – than the 1495 edition.

It will after all be useful to trace a short survey of the printed mediaeval editions of the chronicle: We know for sure, because copies exist, that Gotfred printed it in 1495 and 1508; the latter exists in a unique copy in the Royal Library of Copenhagen.

Further, the existence of editions from 1501 and 1504 are testified by quotations from seventeenth-century authors[10] but no one can tell who printed them. Hellinga find no evidence that Gotfred has been working in Copenhagen between 1495 and 1505 and prove that he has issued books in Leiden between those years; these are unfortunately undated so that we cannot know whether he has spent the whole of this intermediate period in the Netherlands. But it is sure that no dated imprint from a Copenhagen office exists between those two years; in fact, the only issue from a Danish printing office between 1495 and 1505 is the Jutland Law printed in Ribe by Matthæus Brandis in 1504, and it is probable that he also has been active in Denmark, perhaps also in Ribe – or in Slesvig – in 1501 and 1502. Should he be the printer of the lost editions? Or should they have been printed by Gotfred in Leiden as an export article? A question which probably never can be answered for lack of material.

As for the Ålborg fragment it is a tangible fact and thus object of research. Lauritz Nielsen was of the opinion that it was a fragment of the lost 1504 edition, and this opinion was prevailing for about fifty years. Then Helge Toldberg, editor of the critical edition of the Rhymed Chronicle, proposed, as already mentioned, that it could be some years prior to the 1495 edition; not, however, a remnant of a published book but of an attempt which had not been brought to an end. Even if Toldberg pays attention to typographical details, he is in the first hand a philologist, and he is quite aware that a typological study might lead

---

[8] Lauritz Nielsen, "Om Gotfred af Ghemens Udgaver af den danske Rimkrønike," *Nordisk tidskrift för bok- och biblioteksväsen*, I (1914), 252-262.

[9] Helge Toldberg, "Hvornår tryktes der første gang på dansk?" *Fund og forskning*, IX (1962), 53-70.

[10] Helge Toldberg, "De gamle tryk og håndskrifter af Den Danske Rimkrønike," *Nordisk tidskrift för bok- och biblioteksväsen*, XLIII (1956), 85-116. He is opposed to the viewpoint of Lauritz Nielsen (Op. cit. note 8) that the assumption of a 1501 edition should be incorrect and demonstrates further evidence for its existence.

to other results. And here we are back with Lotte and Wytze Hellinga: a detailed study of the frequency of two shapes of the little *a* proves, according to them, that the fragment belongs to the later part of Gotfred's first stay in Copenhagen, that is to 1495, the same year as the editio princeps.

This, in its turn, confirms Toldberg's theory that the fragment is a remnant of a non accomplished book; it is unthinkable that the printer, preparing himself to do what nobody had done before: to print in the Danish language, should envisage to do that both in quarto and in octavo at the same time.

Just the format has played a part in the considerations of all who have discussed the question. According to Hellinga, the Copenhagen imprints of Gotfred have all been quartos until 1495, to which year they also date another undated fragment (of a horarium) in octavo. How should we then explain the fragment? I risk a guess:

Gotfred has come upon the idea to print in the small format in order to reduce the number of impressions, but it turns out then that the composing is becoming proportionately more complicated. He has no smaller types, and as it is a versified text the lines have to be respected. The column is, however, only 67 mm large, and in order to have the lines fit into the narrow format he has to resort to the expedient of abbreviation signs, single consonants instead of double, and so on, and what was worse to the readers – who were after all accustomed to abbreviations – he has to space so closely that many words are not separated at all. No typographical result to be proud of, and we may presume that he has abandoned the experiment.

The understanding of the Ålborg fragment as a not accomplished experiment is supported by the fact that it belongs to the beginning of the text (the sheet is, in fact, the half of the second quire), and that it has not formed part of a book; it has not been sewn but used as a draft paper by some student and later on for propping up a binding. As such it was discovered in a book having belonged to St. Botolph's Monastery in Ålborg in 1817 from where it came to the University Library.

I only pass lightly over other questions concerning the Rhymed Chronicle, e.g. the authorship. It is well known that the Low German manuscript translation mentions the name of Friar Niels in Sorø, while the author's name is not mentioned in the Danish original, perhaps out of monastic modesty. Is he really the author or the only author? In his fundamental treatise[11] Johs. Brøndum-Nielsen maintains, with a slight reservation, that the chronicle is a work of the

---

[11] Johs. Brøndum-Nielsen, *Om Rimkrønikens Sprogform og Tilblivelse*, København 1930.

monastic community which could explain the varying literary quality throughout the poem. The author speaks about himself – or themselves – partly as 'we', that is the community, partly as 'I', that is the individual author of the chapter in question. The part played by Friar Niels – whom Brøndum-Nielsen after all has granted a place in the Dictionary of Danish Biography – should then have been the redactor who has written the beginning and the end and given the whole a final touch.

Hans Brix[12] acknowledges the erudition of Brøndum-Nielsen but does not feel convinced of what he, slightly ironically, calls the "poetical workshop". All that is well known, but I mention the discussion because it is not unique: in several similar cases, philologists with the exactness of Brøndum-Nielsen are opposed to men of letters with Brix's fingertip feeling for poetry. Thus the Rhymed Chronicle shares the fate with much old epic, from Genesis and onward.

Let us then extend the view to all the books known to be printed in Danish during the first period of printing which according to Erik Dal ends with the year of 1522.[13] It stands for a caesura in Danish printing history which ends only in 1528 when the spiritual and political life in Denmark is strongly influenced by the Reformation conflicts; the period 1482-1522 is characterized by the itinerant printers, working only in the same place for a shorter time, the longest stay of all being the second stay of Gotfred of Ghemen in Copenhagen, from 1505 to 1510.

The number of Danish imprints from this first paleotype era – which for books in Danish is further limited to the period 1495-1518 – is 29, but is was not only the Rhymed Chronicle which was published more than once, so that the total number of titles is only 21. Of course we find Danish words and names in Latin texts, e.g. in Henrik Smith's *Hortulus synonymorum*; it would, however, be correct to add to the mentioned number two works of linguistic importance: The proverbs of Peder Laale, Latin and Danish, thus intended for language teaching (3 editions) and Christiern Pedersen's *Vocabularium ad usum Dacorum*, that is a Latin-Danish dictionary (also 3 editions); also the editions of the Jutland Law have some Latin text. Thus the number of imprints in Danish amounts to 35, the number of titles to 23.

During the period we only know of the activity of six printers in Denmark; only three of them printed in Danish: Matthæus Brandis printed the 1504 edition of the Jutland Law; Poul Ræff the three religious poems by Father Michael and

---

[12] Hans Brix. "Til den danske Rimkrønike," *Analyser og Problemer*, III (1936), 132-161.
[13] Erik Dal, "50 trykte bøger 1482-1522," *Bogvennen* 1982, pp. 67-86.

Pfefferkorn's pamphlet against the Jews; Gotfred of Ghemen cares for the rest, 19 imprints including the Ålborg fragment. As already said, we ignore the printers of the two lost editions of the Rhymed Chronicle. Ten further books in Danish are printed in foreign offices in Paris, Cologne, and Leipzig. One may wonder at this fact but it is easily explained: One of the most prolific authors and editors of the sixteenth century, both before and after the Reformation, was the canon of Lund and later reformer Christiern Pedersen; he stayed for years in Paris where he published three devotional books, an edition of Peder Laale, and the first edition of the *Vocabularium ad usum Dacorum* – not to speak of his great achievement, the editio princeps of Saxo's *Gesta Danorum* which does not, however, belong to our subject. The vocabularium and the devotional books were later reissued from German offices.

We should not analyze the Latin book production during the same period; it is no wonder that it is dominated by liturgical books, some few devotional books, and grammars. But just the grammars deserve attention in our context: The three first books printed by Gotfred of Ghemen after his first arrival in Copenhagen are Latin grammars but after that time he almost only printed books in the vernacular. The presumably oldest of the grammars, the Donatus, has no printing year but is dated by Hellinga to 1493, same year as the two other grammars; they have, on the contrary, very exact impressa: *Fundamentum in grammatica* has the date of 28th of June, and the *Regulæ fundamentales* the 9th of July. That is of course a useful knowledge; but what is more interesting is that both of them mention Peder Albertsen; the *Fundamentum* is printed "Hafnye in curia domini doctoris Petri alberti" and the *Regulæ* "Expensis doctoris Petri alberti de Haffnya". That is, Gotfred had his printing office in the house of Peder Albertsen and published at his expenses.

Evidently, the man who was the leading organizer of the young university has also cared for the publishing of books for the students' use. We do not know to what extent he supported the further activity of Gotfred, the Rhymed Chronicle for example, but the fact that the same man was the motive power of the University of Copenhagen and the starter of the printing in the same city really makes him deserve a place of honour in the history of Danish culture.

Now let us leave the Latin aside and turn again to the Danish books. We know of what kind they were but I will stay away from a classification, and for the following reason: Have the contemporaries e.g. read the religious poems by Father Michael mainly as devotional books or have they enjoyed them as poetry? And how have they read the Rhymed Chronicle? After all, how does a modern reader read history books? Is he not fascinated by actions, performed in remote times? That he gets solid knowledge into the bargain is only an advantage. In the late middle ages, history was generally not, according to Elisabeth Mornet[14] read so much for its own sake, and none of the manuscripts Peder Albertsen is known to have donated to the University Library were of historical contents.

It would be interesting if we could know something more exact about the diffusion and the public of the Danish mediaeval books but we have only little knowledge of book collections from the period in question. A certain social stratum was certainly able to read, as schools existed in a certain number of towns, even small. We must, however, take it for granted that books were printed only in small issues; that is also made likely by the fact that e.g. the Rhymed Chronicle and some of the devotional books were reissued only with short intervals. Febvre & Martin[15] give some examples from the great European countries: it is mentioned that some early incunabula were printed only in 100 copies but towards the end of the fifteenth century some great printing offices attain the number of 1500. The modest Danish printers have certainly not come up to that level.

Two other questions must also be answered negatively; not because we do not know but because we know: Did the transition from script to book contribute to the shaping of a more or less consistent Danish written language? Not at least in the early days of printing. It is regrettable that only very few manuscript originals have been preserved; evidently, nobody has cared for them after the printed editions have been available; that is among others the case with the Rhymed Chronicle and Saxo's *Gesta Danorum*. We must also bear in mind that with one exception the printers in Denmark were immigrants and they had to copy the texts as they were available. It is not until the post-Reformation period that the publishing activity of Christiern Pedersen introduces a consistent orthography.

The final question is: Did the libraries care for the conservation of the early Danish books? If the former *no* was given with some reservation – it is after all a truism – no reservation is needed in this case. In two places books were collected to a greater extent in the sixteenth century: in the libraries of the kings and of the university. The king of the Reformation, Christian III, was a very bookish man, and also his son, Frederik II, added to the collection which was in 1605 given to

---

[14] Elisabeth Mornet. "Les livres d'histoire dans les bibliothèques danoises du début du XIVe siècle à la Réforme," *Annales de Bretagne et des pays de l'Ouest*, 87 (1980), 285-318.

[15] Lucien Febvre & Henri-Jean Martin, *L'apparition du livre*, Paris 1958, p. 327-330.

the university by Christian IV, and that collection we know about. It has been thoroughly described by Carl S. Petersen[16] who states that the collection only had five books in Danish, all concerning the Lutheran religion. Luther's works in the original were almost complete; it must be borne in mind that the Danish monarchy was bilingual or multilingual if we include Norwegian and the North Atlantic languages – and that the personal language of culture of several Danish kings was German, and that with very few exceptions the queens of the sixteenth, seventeenth and eighteenth centuries were of German origin. The University Library possesses a twelve-volume edition of Luther's works,[17] read from the beginning to the end by the queen of Frederik II, Sophie of Mecklenburg, in her widowhood.

But if the royal book collection was not remarkable for Danish books, the University Library was not either; in the catalogue of 1603, Ilsøe counts them on one hand.[18]

The mind changed, however, in the seventeenth century, a great period in the research of national history and antiquities. The royal historiographers were ordered to deposit their collections in the University Labrary, and private collectors showed interest in collecting the national literature, such as Professor Peder Hansen Resen who in 1685 donated his library of about 7000 titles to the University Library. Only the catalogue remains,[19] a very awkward tool of research, because the books are enumerated in the more or less accidental order in which they appeared on his shelves, and also because the index is very inaccurate, contrasting with the dignified appearance of the book. But you should not turn over many leaves without having an impression of the riches of the collection, and especially of the great amount of Danish books.

Resen was well aware that many of them were lacking in the University Library: "There were lacking very many books / concerning law and justice / likewise also many concerning the history / law / and other matters of these Northern states and countries... And if the collection is incomplete as all other earthly and human things / it is still more complete than any other library / which has existed up to this time in Denmark / what belongs to books of such

---

[16] Carl S. Petersen. "Christian IV.s Boggave 1605 til Københavns Universitet," *Nordisk tidskrift för bok- och biblioteksväsen*, XXXIV (1947), 115-141, 151-186. Also in: Carl S. Petersen. *Afhandlinger til dansk Bog- og Bibliotekshistorie*, København 1949, p. 1-81.

[17] Copenhagen UL Theol. 11906, fol. (Wittenberg 1568-72).

[18] Op. cit., p. 298.

[19] *Petri Joh. Resenii Bibliotheca Regiæ Academiæ Hafniensi donata...* Hafniæ 1685.

juridical / Northern / Danish and Gothic subjects." 'Gothic' surely means 'Swedish', for there is in fact an astonishing number of Swedish books of all kinds in Resen's library, a feature which was not common in that century, neither in the following. Resen also possessed the 1495 edition of the Rhymed Chronicle, but this as well as all the other books were destroyed in the great fire of 1728.

Fortunately enough, a new Royal Library had been founded by Frederik III shortly after the middle of the seventeenth century; it was in the beginning also mainly of an international scope, but the introduction of the legal deposit in 1697 made it a true national library, and it has since then remained unrivalled in this respect.

Nevertheless the University Library possesses today 77 books older than 1550 printed in Denmark or printed abroad for the Danish market, four of them unique, that is about the fourth of all existing imprints of that period. This is due especially to the great collectors of the eighteenth century whose names appear on a number of titlepages: Arne Magnusson, B.W. Luxdorph, Hans Gram and others. Frederik Rostgaard keeps a special place of honour: he donated the copy of the Rhymed Chronicle which is the library's pride.

It is just that the portait of Rostgaard painted by Johan Hörner adorns the office of the university librarian, and when we look back to Gotfred of Ghemen working in the house of Peder Albertsen there is still a link uniting us with the oldest history of the library, in spite of the catastrophe of 1728. Even if the humanities' section of the University Library is now overshadowed by the Royal Library, it still has an honourable place as a depository of old Danish books.

From script to print

by JOSEPH W. SCOTT

Professor the Right Honourable Friedrich Max Müller[1] published between 1867-1875 a collection of essays in four volumes which he called *Chips from a German workshop*. How right he was! For he had a workshop – a chair in Oxford – he had a splendid set of tools – his deep knowledge of Sanskrit, Pali, comparative religion, comparative philology, philosophy, biography and German – and finally he worked nearly all the time. A thoroughly academic workshop, founded on his Taylorian professorship, and his fellowship of All Souls College, Oxford. By comparison, this paper is more like grains of sawdust found on the floor of an amateur's garden-shed. It is principally based on two books which I catalogued long ago in the Brotherton Collection of rare books and manuscripts, in the Library of the University of Leeds. Two books, similar in nature – one a manuscript, the other a printed book – separated by only some 20 years in time. The manuscript is a roll Chronicle universal history from the Creation of the world to about 1475 (certainly some point in the reign of King Louis XI of France, 1461 to 1483). The printed book is also a universal history from the Creation of the world to the end of the fifteenth century almost. It is Hartman Schedel's *Liber chronicarum*,[2] illustrated by the woodcuts of Michael Wohlgemuth and Wilhelm Pleydenwurff, published by Anton Koberger at Nürnberg in 1493 and popularly known as the Nyremberg Chronicle.

Universal chronicles similar to the manuscript at Leeds became popular in the fifteenth century – particularly the latter half of the fifteenth century – in England and France. I have certainly not yet made a thorough search of the standard catalogues of manuscripts, but even by following up references in the literature I have listed about 30-40 roll chronicles in the U.K. alone. There will obviously be more in France. However, very little has been written about them as a *genre*. There is a paper by M. Büdinger published in 1900, entitled *Die Uni-*

---

[1] Müller, Rt. Hon. Friedrich Max. *Chips from a German workshop*. 4 vols. London, Oxford [printed], 1867-75.

[2] Schedel, Hartman. *Liber chronicarum*. Nuremberg, Anton Koberger, 1493.

versalhistorie im Mittelalter.³ But this deals with the history in these chronicles rather than their form, or connection with each other. Bernhard Bischoff mentions such rolls in a few brief lines, giving as examples "die Rolle des Osterspiels von Muri (XIII Jh), die Frankfurter Dirigier rolle des Balderman von Peterweil (um 1350), und die Rolle des vierter Grabeswächters in Sulmona (XIV Jh)".⁴

Three writers have a little to say about the form of roll chronicles. Firstly, John Henry Middleton in his *Illuminated manuscripts in classical and medieval times* says: "One favourite form of chronicle, giving an abstract of the whole World's history, was in the shape of a long parchment roll, illuminated with miniatures in the form of circular medallions. Some of these great rolls were written and illuminated by English miniaturists, but they appear not to have been as common in England as they were in France; (see p. 139). On these rolls the writing usually continues down the strip, not at right angles to the long sides as on classical papyrus rolls." Middleton continues, "One rather abnormal class of ms. which belongs both to this period [i.e. 14th century] and the following century consists of French and Latin chronicles of the World beginning with the Creation and reaching down to recent times, written and illuminated with numerous miniature paintings on great rolls of parchment often measuring 50 to 60 feet in length. These are usually rather cource in execution."⁵ Secondly, Maso Finiguerra says, "There is another well known class of French ms. chronicles in the form of a long roll, sometimes histories of the world in tabular form, sometimes local chronicles with a brief general history from the Creation prefixed; and these rolls are often adorned with circular miniatures representing the events and personages of the story."⁶ Thirdly, Paul Meyer in his survey of French mss. in Cambridge, says of Cambridge ms. MM 4.44: "Cette chronique, que je n'ai du reste examiné que superficiellement, ne m'a pas paru offrir un grand interêt. Il sutfira d'en rapporter cici les premières et les demières lignes, pour permettre de reconnnaître s'il existe d'autres exemplaires, ce qui est probable."⁷ "Coarse in execution" says Middleton – for the fifteenth century had seen an increase in the

---

³ Büdinger, M. *Die Universalhistorie im Mittelalter*, in Denkschriften d.k. Akademie d. Wiss. zu Wien. Phil.-hist. Klasse XLVI Abh. 1 and 2, 1900.

⁴ Bischoff, Bernhard. *Paläographie*. Sonderdruck aus *Deutsche Philologie im Aufriss* Hgn. von Wolfang Stammler. p. 391.

⁵ Middleton, John Henry. *Illuminated manuscripts in classical and medieval times*. Cambridge, 1892. pp. 125 and 139 and 141.

⁶ Finiguerra, Tommaso di. *A Florentine picture-chronicle*. London, Quaritch, 1893.

⁷ Meyer, Paul. "Les manuscrits français de Cambridge. II. Bibliothèque de l'université," *in Romania* XV. 1886. p. 353.

massproduction of manuscripts which had started in the fourteenth century. Irwin writes in his introduction to *The English Library before 1700*, p. 6.

"By the middle of the century (i.e. XVth) manuscript books were being copied in large numbers for lay readers. Some families such as the Pastons might occasionally employ a scribe of their own: but there were publishing firms such as that of John Shirley (1366-1456) which produced work in quantity. Shirley seems to have lent, as well as sold, mss. to his customers anticipating the latter combination of bookseller and circulating library."[8] Irwin points out in a note to this passage the prefatory verses to B.M. Add. Ms. 16165, quoted by H.S. Bennett, Oxford 1947, p. 116, in his *Chaucer and the fifteenth century*, and more recently by Cheryl Greenberg[9] in her paper on Shirley:

> Yee that desyre in herte and have plesance
> Olde stories in bokis for to rede
> Gode matiers putt hem in remembrance
> And of the other take yee none hede
> Byseching yowe of your godelyhede
> Whan yee this boke have over redde and seyne
> To Johan Shirley restore yee it ageine.

Cheryl Greenberg points out that these verses appear also in mss. Ashmole 59 and Trin. Coll. Camb. 600. Surely this adds up to a fifteenth century lending library of manuscript books.

Lucien Febvre and Henri-Jean Martin mention orders of between 200 and 400 copies of individual mss. in their *L'apparition du livre*, (Paris, 1958, pp. 22-3).[10] Finally, on the mass production of mss. Middleton writes "It is more especially in the cheap *Books of Hours* of the second half of the fifteenth century that the lowest artistic level is reached in France, Flanders and Holland. Education has gradually been extended among various classes of laymen, and by the middle of the fifteenth century it appears to have been usual, not only for all men above the rank of artisans to be able to read, but even women of the wealthy bourgeois

---

[8] Wormald, Francis, and Wright, C.E., ed. *The English library before 1700: studies in its history*. London, Athlone Press, 1958. p. 6.

[9] Greenberg, Cheryl. "John Shirley and the English book trade." *The Library*. Transactions of the Bibliographical Society. Sixth series, vol. IV, no. 4, Dec. 1982. pp. 369-380.

[10] Febvre, Lucien Paul Victor, and Martin, Henri Jean. *The coming of the book*. [Translated from *L'Apparition du livre* by David Gerard.] 2nd impression. London, NLB, 1979, pp. 22-23.

class could make use of prayer books. Hence arose a great demand for pictured *Books of Hours* which appear to have been produced in enormous quantities by trade scribes of towns such as Bruges, Paris and many others. These common manuscript *Horae* are monotonous in form and detail and harsh in colour; and the illuminated borders, with which they are lavishly, though cheaply, decorated, have the same forms of foliage and fruit repeated again and again in dozens of manuscripts, which all look as if they had come out of the same workshop." Jean Porcher describing af fourteenth century family workshop in Paris, writes "After Honoré, the workshop in Rue Boulebrie was controlled by his son-in-law Richard de Verdun ... [it produced] a series of [manuscript] books which crowded the Parisian market, and were doubtless imitated elsewhere until 1330 and even later (Plates XLIX, LII). Simple decorative work, it becomes stereotyped. Some of the books are produced *en masse*, like the many copies of a work then much in demand, the *Bible Historial* of Guiart des Moulins, a French translation of *Historia Scholastica* of Petrus Comestor."[11] The late Neil Ker, whose memorial service was held in Oxford only last Saturday, the 13th November, in his *Medieval Libraries of Great Britain*[12] lists thirty three mss. of Petrus Comestor's *Historia Scholastica* of XII, XIII (the majority) and XIV centuries. Ker also lists four mss. of the *Compendium Historiae* by Petrus Pictaviensis (Peter of Poitiers). Two from the Benedictine abbey of St. Edburga at Pershore in Worcestershire which are now B. M. Royal mss. 10.A.iv, and 11.B.iv. A third from the Benedictine abbey of St. Edmund at Bury St. Edmunds which is now at Cambridge, (Pembroke Coll. 96). The fourth, from the Cistercian abbey of Warden in Bedfordshire is now in Cambridge (Gonv. & Caius Coll. 316). These two Peters – Peter of Poitiers and Peter the Eater (i.e. Petrus Comestor, or Petrus Manducator of Pierre le Mangeur) are the basic texts in Worlds universal chronicles of the twelfth to fifteenth centuries. As P.S. Allen writes: "The *Compendium Historiae* was extended, through its incorporation into a number of universal chronicles. Of these chronicles no two seem to be entirely alike."[13] H. Vollmer has said of them in his *Deutsche Bibelauszüge des Mittelalters*,[14] what St. Jerome once wrote about Latin translations of the Bible: *tot exemplaria, quot codices*. Vollmer also called attention to a number of universal chronicles and the mss. in which they are contained.

---

[11] Porcher, Jean. *French miniatures from illuminated manuscripts* (translated by Julian Brown). London, Collins, 1960. p. 51.
[12] Ker, N.R. *Medieval libraries of Great Britain*. Royal Historical Soc., 1941.
[13] Allen, P.S. *The works of Peter of Poitiers*. Notre Dame, 1936. p. 111.
[14] Vollmer, H. *Deutsche Bibelauszüge des Mittelalters*. Potsdam, 1931.

From script to print

Let us now consider the Leeds ms. in greater detail and some of the mss. which are closely similar to it. It is a French fifteenth century manuscript written in Anglo-Norman French on a long vellum roll of 38 membranes measuring 17.6 metres (57 feet 8¾ ins.) It is written in lettres bâtardes in four columns (mostly), illustrated with 61 circular medallions (56-75 mm., or 2¼-3 inches in diameter). The final medallion is a portrait of Louis XI (1461-83). The prologue begins: "Cy sensuit la genealogie de la bible"; the first double column begins "In principio creavit deus celum et terram." Across the head of the roll stretch contingent miniatures, each 2¾"-70 mm. in diameter giving six unusual days of The Creation:

1. Comment dieu crea / le ciel, la terre & les estoiles.
2. Comment dieu crea la terre / les herbes et les arbres, etc.
3. Comment dieu crea les / eaues et les poissons, etc.
4. Comment dieu crea les / bestes et les oiseaulx, etc.
5. Comment dieu crea les / anges, etc.
6. Comment dieu trebucha / les maulvais anges, etc.
7. Comment dieu de paradis fist adam et eve quant les maulvais anges / furent trebuches. etc.
8. Comment l'ennemy d'enfer se mist en l'arbre en guise de serpent et deceut eve / et comment eve quant elle fist decehue deceut adam son compagnion.
9. Comment adam et eve furent mis en paradis terrestre et leur deffen / dit dieu le fruit de l'arbre et ils trespasserent son commandement, etc.
10. [No title – a miniature of the Expulsion of Adam and Eve from Paradise – Eve in green "hot pants".]
11. Comment adam / commance a la / bourer la terre.
12. Noe qui fist l'arche.
    [Four red lines lead out to the *four* sons of Noah.]
    (a) Sem premier / fils Noe reg / na en Asie Persia seine / fem.
    (b) Cham regna en au / rique Cathalne / femme Cham.
    (c) Jonitam le darnier fils fut / ne XXX ans / apres le de / luge.
    (d) Japhet / iii^e fils noe / regna en / europe.
    [Linked by red lines to these four are the names of thirty eight descendants each in a small red circle (37 mm.). This section occupies 270 mm. (or nearly 1') of the length of the roll.]
13. La tour de Babiloyne.
    [Three red circles (37 mm.) are appended.]

(a) Philistin / nomma les / philistins.
(b) Nonnius / et sa lignee / furent destruiz.
(c) Ananias / et sa lignee / furent destruiz.
14. Abraham patri / arche.
[Followed by 53 red circles (37 mm.) for the length of 680 mm. of the first of the two coll.]
15. Jesue premier preux.
[To save time I shall continue in English.]
16. The destruction of Troy.
17. The departure of the Trojan ships. Four miniatures 2¼" 56 mm.)
(a) eneas (b) priamus (c) turnus (d) helenus.
18. How David was made king over the Children of Israel.
(a) Amon (b) Celeap (c) Salmon/le sage (d) Absalon (e) Adonias (f) Sazacias (g) Jeptain selittam.
Here the roll divides into its four columns.
(a) *Religious history.* beg. Cy sensuit ceulx qui furent / roys de indee apres la mort salmon / que son regne fut divise en deux parties.
(b) *Imperial history.* beg. Cy sensuit ceulx qui furent / roys d'Israel apres la mort salmon / que son regne fut divise en deux parties.
(c) *Roman – then French history* Comment filius / eneas tint le regne des latins.
(d) *English history from Brut* Comment Brut se partit de la / terre latine quant il et son pere tue / et moult de meschief avant qu'il peust / avoir puissance comme vos sera devise.
19. Brut kills the giants.
20. The destruction of Samaria.
21. The foundation of Sincambria.
22. Zedekias king of Judea.
23. The slaughter of Nebuchanezzar.
24. Romulus building Rome.
25. The building of Paris [Lutesse].
26. The fall of Babylon.
27. The rape of the Sabine women.
28. The exile of Queen Vashti.
29. Alexander of Macedon the Fourth Worthy.
30. Judas Maccabeus was the Sixth Worthy.
31. The Nativity.
32. The Ascension.

From script to print

33. How New Troy was named London in England.
34. How Jesus Christ became man as first Pope.
35. The murder of Julius Caesar.
36. How the Sincambrians came to Gaul and named it France.
37. How the French discovered the Roumanians.
38. The first ordination of Archbishops and bishops.
39. Conan, first king of Brittany.
40. Coronation of Pharamand as first king of France.
41. Baptism of King Clovis.
42. How the English king killed 30 Bretons for treason.
43. How Dagobert founded the church St. Denis in France.
44. The death of King Arthur.
45. How Great Britain was destroyed by the Africans and they gave it to the Saxons and named it all England.
46. How Pepin was made King of France.
47. Saint Gregory, Pope.
48. How William the Bastard conquered England and was its king. [Portrait roughly torn out.]
49. How Hue Cappet was made King of France.
50. How Godeffroy de billon in order to go conquer the Holy Land went overseas.
51. Charlemagne elected first emperor of Rome and of France.
52. How Godeffroy de billon conquered Jerusalem and was made its king.
53. St. Louis.
54. Beranger.
55. How Phillipe de Vallois was king of France.
56. Edward King of England.
57. How Jehan King of France was taken prisoner before Poitiers, [1356].
58. Charles, Fifth of that name. [Portrait in centre. 180 mm. $3^{1}/_{8}$".].
59. How Charles Sixth asked for aid from his people to maintain his state. [Here the columns finish and the text is written across the full breadth of the roll.]
60. Charles VIII. A large central miniature.
    Charles VII son of Charles VI reigned 39 years and nine months and passed on [trespassa] 1 an mil IV^c 1Xi [= 1461].
61. Louis, XIth of that name, now rules. A large central miniature.

Looking at other roll chronicles in some ways akin to the Leeds ms. we realize that no two are exact copies but have close similarities. Sometimes in the text, sometimes in the division and arrangement of the columns, sometimes in the list of subjects chosen as illustrations. Montague Rhodes James[15] gives a detailed description of a very similar ms. in The Fitzwilliam Museum. Cambridge "MS. 176. Chronicle of the World in roll-form". Size, 56' 6" long by 1' 8½". Cent. XV (1450). Acquired in 1876, at The Bragge Sale. This is a fair specimen of a very numerous class. These rolls, originally meant, no doubt, to be hung in large halls of castles or private houses, were subsequently replaced by folding plates bound in book form or else by books (notably the "Fasciculus Temporum") containing essentially the same matter and similar pictures. The pictures of this are rough: it comes probably from N.E. France. It begins with the Creation and goes down to The Battle of Agincourt [1415]. Illustrated with 64 medallions.

A comparison of these 64 medallions with the 61 medallions in the Leeds ms. reveals an almost total congruency of subject *and title*. Both contain the non-biblical account of the Fifth and Sixth days of The Creation. The last medallion in Fitzwilliam 176 is Charles VI. (No. 59 in the Leeds ms.) The additional medallions in Fitzwilliam 176 are two extra illustrations of the Garden of Eden story, and the destruction of Troy has five illustrations compared with the two in the Leeds ms. Otherwise, all other illustrations depict the same subject, in the same order, and with exactly the same words in the title. The strongest links between the two mss. is the chain of medallions and their titles. Equally, Moses Tyson's[16] description of MS. R. 14335 in the John Rylands Library show text and medallions very similar to the Leeds ms. The 65 medallions have almost the same subjects and the prologue beginning "Cy S'ensuit la genealogie de la bible .." is identical. Both are arranged in four columns. The history of the Papacy here given ends at 1378; that of the emperors at 1338; that of the Kings of France at 1461 and that of the Kings of England with Henry IV.

Links of authorship are often attributed to either Petrus Comestor or to Petrus Pictaviensis, as BM Add. ms. 41600 (8) shows "Chronicle of the genealogy of Christ from Adam variously attributed to Petrus Pictaviensis and to Petrus Comestor. *Beg*. (f. 846) 'Considerans historie sacre prolixitatem'". The entry for BM Royal ms. 8 c. ix (2) gives "Liber cronicorum (sic) secundum

---

[15] James, M.R. *A descriptive catalogue of the mss. in the Fitzwilliam Museum*. Cambridge U.P., 1895. pp. 381-383.

[16] Tyson, Moses. *Handlist of the collection of French and Italian mss. in the John Rylands Library*, 1930. p. 33.

magistrum Petrum Mandicatorem (80 in table of F. 166) a genealogy of Christ from Adam". – *Preface begins*: "Considerans historie sacre prolixitatem..." – *Text begins*: "Adam in agro Damasceno formatus..."

As a result of the rapid increase in the production of such rolls, and perhaps because of the propaganda needs of the rival factions in the Wars of the Roses, illuminated universal chronicle histories of the world were declining into genealogical rolls of the Kings of England from Adam, through Noah, to Edward IV (1461-1483). Three examples will illustrate the various changes involved in this decline; one manuscript from my own library of University College London, one from Trinity College Cambridge and one from the Lyell collections of manuscripts bequeathed by their collector James P.R. Lyell of Abingdon in the Bodleian Library, Oxford. Dorothy K. Coveney[17] lists in her University College catalogue *MS. Angl. 3*, [which was part of the Gertrude Moseley bequest to University College London in 1918] as a parchment roll of the late fifteenth century. Unrolled, it measures 595.5 x 30.8 (varying to 31.4) cm. and consists of eight lengths of parchment measuring 79.9, 80.6, 82.5, 74.6, 73.1, 83, 76.6 and 56.75 cm. respectively. Lines have been drawn to guide the text, which begins 23 cm. from the beginning of the roll, and is written on both left- and right-hand sides of a genealogical table, which proceeds down the centre. Initial letters of paragraphs are in red and blue alternately, or occasionally green. Names of kings are in red, in medallion, surmounted by a crown, coloured dark yellow. Rubrication appears to have been executed by the scribe. All names appearing in the table are encircled in green, red or blue, and are joined to the table by green, red or blue lines. *Genealogical table of the Kings of England to Edward IV, showing their descent from Adam and Eve. (beg.)* considerans cronicorū plixitatē necnon et difficultatem scolariū --- (*end*) ab illo usque ad henricum sextum originaliter finem perduxi. Adam in agro damasceno formatus ... (end. Henry VI) de quo genuit Edwardum principem qui natus / erat in festo translationis sancti edwardi confesso / ris anno d$\overline{\text{m}}$i m° cccc° / iii°".

Secondly, the Trinity College ms. described by M.R. James[18] is: *"636. Chronological roll* Vellum, or roll folded and bound as a volume, measuring 13$\frac{1}{8}$" x 7" in varying numbers of columns [Given by Th. Whalley, D.D., Vice-Master,

---

[17] Coveney, Dorothy K. *A descriptive catalogue of manuscripts in the library of University College London.* University of London, University College, 1935. p. 21.

[18] James, M.R. *The Western manuscripts in the library of Trinity College, Cambridge.* A descriptive catalogue. Vol. 11. C.U.P. 1901. p. 131.

1637]." The names of the persons in the genealogical tables are written in red circles. *There are no pictures.* The text begins in three columns.

1. Considerans hystorie sacre prolixitatem necnon et difficultatem...
2. Adam in agro damasceno formatus...
3. Prima etas mundi fuit ab adam usque ad noe...

The chronology goes down to Edward IV. The text ends with a notice of him. Edwardus quartus filius et heres Ricardi nuper ducis Eboraci et Cecilie uxoris eius, post decessum patris sui fuit dux Eboraci. Et coronatus est in vegem anglie apud Westmonasterium xxviij° die Junii anno domini M° ccc lxj°. Henry VI, it is noted, was buried at "Cherchessey", so that the date of the MS is after 47".

The third example of a genealogical roll is Ms. Lyell 33:[19] *Genealogical chronicle of Kings of England.* "In English on parchment written in England, c. 1469-1470 in a rather rough textura hand [Pl. VI]. 350 x 215 mm. formed from 15 membranes each measuring c. 100 mm. in length, (the end of the last one has been cut off) joined together and folded into 31½ double leaves, foliated 1-63 (fol. i-ii & 6A-5 are fly-leaves) ... The text from the roundel of Adam & Eve (being tempted by the serpent) to the Ascension of Christ (fol. 42) is linked by a continuous blue and gold band. Biblical names are framed in plum red or green squares, those of the ancestors of the Kings of England in red or blue and gold circles, those of the Kings of England (from Brutus, fol. 11^v) in blue or plum red circles surmounted by gold crowns.

Genealogical chronicle of the Kings of England from Adam to Edward IV. (fol. 1^v, first col.) Prologue, *beg*: Consideryng the length and the hardnesse of holy scripture [and nameli of the ground of the lettir historial] *ends*: and by his grace to be endid ... fro Japhet the son of Noe lyneali descendyng to Brut the first king of that name in the seid land and fro hym to Edwarde the fourth kyng of that name, after the conquest of England (second col.) *beg*. The first age of The World was from Adam to Noe, [ends: and a rewarde for good and yvel.] The Chronicle ends with Edward IV (fol. 63^v): by juste titel of enheritans. And he was crowned kyng at Westmynster in the eight and twenti day of the mone of Iuny in the yere of oure lorde a thousand four hundred sesti. Up to the Ascension of Christ (fol. 42) the main chronicle follows quite closely an interpolated version of the *Compendium Historiae in Genealogia Christi* of Peter of Poitiers, which is found in Naples,

---

[19] De la Mare, Albinia. *Catalogue of the collection of medieval manuscripts bequeathed to the Bodleian Library, Oxford, by James P.R. Lyell.* Oxford, Clarendon Press, 1971. pp. 80-85.

From script to print 29

Bibl. Naz. Ms VIII, C.³, (French c. 1200) and a number of English mss. e.g. – the two closely related mid – 13th century rolls Bodl. Lat. th. b. I (R) and B.M. Royal 14. B. lx;

Bodl. Land misc. 151, fol. 1-6, first half 13th century.
Bodl. Rawlinson C. 563, fol. 1-26ᵛ 14 th cent.
B.M. Add. 11758. 15th cent.
Bodl. Barlow 53. 15th cent. is an English translation.

The number of interpolations varies in each ms. but all the mss. cited include the text on the eight ages of man at the end of the first age.

One of a group of roll chronicles designed to be made up in codex form. The scribe joined his membranes with glue into a roll approx. 13.5 metres in length, and ruled it for writing transversely on one side only in panels, or blocks, of 38 lines (for 3 columns up to fol. 42 [The Ascension] and for two columns for the remainder). Between each panel of writing he legt 40-45 mm. blank, and after writing the text and drawing the lines of the pedigree, he then made a very crisp transverse fold across the middle of each blank space, upwards and downwards alternately so that the roll could be closed up centertina fashion www into a 'book' which is read by turning the volume sideways so that the foredge faces the reader. The text is linked by the continuous pedigree lines which run across the blank margins. Evidently the product of a workshop, presumably in London or Westminster, which produced a number of other genealogical *Chronicles of the English Kings* generally up to Edward IV [1461 - 1483], in English or Latin which are identical in text, script, layout, decoration or all four (nos. (i)-(iii); B; C(i-ii); D(i-ii); E(i) (iv in the list below). Alle have a painted roundel of Adam and Eve and the serpent, unless otherwise stated. This feature probably derives from the interpolated version of the *Compendium* of Peter of Poitiers already mentioned. BM Royal 14. B. IX and Bodl. Lat. th.bI(R) have a series of miniatures including the Adam and Eve pictures in a mandola other mss. in a roundel."

We see at least three developments in these three mss., or rather three deteriorations, from the truly universal chronicles. A concentration upon the kings of *England*, the disappearance of the illuminated medallions which, in so many manuscripts already noted, usually totalled between 61 and 65, and the change from roll form to codex form so well described by the compiler Albinia De la Mare in this strange hybrid form written as a roll and then bound as a codex.

However, the rapid expansion of the printed book, in the last five decades of the fifteenth century, brought the universal histories to an even wider public. The introduction of paper instead of vellum, together with the growth of the general reading public, were powerful aids to this expansion. Lucien Febvre and

Jean-Henri Martin tell us "Vincent de Beauvais' *Miroir Historial* and Rolewinck's *Fasciculus Temporum* still had many readers. The *Mer des Histoires* was re-issued and adapted several times during The 16th century, and Harman Schedel's *Liber Chronicarum*, better known as the Nurmberg Chronicle was immensely popular, as were other similar works *sometimes printed on one side only* so that the leaves could be pasted end to end to form a roll." The exact reverse of the roll of *MS Lyell 33* being turned into codex form.

As we consider these variations in format from the roll to the codex or to a hybrid roll-codex, or, in reverse, a hybrid codex roll we appreciate the value of M.R. James's comment in his detailed description of ms. Fitzwilliam 176 (see above). Here he points out that rolls which were originally hung on walls in large halls, castles or private houses were replaced by folding plates bound in book form. He obviously is referring to that form of concertina folding so lucidly described in the detailed description of MS. Lyell 33 (see above). The assumed clash between manuscript and printed book was for long taken by nineteenth and early twentieth century writers. How many writers have quoted Vespasiano da Bisticci, the Florentine bookseller, telling us that in the library of Federigo III de Montefeltro, duke of Urbino about 1490 "all books were superlatively good and written with the pen; had there been one printed book it would have been ashamed in such company."[20] Better to be reminded by Curt F. Bühler[21] of the opinion of the Abbot Johann Tritheim,[22] abbot of Spanheim – "Scriptura enim si membranis imponitur, ad mille annos poterit perdurare: impressura autem cum res papirea sit quamdiu subsistet. Si in volumine papireo ad ducentos annos perdurare potuerit: Magnum est." For modern writers now agree that there was a natural kinship between the manuscript book and the printed book. Curt F. Bühler, Sandra Hindman and James Douglas Farqhar,[23] and Lucien Febvre and Jean-Henri Martin, establish and document the co-operation and working relationships of scribes and printers between 1450 and 1500. For all the craft and experience of lay-out, margins, line-lengths, decoration and illustration were in the hands and heads of the scribes; the printers – those who had *not* been scribes had to learn it from them, and often with them.

---

[20] Bisticci, Vespasiano da. *Vite di Uomini Illustri*, ed. A. Bartoli. Florence, 1859.

[21] Bühler, Curt F. *The fifteenth century book*. Philadelphia, Univ. of Pennsylvania Press, 1960. p. 35.

[22] Tritheim, Johannes. Abbot of Sponheim. *De laude scriptorum*. Mainz, Peter von Friedberg, 1494.

[23] Hindman, Sandra, and Farquhar, James Douglas. *Pen to press*. Maryland, 1977.

Of the several universal chronicles in printed form, few would disagree that the most successful and the most beautiful was *The Nuremberg Chronicle*. Whatever references to this book I had collected over the years have all been embodied in and extended by Adrian Wilson's *The making of the Nuremberg Chronicle*.[24]

Apart from Bibles, the *Nuremberg Chronicle* was in many ways the greatest production of the incunable period. In Appendix 1 of Wilson's book (p. 238) Peter Zahn estimates that the original Latin edition was 1500 and the German 1000. These are large for the period in comparison with other incunabula. More normal numbers of an edition, according to Ferdinand Geldner,[25] were between 400 and 600. Of the 1500 copies of the Latin edition exactly 800 are recorded in eleven major catalogues of incunables. Only seven are recorded in Great Britain – four in Cambridge and three in The B.M. I myself know of many more in London, Oxford, Manchester, Edinburgh, Glasgow and other university libraries. If we also add on copies in private hands we should reach some 900 extant copies. It certainly establishes the librarian's consolatory slogan "It is very difficult either to steal or to lose a large, heavy book!".

The revolutionary new technique of printing was the only change from the manuscript universal chronicles for most of the text was unchanged. Firstly, as Wilson points out (pp. 19-20) earthly history progresses through the six ages,

---

[24] Wilson, Adrian. *The making of the Nuremberg Chronicle*. Introduction by Peter Zahn. *Nico Israel*, Amsterdam, 1976.

App. 1, p. 238. Recorded copies of the first editions of the Nuremberg Chronicle.

	Latin	German
1. Jahrbuch der Auktimpreise.	71	40
2. GKW.	2.82	269
3. Goff. Incunabula in American libraries 3rd census. N.Y. 1964.	89	44
4. Indice generale degli Incunabuli. Milan. 1972.	124	8
5. Pellechet, M. & Polain, L. Catalogue ... France, Paris 1969-70.	125	5
6. Polain, L. Catalogue ... Belgique. Bruxelles. 1932.	28	2
7. Sajo, beza & Soltész, Erszebet Catalgus ... Hungariae. 1970.	23	22
8. Bohonos, Maria & Szandorowska, Elisa. Incunubula ... Poloniae. Bratislawa. 1970.	48	17
9. Oates, J.C.T. XVth cent. books in Cambridge. 1954.	4	0
10. BMC II.437.	3	1
11. Pellechet, Marie. Catalogue ... Lyon. 1893.	3	0
	800	408

Note: Peter Zahn estimates that the original Latin edition was 1500 and the German 1000.

[25] Geldner, Ferdinand. "Das Rechnungsbuch des Speyrer Druckherrn, Verlegers und Grossbuchhandlers Peter Drach", in *Archiv für Geschichte des Buchwesens*, Vol. 5. (Frankfurt, 1964).

which had been a set pattern since Bishop Eusebius of Caesarea wrote his *Chronicorum Canones* about AD 303. The six ages are: from The Creation to Noah; from Noah to Abraham; from Abraham to David; from David to the Babylonian captivity; from The Captivity to the birth of Christ. Presumably, just as the Seventh of The Creation was sanctified as a day of rest, so shall the Seventh Age bring Eternal Rest.

Secondly, as Wilson says in the compilation of The Chronicle (p. 26), "But as Trithemius had already noted Schedel 'compiled and copied ... from Jacobo Pergomensi and other historians, contributing nothing valuable from the writings of his time'. Indeed, The Chronicle is partly and almost unaltered re-writing of the *Supplementum Chronicarum* of Jacob Philip Foresti of Bergamo. Following the medieval chroniclers, he gives ample space to the curiosities of the middle ages, accounts of epidemics, monsters and comets, and like Vincent of Beauvais, Schedel starts and ends with theological considerations on the Creation and on the Final Judgement. His interest in historical events remains superficial."

Thirdly, "neither did he record the death of the powerful Lorenzo di Medici in the year before the Chronicle was published, nor note, even in the German edition of late 1493, the news of Columbus' first voyage to the New World which ended in March 1493."

However, the illustrations have a life and continuity of their own, with little direct relation to the text. For as Hindman and Farquhar write (p. 86) "The same block was repeated even though the subject differed ... 645 blocks were used for 1,809 illustrations. Blocks were also split into different parts so they could be combined to produce many kinds of illustration." However, the continuity of a series of illustrations based on a long tradition brings me to my final conclusion. I must remind you of my comparison of the sixty-one illustrations of the Leeds ms. with the sixty four illustrations of the Fitzwilliam ms. no. 176. It was not a mere copy, which would have been of little interest, but a different re-drawing of the same subjects for illustration in the same order to the number of over sixty. I am sure we could find parallels in the illustrations before the individual section, of *Book of Hours* (and it may well have been done). Certainly, I have not seen an illustration "*King David praying*" before the *Seven Penitential Psalms* in any Book of Hours I have looked through. Indeed, it is not fanciful to suggest that manuscript universal histories which *shed illustrations*, deteriorated into mere genealogical rolls of The Kings of England; whilst those, which in their printed form, embodied and developed a new vigorous corpus of woodcut engravings of saints, kings, popes, emperors and towns gave a new life to world histories.

The importance of a strong pictorial tradition is well demonstrated by Samuel Claggett Chew the younger, in his book *The virtues reconciled: an iconographic study*.[26] After establishing that the short, truncated pointless sword, which has been frequently carried at Royal coronations in England, is known as the *curtana*, or curtan, or curteyn, as a symbol of Mercy, he turns to lines 239-240 of Chaucer's *Parliament of Foules*.

> Before the temple-dore full soberly
> Dame Pees sat, with a curteyn in her hand

Chew continues "Why should Lady Peace be represented in such wise? Professor Tatlock and Mr. Mackaye in their modernization of Chaucer's text render the passage thus: 'Before the temple-door sat Dame Peace full gravely, holding back the curtain'. This rendering is quite unwarranted, for it suggests a posture and gesture other than those conveyed in the original lines. Chaucer's word is not listed in the glossaries; editors and commentators pass over it in silence; and in the Chaucer *Concordance* it is modernized as our common word 'curtain'. You have a course anticipated the suggestion I am going to make that the symbolic object held by Peace is a *Curtana*, the truncated, pointless sword." Indeed he supports his suggestion with two plates from *Books of Hours* depicting Mercy holding such a sword.

Finally, I think one paragraph on the introduction to Hindman & Farquhar (pp. 3-4) says it all: "The contributions of different disciplines highlight the gaps in the field. Historians have questioned the way in which scholars have separated the books from the milieu in which they were created, and thus have called for a more broadly based use of the extant evidence. *But they seem reluctant to discuss pictorial imagery.*"

Researchers of illumination have provided the history and names of the illuminators, their stylistic and iconographic sources, and vocabulary and techniques for their description, but for the most part graphic media in books contemporary with the manuscript are ignored. Historians of the print [e.g. Schreiber] long ago provided a framework for prints in printed books in the history of visual imagery; however, the broader context of the print – that is, the book itself – was largely ignored. Bibliographers have carefully studied different editions and have provided complete and accurate catalogues on the extant

---

[26] Chew, Samuel Claggett, the younger. *The virtues reconciled: an iconographic study.* Toronto, Univ. of Toronto Press, 1947. pp. 119-123.

imprints from early printing, as well as an impressive array of descriptive tools (e.g. McKerrow, Bowers, Gaskell, Haebler) but the bibliographer is rarely a manuscript experts as well. In short, everyone has carved out a carefully constructed niche in which his own work has a secure place within his own discipline. But the result is that despite the wealth of published material, the relationship between the illuminated manuscript and the illustrated printed book is virtually impossible to define. Until this relationship is clarified, the broader historical context of book production during this century (i.e. XVth] will remain obscure.

Johann Snell

von URSULA ALTMANN

Gutenbergs Erfindung, die Kunst, auf eine neue Weise, künstlich, zu schreiben, wurde in Dänemark erstmals von Johann Snell ausgeübt, der vor 500 Jahren in Odense Bücher durch Drucken vervielfältigte. Nicht mit dem Calamus, dem Stichel oder der Feder, sondern durch das wunderbare Zusammenspiel von Patronen und Formen konnten nun Texte in der ihnen gemäßen Gestalt, in Übereinstimmung von Proportionen und Modul wiedergegeben werden; so sagt es die Schlußschrift des Mainzer Catholicons von 1460.

Für das Schreiben vom Büchern waren bestimmte Normen verbindlich, die sich im Verlaufe von Jahrhunderten entwickelt hatten und von den Skriptorien bei aller Vielfalt regionaler Stileigenheiten streng beachtet wurden, entsprechend dem Zweck, dem die Bücher jeweils zu dienen hatten. Dem erreichten Standard mußten die Jünger der Schwarzen Kunst gerecht werden. Gutenbergs Schüler und deren Nachfolger waren deshalb wiederholt vor neue Aufgaben gestellt, immer dann, wenn sie daran gingen, eine bestimmte Art von Texten erstmals zu drucken, die kommentierte Rechtsliteratur zum Beispiel, die Schriften der antiken Klassiker und der Humanisten, Bücher in den Volkssprachen oder die Bücher für den Gebrauch beim Gottesdienst, um nur einige zu nennen.

Neue Aufgaben ergaben sich für die Drucker auch aus der Buchherstellung im Auflagendruck. Dafür zwei Beispiele. Einzelbogen in großer Anzahl mußten zu Lagen zusammengesetzt und die korrekte Reihenfolge der Bogen und Lagen innerhalb eines Exemplares zunächst für den Verkauf, dann für den Buchbinder, gesichert werden. In der Frühzeit des Buchdrucks wurde jeder einzelne Bogen, nachdem er aus der Presse kam, handschriftlich mit einer Lagenbezeichnung versehen. Diese nötige, sehr aufwendige Arbeit wurde überflüssig, als die Drucker dazu übergingen, auf der ersten Seite eines Bogens unterhalb der letzten Zeile Lagensignaturen zu drucken. Sie gingen damit über den eigentlichen Satzspiegel hinaus, der, vornehmlich in Folianten, das Abbild zweier strenger, geschlossener Säulen bot und in Büchern kleineren Formats als eine Schriftkolumne gestaltet war. Offensichtlich empfanden die Drucker diese nützliche Zufügung als Beeinträchtigung des Schriftbildes. Sie vermieden nämlich die Lagensignatur auf der ersten Seite des Textes, die auch keine Blattzählung trägt. Die Blattzählung war eine Zutat, die von den gelehrten Mitarbeitern der Druckoffizinen für notwendig erachtet wurde, als sie damit begannen, Inhaltsübersichten und Register zu erarbeiten, die gedruckt den umfangreichen Werken beigegeben wurden. Solche Nachschlagehilfen fertigte sich im handschriftlichen Buch der Leser selbst an, insbesondere dann, wenn er die Abschrift eigenhändig vorgenommen hatte.

Schließlich ergänzten die Typographen das Buch des 15. Jahrhunderts durch einen Hinweis auf seine Herkunft. Um auf ihre Offizin aufmerksam zu machen, gaben sie im Druckvermerk ihren Namen an, manchmal sogar mit der Adresse der Werkstatt. Einige von ihnen fügten als Firmenzeichen eine Druckermarke oder ein Verlagssignet hinzu, in Anlehnung an die Schlußschrift der Schreiber am Ende des Werkes. Auch nutzten sie die erste Seite des Buches, die zum Schutz des Textes gegen Verschmutzung beim Transport oft unbedruckt blieb, allmählich als Titelblatt.

Diese und andere Veränderungen gegenüber dem handschriftlichen Buch waren in der Ausbildung und Entwicklung begriffen, als Johann Snell zu drucken begann. Was wir über das Leben und Schaffen des Erstdruckers Dänemarks und Schwedens wissen, verdanken wir in der Hauptsache älteren Forschergenerationen. Sie machten auf die von Snell gedruckten Werke aufmerksam, beschrieben die wenigen noch erhaltenen Exemplare und forschten nach urkundlichen Nachrichten.

Leider ist der Überlieferungsstand noch immer ungünstig. Johann Snell hat sich nur selten als Drucker genannt. Zudem ist ein Teil seiner Druckproduktion lediglich in defektem Zustand auf unsere Tage gekommen, und gerade die letzten Blätter, auf denen ein Impressum zu vermuten wäre, sind nicht erhalten geblieben oder aufgefunden worden. Nachdem Johan Willem Holtrop (1806-1870), Henry Bradshaw (1831-1886), Robert Proctor (1868-1904) und Konrad Haebler (1857-1946) die Methode der exakten Untersuchung der Drucktypen des 15. Jahrhunderts entwickelt hatten, war es möglich, Druckwerke, deren Urheber sich nicht genannt haben, durch Vergleichen mit voll firmierten Drucken einer bestimmten Offizin zuzuweisen. Seitdem haben insbesondere Christian Bruun (1831-1906), Hans Ostenfeld Lange (1863-1943), Isak Collijn (1875-1949) und Bruno Claussen (1880-1958) Druckwerke namhaft gemacht, die aus den Werkstätten Johann Snells hervorgegangen sind. Lebensnachrichten über Snell steuerten Friedrich Bruns (1862-1945) und Bruno Claussen bei.[1] Einige wenige kleine Drucke Snells sind noch entdeckt worden im Zusammenhang mit den Arbeiten am Gesamtkatalog der Wiegendrucke, die 1904 an der Königlichen Bibliothek zu Berlin begonnen wurden und von der Deutschen Staatsbibliothek Berlin/DDR fortgesetzt werden. An diesem großen bibliographischen Unternehmen zur möglichst vollständigen Erfassung und Beschreibung aller Drucke des 15. Jahrhunderts haben Bibliothekare aus den skandinavischen Ländern tatkräftig mitgewirkt. Victor Madsen (1873-1941) von der Königlichen Bibliothek in Kopenhagen hat bis zum Ausbruch des zweiten Weltkrieges Korrekturen für den Gesamtkatalog der Wiegendrucke gelesen, ebenso der schwedische Reichsbibliothekar Isak Collijn, der als Vorsitzender der Gesellschaft für Typenkunde des 15. Jahrhunderts zahlreiche Seiten aus Johann Snells Drucken reproduziert und damit Beispiele von Snells Werk veröffentlicht hat. Die in der Dansk Bibliografi von Lauritz Nielsen niedergelegten Ergebnisse aller dieser Forschungen und der erste Band von Isak Collijns Sveriges Bibliografi sind die Grundlage der folgenden Ausführungen; sie sollen ergänzt werden durch Erkenntnisse über die Verhältnisse im Buchgewerbe des 15. Jahrhunderts, die sich aus der Arbeit am Gesamtkatalog der Wiegendrucke ergeben haben.

Johann Snell begann seine Druckerlaufbahn in Lübeck. 1480 erschien dort ohne Angabe von Ort und Drucker, aber zweifellos in der Hansestadt von Snell hergestellt, die Schrift des Leipziger Theologieprofessors Nicolaus Weigel »Clavicula indulgentialis« (Hain 5403).[2] Snell druckte diese Abhandlung über den Ablaß auf Bogen eines kleinen Folio-Formats noch ohne Lagenbezeichnung in zwei Spalten zu 48 Zeilen je Seite. Als Textschrift verwendete er eine kleine, raumsparende Type, von der 20 Zeilen 81 mm messen, wie sie seit etwa 1480 in Druckoffizinen allmählich in Gebrauch kam, um den Papierbedarf einzuschränken und die Herstellungskosten zu senken. Diese erste Type Snells scheint dem Druckmaterial der Fratres vitae communis in Rostock ähnlich zu

---

[1] Die ältere Literatur verzeichnet Collijn, Isak: Katalog der Inkunabeln der Kgl. Bibliothek Stockholm. T. 2: Schweden, H. 1: Johann Snell 1483-84. Stockholm, 1916, S. 15. – Der gegenwärtige Wissensstand (einschließlich Liste der Snell-Drucke) wird dargelegt von Riising, Anne: Johann Snell. In: Bogvennen 1982 S. 21-30.

[2] Die den Titeln in Klammern beigefügten bibliographischen Nachweise sind zu identifizieren über die »Abkürzungen für angeführte Quellen« im Gesamtkatalog der Wiegendrucke (GW). Bd. 1. Leipzig, 1925, S. XXIII-XXXI bzw. Bd. 8. Berlin (usw.), 1972, S. x14-x38.

sein, das diese in den Jahren 1476 und 1477 benutzten. Deshalb wurde die Vermutung geäußert, der Drucker der Rostocker Fraterherren sei Johann Snell gewesen. Dies ist durchaus möglich. Die beiden Typen unterscheiden sich jedoch grundsätzlich voneinander. Die Rostocker Schrift ist ihrem Charakter nach eine Goticoantiqua mit gotischen und romanischen Buchstabenformen, die von Peter Schöffer als »littera Moguntie« in den Buchdruck eingeführt und in deutschen Druckwerkstätten in vielen Variationen zwei Jahrzehnte lang angewendet wurde. Snell aber druckte sogleich mit der um 1480 modernen Rotunda, der in Norditalien ausgebildeten Form der gotischen Buchschrift. Lukas Brandis hatte diese »littera Venetiana« genannte Schrift, die den Zeitgenossen als gut lesbar galt, 1477 in zwei verschiedenen Größen geschaffen für den Druck des Breviarium Lubicense (GW 5374). An der Ausführung dieses bedeutenden, umfangreichen Druckauftrages im Jahre 1478 war Johann Snell vermutlich beteiligt. Er stand jedenfalls mit Lübecks Erstdrucker in Verbindung, denn von Brandis erhielt er die Lettern der Auszeichnungstype, mit der die Kapitelüberschriften in des Nicolaus Weigel »Clavicula« hervorgehoben sind, und von Brandis auch hatte er jenen großen Initialbuchstaben mit dem Lübecker Wappen, der das ebenfalls in Type 1 hergestellte lateinische Psalterium (Bohatta: Lit. Bibl. 860) einleitet und Johann Snells Drucktätigkeit in Lübeck bezeugt.

Die Lübecker Ausgabe von Weigels »Clavicula« ist der einzige von Snells Drucken, der in mehreren Exemplaren überliefert wurde. Die erhaltenen Exemplare werden in Bibliotheken aufbewahrt, die zum Teil auf Büchersammlungen des 15. Jahrhunderts zurückgehen. Wir können daraus auf die Handelsverbindungen schließen, die Snell für den Absatz dieses Druckes zu nutzen vermochte. Das Buch wurde im Bereich des hansischen Städtebundes verbreitet und gelangte nachweislich nach Hamburg, London, Danzig und Reval, darüber hinaus nach den skandinavischen Ländern, wo es heute in Kopenhagen, in Oslo und in Upsala vorhanden ist. Von Lübeck wurde es landeinwärts nach Köln und Magdeburg geführt, vermutlich über Danzig nach Cottbus und Posen, weiter südlich nach Liegnitz und Breslau bis hin nach Prag und Budweis, also nach Schlesien, Böhmen und Mähren. Johann Snell hat sicherlich lange warten müssen, ehe das Geld für die verkauften Exemplare bei ihm eintraf.

Zu den frühen Lübecker Drucken Johann Snells gehören eine Bulle von Papst Sixtus IV., 1479 zugunsten von Riga gegen Übergriffe des Deutschen Ordens erlassen, die der nach Livland zurückkreisende Kanonikus und Prokurator Degenhard Hillebolt während seines Lübecker Aufenthaltes veröffentlichen ließ (Hain 14804), ferner Ablaßbriefe zum Besten des Kampfes gegen die Türken und der Verteidigung von Rhodos, die der Johanniter Johannes de

Cardona als Ablaßkommissar 1481 in Auftrag gab (Einblattdrucke 785-788), und 1482 weitere Ablaßbriefe für Hinricus Kannengeter, den Subkommissar des von den Franziskanerobservanten verkündeten Türkenablasses (Einblattdrucke 810, 811). In niederdeutscher Sprache druckte Snell um diese Zeit die Legende von der wunderbaren Meerfahrt des heiligen Brandan (GW 5012) und ein Bedebock (Borchling-Claussen 47), in dem er bereits gedruckte Lagensignaturen zur Anwendung brachte. Johann Snells bedeutendste Lübecker Druckwerke sind Diurnalia, Auszüge aus dem Brevier für die Tagzeiten, von denen zwei Ausgaben (GW 8565, 8566) nur in Bruchstücken erhalten sind; das Diurnale Lubicense (GW 8542), 360 Blätter im Oktav-Format stark, läßt Rückschlüsse zu auf den Umfang der nur fragmentarisch überlieferten Ausgaben und beweist, daß Snell innerhalb von zwei Jahren ein leistungsfähiger Drucker geworden war.

Aus diesem Überblick über seine Produktion geht hervor, daß Johann Snell von Anfang an im wesentlichen als Auftragsdrucker gewirkt hat. Er führte die Mehrzahl seiner Druckwerke auf Bestellung kirchlicher Kreise aus, das heißt: Er erhielt die Auslagen für Papier zurückerstattet und wurde für seine Arbeit bezahlt. Zweifellos gehörte Snell zu jenen Druckern des 15. Jahrhunderts, die über eigenes Kapital nicht verfügten. Den aus seiner Arbeit in Lübeck erzielten Erlös verwandte Snell zur Anschaffung einer neuen, 94 mm messenden Texttype im Rotundastil. Er rüstete sich damit für die Übernahme einer neuen Aufgabe, für den Druck des Breviarium Othoniense.

Das Brevier, das liturgische Buch für das kirchliche Stundengebet, das jeder Priester täglich betet und das in Domkirchen und Klöstern als gemeinsames Chorgebet verrichtet wird, setzt sich aus Texten verschiedenen Inhalts zusammen und enthält Anweisungen, nach denen das tägliche Offizium den Festen des Kirchenjahres und den Heiligenfesten entsprechend zusammenzustellen ist. Im handschriftlichen Brevier wurden bestimmte Textstellen von Lesungen, Psalmen und Orationen durch kleinere Schrift abgehoben und die Anweisungen, die Rubriken, ihrem Namen gemäß in roter Farbe ausgeführt. Der Druck eines Breviers stellte hohe Anforderungen an das Können des Druckers und verlangte größte Aufmerksamkeit und Gewissenhaftigkeit beim Satz des Textes. Nicht ohne Grund wurde die Drucklegung eines Breviers meist von einem mit der Herausgabe betrauten Geistlichen überwacht.

Zum Drucke eines Breviers für den Bischofsstuhl Fünens wurde Johann Snell nach Odense berufen. Die von ihm in Lübeck herausgebrachten Diurnalia dürften für seine Berufung mitbestimmend gewesen sein, auch wenn sie – da mit nur einer Type ausgeführt – satztechnisch den Ansprüchen nicht gerecht wurden. Nach dem Vorbild des Lübecker Breviers von 1478 (GW 5374) hat Snell das Brevier für die Diözese Odense der handschriftlichen Vorlage entsprechend in zwei Schriften unterschiedlicher Größe gesetzt und gedruckt (GW 5418). Seine Texttypen haben verschiedene Kegelhöhen, so daß Snell Mühe hatte, die beiden Schriftkolumnen einer Seite auf die gleiche Länge zu bringen. Die für das Brevier obligatorischen Doppelkolumnen einer Seite sind im Erstdruck des Breviarium Othoniense in der Tat gelegentlich unterschiedlich lang, doch ist die Differenz geringfügig und nicht auffällig. Die Technik des Rotdruckes beherrschte Snell noch nicht. Das Buch mußte deshalb für den Gebrauch erst eingerichtet werden. Zu diesem Zweck wurden die Rubriken nachträglich mit roter Tinte unterstrichen.

Vom ersten gedruckten Brevier für Odense ist nur ein einziges Exemplar erhalten geblieben. Es wird in der Königlichen Bibliothek in Kopenhagen aufbewahrt und ist am Anfang und am Ende leider unvollständig. Auf den ersten, uns unbekannten Blättern stand möglicherweise eine Vorrede des Bischofs Carl Rønnow, auf dessen Veranlassung das Brevier zweifelsohne erschien. Vielleicht enthielt das Buch am Schluß ein Impressum mit Snells Namen. Die Druckausführung durch Snell und die Entstehung in Odense sind mit Gewißheit anzunehmen und werden durch einen kleinen Druck gesichert, in dessen Schlußschrift sich Johann Snell nennt.

Dieser Druck ist die »Obsidionis Rhodiae urbis descriptio« von Guillelmus Caoursin (GW 6010), dem Vizekanzler des Johanniterordens, der 1480 Rhodos gegen die Türken verteidigt hatte. Sein Bericht über die Belagerung durch die Türken wurde noch im selben Jahr in Venedig, Parma, Brügge, Löwen und Passau gedruckt, 1481 in Spanien und um 1482 in Rom (GW 6004-6009). Snells Ausgabe, laut Druckvermerk 1482 in Odense erschienen und mit der neuen Texttype, die für das Brevier angeschafft worden war, hergestellt, steht wie die anderen Ausgaben auch im Zusammenhang mit der von Sixtus IV. am 12. Dezember 1479 erlassenen Ablaßbulle zugunsten der Johanniter. Die Schrift des Caoursin sollte die Ablaßverkündigung und den Absatz der Ablaßbriefe gewissermaßen publizistisch unterstützen. Der Ablaßkommissar für Deutschland und seine Nachbarländer Johannes de Cardona hatte, wie bereits erwähnt, 1481 während seines Aufenthaltes in Lübeck von Johann Snell Ablaßbriefe drucken lassen, die in vier verschiedenen Ausführungen vorliegen. Es ist anzunehmen, daß Snell die Anregung zur Drucklegung des Berichts, vermutlich auch die Druckvorlage aus kirchlichen Kreisen erhielt. Seine Ausgabe zeigt gegenüber den vorangegangenen Drucken eigenständige Züge. Durch jüngste Entdeckungen in der Königlichen Bibliothek zu Kopenhagen ist erwiesen, daß die Obsidionis Rhodiae urbis descriptio des Caoursin, laut Impressum von Snell 1482 in Odense gedruckt, während einer Unterbrechung in der Drucklegung des Breviarium Othoniense entstanden ist.[2a] Firmierung und Datierung dieses Breviers, im Gesamtkatalog der Wiegendrucke 1932 auf der Grundlage der scharfsinnigen Überlegungen skandinavischer Forscher formuliert (GW 5418: [Odense: Johann Snell, um 1482/83]), sind damit bestätigt.

Neben dem Brevier hat Johann Snell für das Bistum Odense noch eine Agenda[3] gedruckt, wahrscheinlich auch die kleine Sammlung von Predigten für die Sonntage und Heiligenfeste im Laufe des Kirchenjahres, die sich »Vademecum« nennt (Oates 1196).[4] Seine Tätigkeit in Odense stand, soweit wir wissen, ganz im Dienste der Kirche.

Zu derselben Zeit wurde ein Missale Othoniense in Lübeck gedruckt (Copinger 1283a). Ein Exemplar ist nicht erhalten. Nur einzelne Blätter in Stockholm, Kopenhagen und Upsala, alle auf Pergament gedruckt, geben uns Kunde von den Bemühungen des Bischofs Carl Rønnow um die würdige Feier des Gottesdienstes in seiner Diözese. Zu den knapp 40 überlieferten Blättern gehört glücklicherweise das letzte bedruckte Blatt. Der Schlußschrift ist zu entnehmen, daß das Missale unter dem Bischof Carl Rønnow für Odense 1483 in Lübeck mit der Presse gedruckt worden ist.

Die hier verwendeten Typen weisen den Druck als das Werk von Lukas Brandis aus. Es sind die Schriften, die er für das Missale Magdeburgense von 1480 (Hain-Copinger 11321) geschaffen hat: eine kleinere und eine größere Textura, die auf den gleichen Kegel gegossen sind und deshalb selbst innerhalb einer Zeile nebeneinander gesetzt werden können. Die Anforderungen, die an den Drucker eines Meßbuches gestellt waren, müssen mindestens so hoch eingeschätzt werden wie die Aufgabe, ein Brevier zu drucken. Neben den gekuppelten Missaleschriften war die Anfertigung einer großen Kanonschrift erforderlich, und die Schwierigkeiten des Druckens mit zwei Farben mußten gelöst werden. Die Schlußschrift des Magdeburger Missale von 1480 nannte die Drucklegung eines Meßbuches eine rühmenswerte Tat und würdigte die Leistung von Lukas Brandis in poetischen Worten, ebenso den Beistand, den er dem Drucker

---

[2a] Laursen, Michael: Tekniske undersøgelser af Danmarks to ældste trykte bøger: Breviarium Othoniense og Descriptio obsidionis urbis Rhodie. In: Nordisk tidskrift för bok- och biblioteksväsen 70 (1983) S. 77-81.

[3] Den Hinweis darauf verdanke ich cand. theol. Merete Geert Andersen, Kopenhagen. – Vergleiche auch Rüsing, Johann Snell, S. 27. – Exemplar vorhanden in London, British Library. – Nach freundlicher Mitteilung von Dr. Lotte Hellinga, London, handelt es sich dabei um GW 465.

[4] Exemplare in Cambridge, University Library, und in Wolfenbüttel, Herzog August Bibliothek.

Bartholomäus Ghotan zuteil werden ließ. Ghotan, Inhaber einer Vikarie am Dom, war vom Magdeburger Domkapitel mit der Drucklegung des Meßbuches für die Erzdiözese beauftragt worden. Zu seiner Ausbildung berief das Domkapitel Brandis nach Magdeburg, wo zunächst 1479 ein Missale für die Prämonstratenser (Weale-Bohatta 1669) hergestellt wurde. Bei der Arbeit an dem Prämonstratensermissale, dem ersten in einer deutschen Offizin gedruckten Meßbuch, konnten und mußten Brandis und Ghotan die nötigen Erfahrungen sammeln. Ein neuer Schritt auf dem Wege von der Handschrift zum gedruckten Buch war zu tun. Über eine noch unbekannte Einzelheit kann ich hier berichten. Vermutlich im Spätherbst 1479 hat Lukas Brandis seine Heimatstadt Delitzsch bei Leipzig aufgesucht und der Pfarrkirche St. Peter und Paul ein auf Pergament gedrucktes Exemplar des Prämonstratensermissale für 14 Gulden zum Kauf angeboten. Sein Angebot wurde angenommen. Brandis erhielt 6 Gulden Anzahlung und die Auflage, das Buch gebunden und mit Beschlägen versehen sowie mit einem Kanonbild ausgestattet zu liefern. Die Beschreibung des Missale Praemonstratense von 1479 im Manuskript des Gesamtkatalogs der Wiegendrucke enthält keine Notiz darüber, ob ein Kanonbild gedruckt worden ist. Dem Exemplar, das dieser Beschreibung zugrunde lag, fehlte das entsprechende Blatt; es war herausgerissen worden. Unabhängig davon, ob der Druck von 1479 ein Kanonbild vom Miniator oder vom Holzschneider erhalten hatte – mir scheint aus der dem Lukas Brandis erteilten Auflage hervorzugehen, daß ein gedrucktes Kanonbild zunächst nicht vorgesehen war. Das Missale Magdeburgense von 1480 jedoch enthält ein gedrucktes, im Holzschnitt ausgeführtes Kanonbild.

Unter den bisher aufgefundenen Blättern des Missale Othoniense von 1483 ist offenbar keins, das dem Kanon entstammt. So kennen wir die Kanontype dieses Druckwerkes nicht. Wir dürfen uns jedoch eine Vorstellung von ihr machen nach dem Kanon im Missale Upsalense vetus, das von Johann Snell um 1484 in Stockholm gedruckt wurde (Copinger 4260), besser noch nach dem Kanon im Missale Aboense, das Bartholomäus Ghotan 1488 in Lübeck druckte (Hain-Copinger 11253). Brandis hat nämlich bei der Herstellung des Schriftmaterials für die in Magdeburg gedruckten Missalien sowohl für Ghotan als auch für sich selbst Typen hergestellt, die er auch zur Nutzung an andere, zum Beispiel an Snell, weitergab. Bevor Snells Drucktätigkeit in Stockholm behandelt wird, soll kurz erwähnt werden, daß Lukas Brandis 1497 zusammen mit seinem Bruder Matthäus Brandis in Lübeck die zweite Ausgabe des Breviarium Othoniense (GW 5419) gedruckt hat. Selbstverständlich ist dabei in Rot und Schwarz gedruckt worden.

Johann Snell

Johann Snells Brevier-Druck für Odense, um 1482/1483 in dieser Stadt ausgeführt und Teil eines umfangreichen Publikationsprogrammes des Bischofsstuhles von Fünen, war durchaus mit Mängeln behaftet und bedurfte darüber hinaus der nachträglichen Rubrizierung. Trotzdem wird der Bischof von Odense zufrieden gewesen sein, konnte er doch die Priester seiner Diözese mit einheitlichen, korrekten Büchern versorgen. Mit dem Breviarium Othoniense hatte sich Snell ein weiteres Mal als Drucker liturgischer Bücher empfohlen. Wir wissen nicht, ob Snell nach Schweden berufen wurde oder aus eigener Initiative nach Stockholm ging, wo er die große Aufgabe übernahm, ein Missale für Upsala zu drucken.

Zunächst jedoch brachte Snell am 20. Dezember 1483 in Stockholm den »Dialogus creaturarum optime moralisatus« des Mailänders Maynus de Mayneriis (Hain-Copinger 6128) heraus. Dies ist eine der im Mittelalter so beliebten Sammlungen von Fabeln und Erzählungen mit Nutzanwendungen. Jeder der 122 Dialoge ist nach einem einheitlichen Schema aufgebaut: Der Fabel, die mit einer gereimten Sentenz schließt, wird die moralitas, die Nutzanwendung gegenüber gestellt, die Zitate und Beispiele aus der Bibel, den Kirchenvätern, aus klassischen und mittelalterlichen Autoren anführt. Solche Exemplasammlungen wurden für Predigtzwecke zusammengestellt und dienten auch der eigenen erbaulichen Lektüre, sofern der Leser zu den »litterati« gehörte, die Latein verstanden. Snell hat dieses Buch mit einer neuen, sehr großen Textschrift gedruckt, von der 20 Zeilen 128 mm messen. Der Umfang beträgt 157 Blätter im Quart-Format. Ersichtlich hat Snell mit dem »Dialogus« ein Buch schaffen wollen, das hohen Ansprüchen gerecht werden sollte, das für ein kaufkräftiges, zahlungsfähiges Publikum bestimmt war. Die Type ist eine schöne Textura von Lübecker Schnitt. Bedeutende Holzschnittinitialen in drei verschiedenen Größen, originelle Lombarden und 18 verschiedene Rubrikzeichen werden als reicher Schmuck zur Anwendung gebracht. Jede Fabel wird durch einen Holzschnitt versinnbildlicht. Als Vorlage diente Snell eine der lateinischen Ausgaben, die Gerard Leeu 1480 und 1481 in Gouda herausgebracht hatte (Hain 6124, 6125). Auch die Holzschnitte der Goudaer Ausgabe sind kopiert und verkleinert wiedergegeben worden. Dabei hat der Zeichner das Bild seitenrichtig kopiert. Infolgedessen haben die dargestellten Figuren, zum Beispiel Mond und Sonne auf Blatte 13a, dem Textbeginn, die Plätze getauscht, und die Dialogüberschrift befindet sich im Widerspruch zur Darstellung des Holzschnittes. Dieser Fehler wird den Absatz des Buches gewiß nicht geschmälert haben; er zeigt aber, daß sich jeder Drucker des 15. Jahrhunderts vor immer neue Aufgaben gestellt sah, wenn er eine für ihn neue Buchgattung, in diesem Falle ein Holzschnittbuch, herausbringen wollte.

Einer solchen neuen Aufgabe, der kompliziertesten, die es gab, stellte sich Johann Snell, als er den Druck eines Missale für Upsala in Angriff nahm. Auch von diesem bedeutenden, umfangreichen und großen Buch ist kein Exemplar erhalten geblieben. Gustaf Edvard Klemming hat 1860 und später aus alten Archivalien-Umschlägen Exemplare, wenn auch unvollständig, rekonstruieren können. Diesen seinen Bemühungen sind übrigens auch die Blätter aus anderen liturgischen Büchern der nordischen Diözesen zu verdanken. Wir wissen also nicht mit Sicherheit, wer der Drucker des Missale Upsalense vetus (Copinger 4260) gewesen ist. Wenn Johann Snell der Drucker des Missale Upsalense war, – und ich stimme mit Collijn überein, daß kein anderer Drucker mit größerer Wahrscheinlichkeit namhaft gemacht werden kann – dann hat er eine bedeutende Leistung vollbracht, wenn er auch die Aufgabe nicht ganz dem Standard entsprechend löste, der inzwischen im Druckgewerbe erreicht war.

Alle wichtigen, die wesentlichen Anforderungen sind erfüllt: Das Missale Upsalense ist mit zwei gekuppelten Missaletypen,[5] die auf den gleichen Kegel gegossen sind, ferner einer großen Kanontype und in Rot und Schwarz gedruckt. Die kleinen Mängel bestehen in der Ausführung des Rotdruckes und in der Satzgestaltung, was den einheitlichen Zeilenschluß betrifft. Der Rotdruck war allerdings kompliziert genug. In der Regel haben die Drucker des 15. Jahrhunderts rot und schwarz in zwei Druckgängen gedruckt. Sie setzten zuerst die Textstellen, die in Rot erscheinen sollten, und druckten sie auf der entsprechenden Stelle der Seite ab. Danach setzten sie den Text, der schwarz erscheinen sollte. Das richtige Einpassen war in der Tat ein Problem. Snell half sich, indem er für die roten Textstellen ein wenig mehr Platz vorsah, als nötig gewesen wäre. Merkwürdigerweise sind im Meßbuch für Upsala die Zeilen am rechten Rand nicht einheitlich ausgeschlossen. Am auffälligsten ist diese Erscheinung im Kanon. Er ist in zwei Spalten gesetzt; bei der Größe der Kanonschrift stehen deshalb verhältnismäßig wenig Lettern in einer Zeile. Da inzwischen die Anzahl der Ligaturen und Abbreviaturen, die zu einer Schrift gehörten, bedeutend verringert worden war – zu verdanken den Normierungsbestrebungen der Typographen –, gab es wenig Möglichkeiten zur Variation. Der Wortzwischen-

---

[5] Collijn, Johann Snell, S. 61 f. verweist auf einen Probeabzug mit Text und Typen des Missale Upsalense vetus, der die Sequenz, abweichend von dem fertigen Druck, in der größeren Missaletype zeigt; mit Collijn meine ich, daß diese Probe zurückgewiesen und statt dessen verlangt wurde, die Sequenz wie üblich in kleinerer Schrift wiederzugeben. Mit diesem Probedruck liegt uns ein indirektes Zeugnis vor für einen der Schritte, die zu tun waren bei der Umsetzung des handschriftlichen Kodex in das gedruckte Buch.

raum wurde nämlich noch nicht verändert, um den gleichmäßigen Zeilenschluß zu erreichen. Als Bartholomäus Ghotan wenige Jahre später das Meßbuch für die Diözese Abo druckte (Hain-Copinger 11253), setzte er den Kanon einspaltig und erzielte damit die im Catholicon von 1460 (GW 3182) gepriesene Harmonie der Proportionen.

Nun war aber Johann Snell durchaus fähig, einen gleichmäßigen Zeilenschluß beim Setzen zustandezubringen, wie seine Drucke beweisen, selbst bei der Verwendung der großen Textura. Er hat in Stockholm – außer Ablaßbriefen für Bartholomaeus de Camerino (GW 3436) – mit der größeren der beiden Missaleschriften ein Schulbuch zum Unterricht in der lateinischen Sprache herausgebracht (Collijn: Sveriges bibliogr. 1, S. 38 ff.). Soweit das kleine Bruchstück dies erkennen läßt, ist die Schulgrammatik vorzüglich gesetzt und gedruckt. Man kann deshalb annehmen, daß beim Satz des Missale Upsalense ein ungeübter Setzer, möglicherweise ein Kleriker, beteiligt war, der Johann Snell bei der Drucklegung des Meßbuches zur Hand ging.

An dieser Stelle ist es notwendig, etwa über den Einfluß kirchlicher Kreise auf die Entstehung von Druckoffizinen im 15. Jahrhundert zu sagen. Die Erfindung des Buchdrucks ist gerade von den geistlichen Behörden lebhaft begrüßt worden. Die neue Kunst setzte die Kirche in den Stand, die liturgischen Bücher nach entsprechender Überarbeitung nunmehr unter ihrer Aufsicht in ausreichender Zahl vervielfältigen zu lassen. Die Bestrebungen des Kardinals Nikolaus von Kues um die Reform des Meßbuches sind allgemein bekannt. Erneut wird gegenwärtig die Frage untersucht, ob der Kusaner mit Johann Gutenberg in Verbindung stand, ob nicht als erstes großes Druckwerk ein Missale erscheinen sollte. Einer solchen Aufgabe standen jedoch beträchtliche technische Schwierigkeiten gegenüber. Das Verfahren, mit roter und schwarzer Farbe drucken zu lassen, hatte Gutenberg erfolgreich entwickelt, wie einige Seiten in der Gutenberg-Bibel (GW 4201) beweisen; er mußte den Rotdruck jedoch nach wenigen Bogen aufgeben. Die Mainzer Psalterien von 1457 und 1459 aus der Fust-Schöfferschen Offizin (Hain 13479, 13480) haben außer Rotdruck noch mehrfarbig ausgeführten Initialschmuck. Aber diese technische und künstlerische Höchstleistung blieb eine Ausnahme und ist nicht wieder erreicht worden. Rotdruck verlangten auch die Rubriken der römischen und kanonischen Rechtsbücher, jedoch nur gelegentlich. Der ständige Wechsel zwischen schwarzen und roten Textstellen nicht nur auf jeder Seite, sondern manchmal auch innerhalb einer Zeile entsprach in Brevieren und Meßbüchern nicht nur der Tradition, er war für die richtige Gestaltung des Offiziums unentbehrlich. Erst Ende der 70er Jahre des 15. Jahrhunderts sind in Italien einige wenige

Meßbücher gedruckt worden. Die ältesten gedruckten Missalien diesseits der Alpen entstanden 1479 und 1480 in Magdeburg (Weale-Bohatta 1669, Hain-Copinger 11321) unter wesentlicher Hilfe von Lukas Brandis, dem Lehrmeister von Johann Snell.

Es ist bemerkenswert, mit welchem Eifer die Bischöfe der skandinavischen Diözesen die Möglichkeit ergriffen, liturgische Bücher drucken zu lassen, und welche Wege sie dabei beschritten. Zum Druck des Breviers (GW 5418) war Johann Snell 1482 nach Odense berufen worden, ein Missale für diese Diözese (Copinger 1283a) wurde etwa gleichzeitig in Lübeck bei Brandis in Auftrag gegeben; dort erschien 1497 auch die zweite Ausgabe des Breviers (GW 5419). Nachdem Snell 1484 in Stockholm das Missale für Upsala (Copinger 4260) gedruckt hatte, schloß Bartholomäus Ghotan 1487, wahrscheinlich in derselben Stadt, den Druck eines Rituale und eines Meßbuches (Copinger 4234) für Strängnäs ab und druckte ferner ein Psalterium und ein Rituale für Upsala (Collijn: Sveriges bibliogr. 1 S. 75 ff., S. 82 ff.). Um 1493 wurde vermutlich in Lübeck ein prachtvolles Graduale für den Gottesdienst der Kirche Schwedens (Copinger 2765a) hergestellt, dessen Drucker ein Höchstmaß von Können bewies. Bei Georg Stuchs in Nürnberg, der sich auf den Druck von Liturgika spezialisiert hatte, erschien 1493 ein Brevier für Linköping (GW 5373), 1498 ein Brevier für Skara (GW 5458), während die Breviere für Strängnäs (GW 5467) und Upsala (GW 5499) 1495 und 1496 in Stockholm in der Werkstatt von Johannes Fabri gedruckt wurden. Für Dänemark druckte Matthäus Brandis um 1504 ein Missale in Ribe (Nielsen 184) und 1510 in Kopenhagen ein Missale Hafniense (Nielsen 179). Die Sorge der skandinavischen Bischöfe, die in ungenügender Anzahl vorhandenen, dazu durch häufiges Abschreiben verderbten liturgischen Bücher durch korrekte, dem Offizium angemessene neue Ausgaben zu ersetzen – wie es in der Vorrede des Missale Aboense von 1488 (Hain-Copinger 11253) heißt –, hatte selbstverständlich Auswirkungen auf das geistige, literarische und kulturelle Leben, zunächst der Städte und in der Folge auch des umliegenden Landes.

Johann Snell hat in Odense und in Stockholm nicht nur liturgische Bücher gedruckt, sondern auch Bücher für Laien, wenn auch vorerst noch für gelehrte Laien. Bei der Auswahl der Texte, die er neben Brevier und Meßbuch drucken konnte, war er abhängig von den Drucktypen, die ihm zur Verfügung standen, denn für die Wiedergabe bestimmter Texte war eine entsprechende Schrift verbindlich.[6] Der Einsatz der richtigen Mittel entschied über Erfolg oder Mißer-

---

[6] Altmann, Ursula: Zur Schriftentwicklung bei deutschen Inkunabeldruckern. In: Studien zur Buch- und Bibliotheksgeschichte. Hans Lülfing zum 70. Geburtstag. Berlin, 1976, S. 60-72.

folg einer Druckauflage, da der Leser sein Buch in der gewohnten Ausführung erwartete. Erst nachdem Snell Missaleschriften, also Texturschriften angeschafft hatte, die von der Kirche bestellt und sicherlich auch bezahlt worden sind, konnte er daran gehen, den Dialogus moralisatus seiner Vorlage gemäß zu drucken, nämlich in der sogenannten »black letter«. Auch für die Herstellung der lateinischen Schulgrammatik war die gotische Textura üblich.

Sodann ließen die Drucker am Ort ihrer Wirksamkeit einen Teil ihres Druckmaterials zur späteren Nutzung zurück. Johann Snell hat, soweit wir wissen, als Drucker in Dänemark oder Schweden nach 1485 nicht mehr gearbeitet; sein Druckmaterial jedoch wurde von 1510 an von Paul Grijs in Upsala benutzt. Schriftmaterial von Bartholomäus Ghotan und eine Druckerpresse waren im Kloster Vadstena aufbewahrt und wurden 1495 ein Raub der Flammen, als in der Krankenstube des Klosters ein Brand ausbrach. Lettern aus vier Schriften des Matthäus Brandis gingen in den Besitz von Poul Raeff in Kopenhagen über, der seit 1513 damit druckte.

Schließlich kamen die Drucker nicht ohne Bücher an ihren neuen Tätigkeitsort. Bei dem Schadensfeuer in Vadstena verbrannte auch eine Tonne mit Büchern, die Bartholomäus Ghotan gehörte. Als Ghotan 1493 über Åbo nach Nowgorod reiste, führte er eine Kiste mit Büchern mit sich. Sowjetische Sprach- und Literaturwissenschaftler und Slawisten der DDR haben eine Anzahl jener Bücher ermitteln können: die Kölner niederdeutsche Bibel von 1478 (GW 4307 oder 4308), ein 1492 in Lübeck gedrucktes Kräuterbuch (Hain-Reichling 8957) und ein sonst verschollenes, von Ghotan gedrucktes »Zwiegespräch zwischen dem Leben und dem Tod« (Borchling-Claussen 82), vielleicht auch die niederdeutsche Ausgabe der Historia destructionis Troiae, gedruckt von Lukas Brandis (GW 7240), und den Lucidarius in Niederdeutsch, Lübeck 1485 (Hain 8815).[7] Ghotan hatte sich dem russischen Großfürsten Iwan III. zu Diensten verpflichtet und war auch in Beziehungen getreten zum Erzbischof von Nowgorod. Ghotan kam in Nowgorod ums Leben, vermutlich im Zusammenhang mit Tumulten bei der Schließung des Hansekontors 1494; die von ihm eingeführten Bücher wurden in Rußland nachweislich benutzt: Die niederdeutsche Bibel diente neben einer lateinischen Vulgata als Grundlage für die erste vollständige russisch-slawische Bibelübersetzung um 1500, die russische Übersetzung des Kräuterbuches wurde 1533 in Moskau von dem Lübecker Arzt Nikolaus Bülow abgeschlossen, von dem Zwiegespräch zwischen dem Leben und dem Tod existiert eine in Nowgorod angefertigte Übersetzung in die altrus-

---

[7] Raad, Harald: Zu einigen niederdeutschen Quellen des altrussischen Schrifttums. In: Zeitschrift für Slawistik 3 (1958) S. 323-335.

sische Sprache, die jetzt in der Saltykow-Schtschedrin-Bibliothek in Leningrad aufbewahrt wird – dies als ein Beispiel für die Wirkung gedruckter, eingeführter Bücher.

Als Buchführer und Buchbinder hat sich Johann Snell seit 1485 hauptsächlich betätigt, abgesehen von einem Breviarium Dominorum Teutonicorum (GW 5234), das er nach seiner Rückkehr aus Dänemark und Schweden noch druckte. Liturgische Bücher hatten einen festen, regional begrenzten Abnehmerkreis; um den Absatz aller anderen Werke mußten sich die Drucker sehr bemühen. Sie nutzten zunächst bereits bestehende Handelsbeziehungen und übergaben ihre Erzeugnisse Fernhandelskaufleuten. Bedeutende Druckoffizinen bauten ihren eigenen Vertrieb auf. Schon die Firma Fust und Schöffer hatte ihre Drucke über weite Entfernungen hin bis nach Frankreich und, über Mittelsmänner, von Lübeck aus nach Riga und Reval abgesetzt. Ausgedehnte Buchführerrouten entwickelten Adolf Rusch in Straßburg, Anton Koberger in Nürnberg und Peter Drach in Speyer. Die große Druck- und Buchhandelsgesellschaft Johann von Köln, Nicolas Jenson und Genossen, zu der Peter Ugelheimer aus Frankfurt gehörte, verfügte um 1480 nicht nur über weitreichende Geschäftsbeziehungen in Italien, sondern mit dem Buchführer Johann Ewiler über Handelsverbindungen bis hinauf nach Lübeck. Ewiler ließ sich 1482 in Lübeck nieder und beschäftigte zwei ebenfalls zugewanderte Gesellen mit dem Einbinden von Büchern; das führte zu einer Klage der Lübecker Buchbinder vor dem Rat der Stadt wegen des Schadens, den diese Konkurrenz verursachte. Seit 1486 übernahm Ewiler Bücherlieferungen von Johann Koelhoff aus Köln. Nach eigenen Aussagen hat Ewiler große Mengen Bücher nach Dänemark, Schweden und Livland ausgeführt.[8]

Bücher, die von Johann Snell eingebunden und von ihm nach Dänemark oder Schweden gebracht wurden, sind bisher nicht benannt worden. Da Snell die beim Drucken angefallene Makulatur aufbewahrte und diese nachweislich als Einbandmaterial verwendet worden ist, könnten weitere Forschungen mit der Untersuchung der historischen Bucheinbände einsetzen. Unter den von Paul Schwenke (1853-1921), Erstem Direktor der Königlichen und Staatsbibliothek Berlin, zu Beginn des Jahrhunderts gesammelten Durchreibungen

---

[8] Grimm, Heinrich: Die Buchführer des deutschen Kulturbereichs und ihre Niederlassungsorte in der Zeitspanne 1490-1550. In: Archiv für Geschichte des Buchwesens 7 (1966) Sp. 1153-1772.

von spätgotischen Bucheinbänden[9] findet sich eine Gruppe von Blindstempelmaterial, das einem »schwedischen Buchführer« zugeschrieben wird. Wahrscheinlich lassen sich solche Bucheinbände in Dänemark und Schweden nachweisen. Es könnten auch die Provenienzen der in Dänemark und Schweden vorhandenen Inkunabeln und alten Drucke zum Ausgangspunkt neuer Untersuchungen gemacht werden, um die Wirkungsgeschichte dieser Bücher zu erforschen. Auch nach Gründung der Universitäten in Kopenhagen (1479) und Upsala (1477) haben junge Nordländer die Universitäten auf dem Festland bezogen und Bücher aus Paris, Rom und Prag, aus Erfurt, Leipzig und Rostock von ihren Studien in die Heimat mitgebracht. Von diesen Büchern, die für Unterricht, Lehre und Verwaltung genutzt wurden, ging zweifellos ein tiefgreifender Einfluß aus, der sich erst später zeigte.

Um mit Odense zu schließen: Um 1478 wurde von Lukas Brandis in Lübeck als Erstausgabe der Marien-Psalter des Alanus de Rupe (Ce^3 R-360) gedruckt, vorgesehen als Anleitung zur Meditation beim Beten des Rosenkranzes; 1515 erschien in Kopenhagen bei Poul Raeff, gedruckt mit Typenmaterial von Matthäus Brandis, »en moghz nytthaelig bog paa danckae« (Nielsen 177), die Übertragung des Psalters in dänische Verse, die Michael (Nicolai), Priester an St. Albani zu Odense, 1492 gedichtet hatte.

---

[9] Schunke, Ilse: Die Schwenke-Sammlung gotischer Stempel und Einbanddurchreibungen, nach Motiven geordnet und nach Werkstätten bestimmt und beschrieben. T. 1: Einzelstempel. Berlin, 1979. (Beiträge zur Inkunabelkunde, 3. Folge; 7)

The Breviarium and the Missale Nidrosiense (1519)

by LILLI GJERLØW

The history of the Nidaros Breviary and Missal is bound up with the history of one man, Erik Valkendorf.[1] He was a younger son of the nobleman Axel Valkendorf of Glorup in Funen. In the 1490s, after university studies in Greifswald, he made his career, not through the ministry, but in the chancery of King Hans of Denmark-Norway († 1513), where he was highly appreciated. From 1506 he was the crown prince, the future King Kristian II's counsel in Norway.

In 1510 Erik Valkendorf was provided with Nidaros, metropolitan See of Norway. The chapter had chosen one of their own, but they were overruled by the King. However, Erik Valkendorf came, saw, and won. Things began to happen. Under his rule the restoration of the octagon of the cathedral, damaged by fire, got under way. In 1512 he visited his huge diocese, sailing to the utmost north, to the fortifications of Vardø *juxta paganos*. The Church of Vardø had been consecrated by Archbishop Jørund in 1307, but since then no archbishop had sailed that far. During his visitation he had occasion to study the liturgical

Abbreviations:
 AV VI = *St. Olav, seine Zeit, und sein Kult* = Acta Visbyensia, VI. Das Visby Symposion 1979 (Uddevalla, 1981).
 BN = *Breviarium Nidrosiense* (Parisius 1519). Facsimile edition by Børsum's Forlag (Oslo, 1964).
 Børsum = B.M. Børsum, *Appendix to Breviarium Nidrosiense...* 2. Bibliographical Survey (Oslo, 1964), pp. 127-221.
 DN = *Diplomatarium Norvegicum*, 1- (Christiania, 1849-)
 LN = Lauritz Nielsen, *Dansk Bibliografi 1482-1550*, I-II (København og Kristiania, 1919).
 MN = Missale Nidrosiense (Haffnie, 1519). Facsimile edition by Børsum's Forlag (Oslo, 1959).
 NTBB = Nordisk Tidskrift för Bok- och Biblioteksväsen, I- (Uppsala, 1914-).
 Ordo = *Ordo Nidrosiensis Ecclesiae* (Ordubók), ed. Lilli Gjerløw (Libri liturgici Provinciae Nidrosiensis medii aevi, II, Osloiae, 1968).
 Renouard = *Imprimeurs et libraires parisiens du XVI*[e] *siècle*. Ouvrage publié d'après les manuscrits de Philippe Renouard, I (Paris, 1964), II (1969), III (1979).

[1] See the monograph of L. Hamre, *Erkebiskop Erik Valkendorf* (Bergen, 1943); for the historical background: O.J. Benedictow, *Fra rike til provins* 1448-1536 (Norges historie, 5; Oslo, 1977).

manuscripts of the churches, and he must very soon have decided to provide them with printed service books.

In the collection of manuscript fragments of the State Archives in Oslo, there are service books destined for use in church, written in the late medieval quadrangular "missal" hand. For the private recitation of the Canonical Hours, the clergy were in duty bound to write their own breviaries. What breviary fragments we have, are written in a rapid cursive "bastard" style, not in the least spectacular. The breviary became Erik Valkendorf's first concern.

Only eight copies are known to exist. There are three in Norway, one in Universitetsbiblioteket, Oslo, another in the Deichman Library of Oslo, a third one in the Library of Videnskabsselskapet in Trondheim. There are two in Sweden, one in Kungliga Biblioteket, Stockholm, which once belonged to Johannes Messenius, another in Läroverksbiblioteket, Skara. There are also two in Denmark, both in Det kongelige Bibliotek, Copenhagen, which once belonged to the collectors Klevenfeldt and Hjelmstjerne. nos. 28 a and b, respectively. And there is one in the University Library of Greifswald which in 1602 belonged to Henning Valkendorf, a scion of the same family. As a civil servant in Bergen, Henning Valkendorf administered the property which before the Reformation belonged to the monasteries of St John and St Michael (Munkeliv) in Bergen.

There is no complete copy, except that of the University Library of Oslo, which, however, is partly a reconstruction, made at the instigation of Oluf Kolsrud. In 1910 an incomplete copy was bought in Denmark. In 1914 leaves from this copy were used to supplement the Oslo University Library copy; the remainder of it was ceded to Trondheim. Forty-six leaves were reproduced from Messenius' copy, from Copenhagen 28 a, and from Henning Valkendorf's copy.[2] This reconstructed copy was used by the antiquarian B.M. Børsum for his facsimile edition of 1964. Together with it went an Appendix in two parts: a general introduction by H. Buvarp, and a study of the printing and the decoration of the Breviary by Børsum himself.

For the typographical description of the Breviary, see LN no. 28, and Renouard III, no. 599. As regards the contents of the book, the following survey may be useful. In my editions of the Nidaros liturgy, I have referred to my (invisible) pagination of the Breviary and the Missal.[3]

---

[2] Oluf Kolsrud, "Vår eldste trykte bok. Breviarium Nidrosiense Paris 1519," in *Norsk Boktrykkalender 1919* (Kristiania, 1919), pp.133 sq.

[3] For a concordance, see the bibliography of the *Ordo*, p. 18 and p. 22.

p. 1: title page;

p. 2: woodcut of St Olav;

pp. 3-6: Erik Valkendorf's foreword, dated April 1, 1516;

pp. 7-13 (red + j. recto – iiij. recto; in the Breviary wrongly: iij): *De officio diuino et horis canonicis per aduentum annuatim dicendis... Dominica die. Littera dominicalis. E...*

Such tables appear in the late twelfth century, but their general spread was due to the Franciscans, who incorporated them in their service books; see S.J.P. van Dijk & J. Hazelden Walker, *The Origins of the Modern Roman Liturgy*, pp. 354 sqq. However, in our case the Sarum *pica* seems to be the relevant model; see *Breviarium Ecclesiae Sarum*, ed. F. Procter & Chr. Wordsworth, I (Cambridge 1882/1970), pp. i-iv; III (1886/1970), pp. lxiij sqq.

pp. 13-14 (red +.iiij). A *nota* that the gradual psalms, by five and five, followed by a prayer, should be used at the Little Hours of St Mary's feasts and at the Saturday Marian Office, actually as found in most fifteenth-century Hours of Our Lady; next, four mnemotechnical hexameters of catchwords for the inception of the Old Testament Offices from Trinity to Advent;

pp. 15-338 (A.j – T.viij + U.j-x): The Temporal from Sunday 1 in Advent to Sunday 25 after Trinity;

pp. 339-340 (black +.j): *Swo skulo helgor och fastor haldas i Nidros biscopsdøme*, a list of holidays and fastdays to be observed, which is actually the first Norwegian text to appear in print;

pp. 341-356 (black +.ij-viiij, in the Breviary wrongly: vij): Calendar with pascal tables, etc. At the end of most pages containing the calender, a *nota* gives rules for the celebration of certain feasts;

pp. 357-358 (black +.x): *De laude virtute et efficacia psalmorum. Regius sic inquit propheta dauid... Et hec de laude et virtute psalmorum sufficiunt.* This is Alcuin's *De Psalmorum Usu*, see *Patrologia latina*, CI, cols. 465 sqq. For the manuscript tradition, see J.-B. Molin, "Les Manuscrits de la *Deprecatio Gelasii*," *Ephemerides Liturgicae*, XC (Roma 1976), pp. 113-148. Part of it is found in Icelandic translations *c.*1500, ed. Oluf Kolsrud, *Messuskýringar* (Oslo 1952), pp. 79 sq. It also appears quite often in the early printed service books, e.g. *Psalterium Upsalense* 1510; see I. Collijn, *Sveriges bibliografi indtil 1600*, I (Uppsala 1934-38), pp. 202 sqq.; and also in the Sarum Breviary, op. cit., II (1879/1970), pp. xxiii sq.;

pp. 359-489 (a.j – i.ij): the liturgical Psalter, followed by *Memorie beate virginis Marie post completorium*; *Benedictiones matutinarum*; *Letania*; *Vigilie mortuorum*;

pp. 491-552 (aa.j – dd.vij): the Common of the saints, followed by *Commemoratio crucis per annum*, and *Commemoratio beate Marie virginis per annum*;

pp. 553-882 (dd.viij – zz.viij + aaa.j – bbb.iiij): the Sanctoral from the Vigil of St Andrew, 29 November, to St Katherine, 25 November, followed by the Office *In dedicatione ecclesie*;

pp. 882-898 (bbb.iiij –ccc.iiij): the proper Offices of St. Joseph, St Canute of Denmark, and St Suithun, patron of Stavanger;

p. 899 (ccc.v.recto): *Quicumque orationem sequentem deuote quotidie dixerit: sine penitentia et mysterio corporis christi non decedet: sic fertur reuelatum beato bernhardo: cui a angelo data est. Aue nobilissima virgo maria ancilla sancte trinitatis...*

This prayer appears in fourteenth-century manuscripts, beginning *Ave Maria ancilla trinitatis*; see G.G. Meersseman, *Der Hymnos Akathistos im Abendland*, II (Spicilegium Friburgense 3, Freiburg S. 1960), p. 172. With the same rubric it also appears in the Danish prayer books *c*.1500, e.g. *Middelalderens danske Bønnebøger*, ed. K.M. Nielsen, III (Copenhagen 1957), no. 421; in Danish, ibid., I (1946), no. 117; and there is a Swedish translation of it in the late medieval Swedish prayer books, ed. R. Geete, *Svenska Böner från Medeltiden* (Samlingar utgifna af svenska Fornskrift-Sällskapet, 38, Stockholm 1907-1909), no. 98.

p. 900 (ccc.v.verso): Joannes (Hans) Reff's account of the printing to the Archbishop, dated July 1, 1519;

p. 901 (ccc.vj.recto): The printers' colophon, dated July 4, 1519, and collation of the quires: *red+*; *A-U*; *black +*; *a-i*; *aa-zz*; *aaa-ccc*; all *quaterni*, except *red +*, which is a *duernus*; *U* and *black +* are two *quinterni*; *i* has two leaves; and *ccc* is a *ternus*.

The title page has survived only in the Greifswald copy. It was discovered by Lauritz Nielsen in 1912.[4] In the lower margin is an owner's note in Danish: This book belongs to me Henning Walkendorff, Anno 1602. The title itself is unusual, with *breviaria* in the plural; it says that these *breviaria*, now printed for the first time, with the utmost care, by the very best craftsmen, by order, and on the costs of Archbishop Erik Valkendorf – these *breviaria accipiunt exordium*. Below are the Archbishop's *insignia* with his coat of arms, a rose surrounded by three

---

[4] Lauritz Nielsen, "Nye Oplysninger om to danske Palæotyper," in *NTBB*, I (Uppsala, 1914), pp. 38-39.

Plate 1. *Breviarium Nidrosiense* 1519. Title page.

wings of swans. Further below four hexameters sing the praise of the Archbishop. It says about this: Behold the *insignia* of the *presul* of Nidaros. Pray do contemplate this great man. For in the whole realm of Denmark there is no nobler or worthier *presul*.

On the verso of the title page is a woodcut of St Olav in Maiestas Domini-style with his axe and the globe surmounted by the cross. He rests his feet and the shaft of his axe on a monster with a crowned head, in fact, a *replica* of the Saint's own head. Underneath, E(ricus) W(alkendorf) A(rchiepiscopus) N(idrosiensis), his coat of arms, and A(postolice) S(edis) L(egatus). Three small woodcuts, Christ in Majesty, with Veronica on his left, another female saint, probably Appollonia, on his right, do not quite fill in the vacant space at the base of the image.

Erik Valkendorf's foreword follows on the next page (3). It takes up two leaves without foliation. This foreword is extant only in Copenhagen 28 a, where it is found attached with glue. But the first page of the foreword also shows the imprint of the frame of the woodcut on the verso side of the title page, now lost.

His foreword is addressed to the clergy of the whole Province of Nidaros, *nostre diocesis et prouincie ubilibet*. With a series of citations from canon law the Archbishop emphasizes his right, and his duty, to uphold the liturgical use of his province. He had realized, he says, that the liturgical books of the churches were in a very bad shape, and for that reason printed liturgical books from foreign uses had been adopted. He mentions those of Rome, Cologne, Utrecht, Lund, Uppsala, Sarum, and also Cistercian, Franciscan, and Dominican books. Therefore he had charged his dean, Petrus Stuth, and his archdeacon, Ericus Johannis, with presenting a corrected and revised copy of the *breviaria*, and his secretary, the canon Johannes Reff, with having the *breviaria* printed in Paris while studying there. This task is now *bene expeditum*; the *breviaria* have been printed with the utmost care, and they are beautifully bound, thanks to great expenditure on his part, and also thanks to the printers, who had worked overtime to accomplish their task. He enjoins all the clergy of his province to acquire a copy of the *breviaria* and grants all the buyers 40 days of indulgence. His foreword is dated: *In Palatio nostro archiepiscopali Nidrosiense ad kalendas Apriles Anno ab incarnatione redemptoris nostri. Mccccxvj.*

On the second-last page of the book Hans Reff accounts for his work to the Archbishop. Now he styles himself *baccalareus utriusque*. He says that as he was himself ignorant of the art of printing, he had addressed himself to the learned Jodocus Badii Ascensii, who had secured for him the services of the skilled printers Johannes Kerbriant, alias Huguelin, and Johannes Bienayse. He dates his account: *Ex chalcographia prescriptorum impressorum apud parrhisiorum Luteciam ad Calendas Julias anno salutis M.d.xix.* He calls the book *breviarium*.

And on the next, the last page of the book, there is the printers' colophon, *Finit breviarium iamprimo impressum... Anno domini millesimo quingentesimo decimonono. die vero Julii quarta,* and their collation, which, however, does not include the two leaves containing the Archbishop's foreword (pp.3-6).

This is the unsolved problem of the Nidaros Breviary. Was a first edition finished, and bound, ready for the Archbishop's inspection, on April 1, 1516?

In his article written in 1919 Oluf Kolsrud says that the problem remains unsolved. Later, in his lectures on the history of the Medieval Church in Norway, he says that the book was printed in 1516, but the edition was held up because three proper Offices should be added to the Sanctoral at the end of the book, those of St Joseph, of St Canute, the national saint of Denmark, and of St Suithun, patron saint of the Church of Stavanger. These lectures, however, were edited posthumously.[5]

Kolsrud probably thought that the addition of these Offices had something to do with the balance of the book. The proper Office of St Erik of Sweden had been included, but not that of St Canute of Denmark; the proper Office of the Saints of Selja, patrons of the Church of Bergen, but not that of St Suithun of Stavanger. It could also be argued that the proper Office of St Anne, Mary's mother, had been entered, but not that of St Joseph, *nutritor Christi*.

The choice of Paris for the printing of the Breviary was not fortuitous. From 1510 to 1515 Christiern Pedersen, canon of Lund, resided in Paris in order to organize the printing of a whole series of books, in Latin and Danish, the latter partly his own works.[6] When Erik Valkendorf and Christiern Pedersen met at the Assembly of the Estates in Copenhagen in 1513, the former contributed to the costs of Christiern Pedersen's edition of Saxo, which appeared in 1514, and

---

[5] See Oluf Kolsrud, *Noregs kyrkjesoga*. I. Millomalderen (Oslo, 1958), pp. 367 sq.

[6] Christiern Pedersen, canon of Lund, publisher and author, though not a printer himself, takes pride of place in Danish printing of his time. His work as a publisher falls into three periods. After his Paris years he returned to Lund. In 1526 he joined King Kristian II, exiled since 1523, espoused the Protestant cause, and served it as a publisher in Antwerpen from 1529 to 1531. After Kristian II's defeat and imprisonment in 1532, he was allowed to settle in Malmø where he could realize his lifelong dream of setting up his own workshop in 1533. It came to an abrupt end in 1335, when, true to the imprisoned King, he made common cause with the burghers of Malmø who rebelled to have him re-instated. See Lauritz Nielsen, "Christian Pedersen og Bogtrykkerkunsten," in *NTBB*, V (1918), pp. 45-60.

the printer was Josse Bade. The same year Christiern Pedersen also brought out the Missale Lundense, the work of a very distinguished printer, Wolfgang Hopylius from Utrecht, by far the most beautiful of the Scandinavian missals (LN no. 181).[7]

A list of the books printed or marketed by Bienayse and Kerbriand, jointly, separately, or with other partners, was compiled by Børsum (pp. 150-175) from Bohatta's bibliography. As regards Bienayse, this list has been superseded by the edition of Renouard's manuscripts, III, nos. 583-600.

Jean Bienayse, a citizen of Rouen, "libraire, imprimeur, et fondeur de caractères", is on record as an exporter of books to England in 1503. In 1506 he has his first book, a Sarum Portiforium (Breviary) printed in Rouen. From 1507 onwards he works exclusively in Paris, for himself or in association with others. From 1516 to 1519 he is associated with Kerbriand for the printing of six books, of which the three last ones, a Cistercian breviary (Renouard III, no. 598), the Nidaros Breviary (no. 599), and a Dominican missal (no. 600), are all dated 1519. His last recorded venture is the printing of a Sarum missal, August 30, 1521, together with two associates (Renouard I, no. 12).

Jean Kerbriand, alias Huguelin, is on record as a printer from 1516 to 1555. The production of both printers consists exclusively of theological and liturgical service books, missals, and, in particular, breviaries.

The Nidaros Breviary has been described as 'one of the most beautiful specimens of its kind', a verdict approved even by Lauritz Nielsen (LN p. XXXI). Some writers have run to the conclusion that our printers belonged to the *élite* of the Paris printers. To the *élite* belonged Josse Bade, who ushers in the golden age of French printing, the epoch of the Humanist scholar-printers who introduced the exclusive use of roman and italic founts for their Latin, Greek and French books. But tradition willed that the liturgical books should follow the late medieval pattern; missals should be set in the style of Gutenberg's Bible, breviaries in a somewhat rounded French-Gothic type.

Børsum (pp. 145 sqq.) is very hard on our printers. Certainly, there are faults in the foliation, as in nearly all the printed books with that complicated foliation, and sometimes, in the transition between red and black print, the masking is not perfect. These defects however, do not spring to the eye from the 451 leaves or the 901 pages of the Breviary. Our printers were conscientious, honest-to-God craftsmen.

The Nidaros Breviary owes its reputation to the great number of woodcut

---

[7] Edited in facsimile by Bengt Strömberg (Malmö, 1946).

initials, frames, and pictures found in it. The initials have all been reproduced by Børsum, pp. 184-187, and so have all the illustrations, pp. 189 sqq.

There are four great heraldic initials (47 x 38 mm), together used twelve times, which must have been cut especially for the occasion:

Plate 2. *Breviarium Nidrosiense 1519. Heraldic initials.*

A (p. 51 = C.iij. recto), with the ARMA S. NIDRO(SIENSIS) ECCLESIE, is used twice;

B (p. 359 = a.j), with ERI. WAL. AR. NI. A. S. L., Valkendorf's *insignia* and coat of arms, is also used twice;

D (p. 390 = b.viij. verso), fourpartite, with the Nidaros arms and Erik Valkendorf's arms diagonally juxtaposed, is used four times. Valkendorf's initials apart, there are also the letters I.R.C.N. in the left-hand corner. What do they mean?
S (p. 86 = E.iiij. verso), with ARMA REGNI NORVE(GIE), is also used four times.

The great *A* may have belonged to Christiern Pedersen, known as a collector of heraldic letters. It turns up in "Det gotlandske Vaterret", printed in 1545 by Hans Vingaard, the printer who bought Christiern Pedersen's material when the latter had to close his Malmø office in 1535 (LN p. 206, Init. æ).

There are seven initials in the next-largest size (*c.*30 x 30 mm), three of them with figures:

Plate 3. *Breviarium Nidrosiense* 1519. Initials.

E (p. 3), with the portrait of a man, is used thrice;
C (p. 444 = f.iij. verso), with St Christopher carrying the Christ-child on his right shoulder, while he feels his way across the stream with his staff, is used twice;
S (p. 264 = Q.v. verso), a bishop with staff and book, is used once;
G (p. 258 = Q.ij. verso), *K* (p. 479 = h.v), and *T* (p. 491 = aa.j), with vegetal ornaments, are used once. Of these, *G* is particularly interesting as it turns up in a print by Johan Hoochstraten, Christiern Pedersen's printer in Malmø from 1533 to 1535 (LN p. 227, Init. u).
U (p. 16 = A.j. verso), slighty bigger than these six, with Erik Valkendorf's initials and coat of arms, used once, must have been cut for the Breviary; there is also a smaller *U* (p. 15 = A.j), used twice, a *replica* of the bigger one, however, without initials and coat of arms.

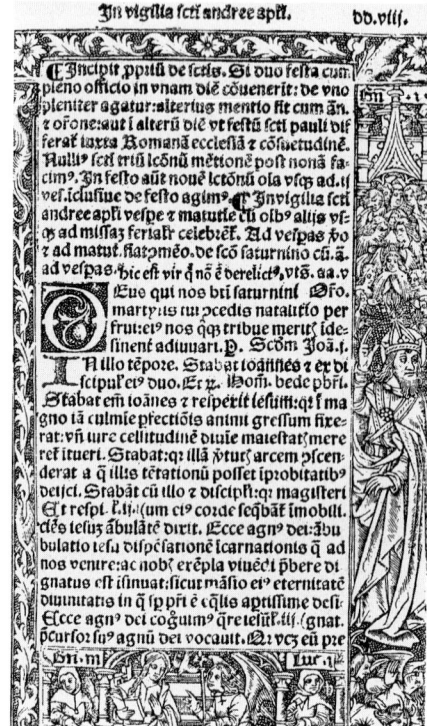

Plate 4. *Breviarium Nidrosiense 1519*,
p. 553 = dd.viij.

The three series of small-sized initials probably belonged to the printers; Børsum found the initial *D* of the third size in their Cistercian breviary of 1519, which is also set in the same type as our Breviary.

The title page apart, there are woodcut frames at the beginning of the Temporal (p. 15 = A.j.), of the Psalter (p. 359 = a.j.), and of the Sanctoral (p. 553 = dd.viij.).

The frame of the title page is decorated with vegetal ornaments where fabulous creatures and animals display themselves. The left-hand stock reappears in the frame at the beginning of the Sanctoral; it is also used in the printers' Cistercian breviary of 1519 together with the end-piece.

The frame at the beginning of the Sanctoral alone has illustrations from the Bible. The right-hand stock shows God the Creator with, above him, the good angels; under his feet, the bad angels ejected from heaven. At the top of the stock is the reference *Gn. i*. The end-piece shows in the middle the Annunciation with

Plate 5. Breviarium Nidrosiense 1519, p. 490 = i.ij. verso.

the Virgin holding a book in her right hand; the scene is flanked by two figures placed between columns. Over the left-hand figure is the reference *Gn. iii*, over the right-hand one, *Luc. i*. The references would seem to bear upon the fall of Eve and the redemption through Mary. But who are the two figures sensed to represent?

The frames at the beginning of the Temporal and the Psalter, without figures, have some stocks in common.

A full-page fourpartite woodcut introduces the Common of the saints (p. 490 = i.ij. verso). It shows Christ with his disciples, the Holy Martyrs, Confessors, and St Mary with the Holy Virgins. The same woodcut, but reversed, and in a smaller size, introduces the Common of the saints of the Lund Missal of 1514, and its printer, Wolfgang Hopylius, also re-used it for his Dominican missal of 1517. Sinding found it in a missal of Cologne, printed in Paris in 1520,[8] and it is also found in Bienayse's and his associates' Sarum missal of 1521.

[8] See O. Sinding, "Breviarium Nidrosiense og dets kunstværd," in *Kunst og Kultur*, 6 (Kristiania 1916-17), p. 100.

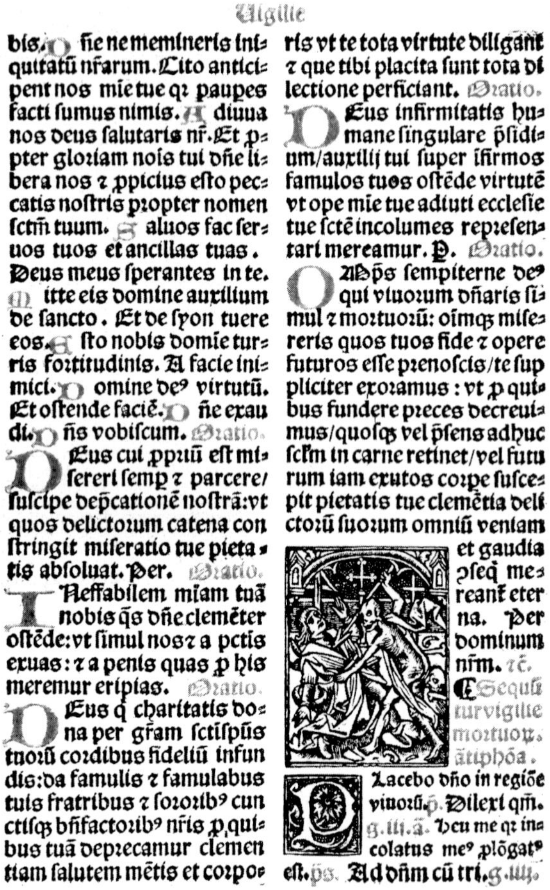

Plate 6. *Breviarium Nidrosiense* 1519, p. 482 = h.vj.

The Commemoration of the Holy Cross *per annum* is also introduced by a full-page, highly dramatic crucifixion scene (p. 530 = cc.iiij.verso).

A small vignette (30 x 23 mm) introduces the Office of the dead (p. 482 = h.vj. verso), Death penetrating a young man with his spear.

"St Bernard's prayer" (p. 899 = ccc.v) is illustrated with a representation of the Virgin with the Child under a canopy between a flute-playing and a singing angel. It measures 80 x 58 mm.

The Breviarium and the Missale Nidrosiense (1519)

Plate 7. Breviarium Nidrosiense, p. 899 = ccc.v.

Sinding and Børsum in their study of the Breviary, as also Strömberg in his study of the Lund Missal, all arrive at the same conclusion: that, in general, the frames and the woodcuts were procured in the Paris market by the printers, who owned them, and re-used them.[9]

There are, however, two more full-page woodcuts in the Breviary which stand apart, executed in another style.

"St Mary in the Sun" introduces her *Commemoratio per annum* (p. 536 = cc.vij. verso). In the late Middle Ages this image must have been familiar to everybody, in particular from the mid 1470s when Pope Sixtus IV published a letter of indulgence carrying this picture with a prayer. A reprint of this letter by Martin Tretter of Danzig, made in 1506, found its way at least to Linköping in

---

[9] For their Roman Missal of 1518, Bienayse and Kerbriand with Jean Adam used a great many illustrations, copied from the Books of Hours of Simon Vostre (Renouard I, no. 10); Bienayse and Kerbriand with Jean II de Marnef and Jean Petit re-used the same illustrations for their Dominican Missal of 1519 (Renouard III, no. 600).

Plate 8. *Breviarium Nidrosiense 1519*,
p. 536 = cc.vij. verso.

Sweden.[10] Hans Reff seems to have had a special relationship to this woodcut, with his name added under the invocation *Succurre virgo Maria*.

The woodcut of St Olav at the verso of the title page also introduces his feast, 29 July (p. 732 = qq.j. verso). Only the small woodcuts at the base are different; here they fill in the whole space. There are five, Christ in glory and the four evangelists with their symbols. St Olav with the crowned human-headed monster under his feet appears in Norwegian monuments around 1400. It was destined to a great future. Up till the Reformation it is the standard representation of St Olav, most often standing, but also seated, carved in wood on the corpus of the altars, painted or carved on their wings.[11] We meet with it in all the

---

[10] See I. Collijn, "Madonna i solen med Sixtus IV:s aflatsbön," in *NTBB*, VI (1919), pp. 62-67; for further bibliography, S. Ringbom, "Maria in sole and the Virgin of the Rosary," in *Journal of the Warburg Institute*, 25 (1962), pp. 326-330.

[11] See E. Engelstad, *Semiddelalderens kunst i Norge* (Oslo, 1936), *passim*. For a modern appreciation, limited to West Norway, see H. von Achen, "Sengotiske Alterskabe i Hordaland. Studier i

Plate 9. *Breviarium Nidrosiense* 1519,
p. 732 = qq.j. verso. See p. 66.

Scandinavian countries and all along the North Sea and the Baltic littoral, which seems to imply that it must have spread from Lübeck. In Norway, we take leave of it on the coins and the seal of Olav Engelbrektsson, the last Archbishop of Nidaros, who died in exile in Brabant in 1538.[12] In Iceland it had a late flowering. We find it in the law-books of the mid-century, but that was in the order of things. The Reformation did not touch Iceland before 1550, and Olav always stood for the law. It is more surprising to find it, in the second half of the seven-

---

senmiddelalderens kunstmiljø," in *Foreningen til norske Fortidsminnesmerkers bevaring. Årbok 1981* (Oslo, 1981), pp. 13-58. With a German Summary.

[12] See C.I. Schive, *Norges Munter i Middelalderen* (Christiania, 1865), Plate XVIII, no. 17 K. Skaare, *Moneta Norwei* (Oslo, 1966, p. 20 (coins); for Olav Engelbrektsson's seal, see Grethe Auténh Blom, *St. Olavs by ca. 1000-1537* (Trondheim bys historie, 1; Trondheim, 1956), p. 472. The seal of the parish church of Löderup in south-east Sweden, dedicated to St Olav, in the first half of the sicteenth century carries the same picture; see T. Eriksson, "Löderupfuntens ikonolavografiska problematik," in *Fra Sankt Olav til Martin Luther*, ed. M. Blindheim (Oslo, 1975), pp. 9-35.

teenth century, painted on the corpus of the alter of the Church of Berufjördur in east Iceland; only the small woodcuts at the base have been replaced by an inscription.[13]

Olav with the crowned monster under his feet has been much discussed. Harry Fett and others with him thought it might symbolize the Saint's old sinful self.[14] Other interpretations are founded upon the two late-medieval "apocryphic" legends, which both quote part of the Nidaros legend verbatim while giving it a new twist.

The so-called Ribe legend, copied by Peder Madssøn, vicar of Ribe in south Jutland, between 1460 and 1465, introduces Olav's heathen brother Harald.[15] After their father's death, Olav, designated heir, and Harald both sail for Nidaros, Harald in the evil intent of robbing his brother of his heritage. Harald gets the advantage of an early start; it is Sunday, and Olav, trusting to God, refuses to leave before the end of the Divine Office. With God's help he sails right through the mountains and arrives in Nidaros three days before his brother. The heathen brother is also the instrument of Olav's exile and death at Stiklestad. The crowned monster, it has been argued, represents Harald, also a king, in the shape of a dragon, symbol of heathendom, of the devil, as expressed in the Norwegian sequence in honour of St. Olav. *Postquam calix Babylonis/ illudentis fel draconis...*[16]

The sail race between Olav and Harald is probably the most popular and the most widespread of the St Olav tales. In Denmark it is represented on the wings of an altar with St Olav carved on the corpus c. 1310 and on wall-paintings both from the fourteenth and the fifteenth century;[17] in Sweden, it is frequently found on the wall-paintings of the second half of the fifteenth century.[18] It is also celebrated in the vernacular ballads and tales which survived the Reformation, with

---

[13] See Elsa E. Gudjónsson, "Sammenhængen mellem nogle islandske religiøse billeder og udenlandske tryk," in ICO = *Den ikonografiske post* 1979 (Stockholm, 1979), no. 4, pp. 22-29. With an English Summary.

[14] See H. Fett, *Hellig Olav Norges evige konge* (Oslo, 1938), which also includes the classic Norwegian statuary of St. Olav.

[15] Ed. G. Storm, "Om en Olavs-legende fra Ribe," in Videnskabs-Selskabets Forhandlinger 1885 (Christiania, 1885), no. 3.

[16] *Analecta hymnica*, 55 (Leipzig, 1922), p. 303, no. 272.

[17] See Ulla Haastrup, "Olav der Heilige in dänischen Wandmalereien," in AV VI (1981), pp. 151-160.

[18] See Mereth Lindgren, "Die Legende vom heiligen Olav in der mittelalterlichen Malerei Mittelschwedens," in AV VI (1981), pp. 135-150.

reminiscences of the pilgrim roads to Nidaros, Compostela of the North.[19]

The so-called Hanseatic legend was described and partly quoted by the Bollandists from a now lost legendary, formerly belonging to St Salvator's Church in Utrecht.[20] The text was first printed in the late medieval "Golden Legends" by Ulrich Zell (Cologne 1483), and by John of Westphalia (Louvain 1485), which latter was reprinted by Storm.[21] In Low German translation, as *Passionael efte Dat Leuent der Hyllighen*, it was printed in Lübeck by Stefan Arndes in 1492, 1499, and 1507, and it was reprinted by Adam Petri of Basel in 1511 and 1517. The Low German text was reprinted by J. Langebek from Stefan Arndes' *Passionael*, printed, according to Langebek, in Lübeck 1505.[22] Could Langebek have read 1505 for 1507? By courtesy of Dr. Ursula Altmann, of the Inkunabelabteilung, Deutsche Staatsbibliothek, it appears that a 1505 edition "lässt sich bibliographisch nicht nachweisen".[23]

The Hanseatic legend improves upon the Ribe legend: there are two sail races. The prize of the second race is the crown of Denmark. Olav sails in a small boat with God's angel as only companion. The Latin texts are not illustrated, while in all the Low-German editions, every single legend is preceded by a woodcut. The Lübeck editions of 1492, 1499, and 1507 all present the same woodcut: Olav in a small boat together with the angel and, over them, in the left-hand corner, God's blessing hand. The height of the woodcut varies from 64 to 72 mm, the width from 63 to 70 mm. In the Basel edition of 1511 it was reworked to fill in the written space of two columns with an ornamental stock on the left; that of 1517 improves on the former in some details.

In the Hanseatic legend Olav, on his return to Denmark (!) from his exile, is captured by Harald and his heathen followers and crucified by them.[24] He

---

[19] St. Olav's sail race even appears in a liturgical hymn, *Procul pulso iam torpore*, used at matins in the Lund and Roskilde breviaries of 1517, with strophe five beginning *Largum iter naviganti rupes scissa prebuit...* See G. Storm, *Monumenta historica Norvegiae* (Kristiania, 1880/Oslo, 1973), pp. 262-263; *Analecta hymnica*, 11, p. 207, no. 381.

[20] *Acta Sanctorum*, Julii, t. VII (1731), p. 89.

[21] G. Storm, *Monumenta*, op. cit., pp. 277-282. See also the Introduction, pp. XXXVIII-XXXXI.

[22] *Scriptores Rerum Danicarum medii aevi*, II (Hafniae, 1773), pp.535-539.

[23] Letter of December 31, 1982.

[24] The crucifixion of St Olav is represented on the wings of a reredos, made in the Hanseatic area (Lübeck?) c. 1500 for the Church of Andenes in North Norway, now in the Tromsø Museum. See P. Reuterswärd, "Mysteriet med de dubbla passionerna," in ICO, op. cit., 1980, no. 4, pp. 21-25. With an English Summary.

submits Christ-like to his fate, revealed to him beforehand by God. After three days on the cross, in the perfect *imitatio Christi*, his body was placed on a pyre by his executors, but when the fire abated, Olav's body was intact. Out of the ashes arose a dragon, *draco terribilis, en groet drake*, who killed Olav's enemies. Therefore, it has been argued, this friendly dragon is represented with Olav's crowned head.[25]

The Low German translator at least had honest doubts about the death of St Olav. After the passage about the crucifixion, the 1492 and all the other prints lodge a mild protest, in short: It is also told that Olav died fighting in the battle of Stiklestad in Norway.[26] However, we have better leave the problem of the crowned monster in the hands of the art historians.[27]

Thus great care was lavished on the Breviary, a small octavo for private recitation, small enough to go into a priest's pocket. The Nidaros Missal, in folio size, destined for the altar, does not seem to have benefited from so much care on the part of the Archbishop. His ever increasing difficulties with the King, and the King's functionaries, may have had something to do with it.

Fifteen copies are known, and there is probably one more, privately owned. Oslo, Trondheim, and Copenhagen have each one complete and two defective copies; the Deichman Library of Oslo has two defective copies; Bergen, London, Paris, and the Villafranca Library in Nice have each one defective copy. They usually have annotations from the churches to which they once belonged. A facsimile edition was issued by B.M. Børsum in 1959, based on the complete copy of Oslo.

There is no mystery about the printing of the Nidaros Missal. It was the work of Poul Reff, canon of Copenhagen, the first native printer of Denmark, and brother of the Nidaros canon, Hans Reff, who supervised the printing of the Breviary in Paris from 1515 to 1519. His activity as a printer comprises three periods; his first, and best, in Copenhagen from 1513 to 1519, culminating with the printing of the Nidaros Missal; a second period in Nyborg, in 1522; and a third period in Århus from 1530 to 1533. During the troubled 1520s and 1530s he kept his faith with the Old Church (see LN pp. XXX sqq.).

---

[25] See M. Blindheim, "St. Olav – ein skandinavischer Oberheiliger. Einige Beispiele der Literatur und der Bildkunst," in AV VI (1981), pp. 53-68: Idem, "Hellig Olav – En skandinavisk overhelgen," in *Olav konge og helgen myte og symbol* (Oslo, 1981), pp. 105-135.

[26] Cited by Storm, *Monumenta*, op. cit., p. XXXX.

[27] For the bibliography of St Olav in general, see *Kulturhistorisk Leksikon for nordisk Middelalder*, XII (1967), pp. 544-550; 561-588; in particular, the article "Ikonografi," pp. 568-579. For more recent contributions, see AV VI (1981), *passim*.

For the typographical description, see LN no. 182. The quires of eight leaves have signatures below the text on the recto of the first four leaves, while the foliation on the top of the leaves, beginning after the first quire, runs from .j. to .xxiv. This is the list of the contents of the book, with my pagination:

p. 1: title page;
p. 2: Poul Reff's foreword;
pp. 3-14: Calendar January-December;
p. 15: *Notata omnium mensium*, identical to those added at the end of the pages containing the calendar of the Breviary, pp. 341 sqq.;
p. 16: *Oratio ante missam dicenda. Oratio post missam*;
pp. 17-352 (a.j. – g.xxiiij. verso): The Temporal, from *Dominica prima aduentus*, to *Dominica antequam aduentus domini incipiatur*;
pp. 353-365 (h.j. – h.vij. recto): *Preparamenta ad missam*, *Gloria*, Credo, *Prefationes*.
p. 366 (h.vij. verso): full-page woodcut of the crucifixion;
pp. 367-382 (h.viij. – h.xv. verso): *Canon missae*;
p. 383-384 (h.xvj.): *Orationes post missam legende*; *Ite missa est*;
pp. 385-490 (h.xvij. – k.xxj.verso): The Sanctoral, from *Vigilia beati Andree*, 29 November, to *Sancte Katherine virginis et martyris*, 25 November;
pp. 490-491 (k.xxj. verso – k.xxij. recto): *Hiis diebus Credo in unum deum cantatur*;
pp. 491-492 (k.xxij. recto verso): *Qualiter officium beate marie ad altare eiusdem celebrandum sit*:
pp. 493-539 (A.j. – A.xxiiij. recto): *Commune sanctorum*;
pp. 539-542 (A.xxiiij. recto – B.j. verso): *In dedicatione ecclesie*; *In dedicatione altaris*;
pp. 542-543 (B.j. verso – B.ij. recto): *In commemoratione sancte Crucis*;
pp. 543-548 (B.ij. recto – B.iiij. verso): *In commemoratione beate marie virginis (per annum)*;
pp. 548-555 (B.iiij. verso – B.viij. recto): *Ordo collectarum tempore quadragesimali*;
pp. 555-562 (B.viij. recto – B.xj. verso): *Ordo collectarum specialium per totum annum*;
pp. 562-568 (B.xj. verso – B.xiiij. verso): *Missa pro defunctis*; *Ordo collectarum pro defunctis*;
pp. 569-570 (B.xv. recto-verso): *In festo visitationis beate marie virginis*;

pp. 570-579 (B.xv. verso – B.xx. recto): *Missa de sancto spiritu*; *Pro paganis et turcis*; *Pro pestilentia*; *In commemoratione omnium sanctorum*; *De Angelis*; *De tribus magis pro peregrinantibus*;

pp. 579-581 (B.xx. recto – B.xxj. recto): *Exorcismus salis et aque*;

pp. 582-605 (B.xxj. verso – C.ix. recto): *Sequentiae* (there are forty-two);

pp. 605-606 (C.ix. recto – verso): *Accidentia circa missam*;

p. 606 (C.ix verso): *Missale secundum usum ecclesie Nidrosiensis finit feliciter. Impressum Haffnie arte magistri Pauli Reff: ibidem Canonici ac sanctissimi domini nostri Pape ad titulum Nidrosiensis ecclesie Accoliti. Anno domini M.CCCCC. xix. Die vero .xxv. Maij.*

The Nidaros Missal distinguishes itself by an almost modern title page. The Archbishop's hand is apparent in the title: *Missale pro usu totius regni Noruegie*, etc.; his coat of arms is the only ornament. However, the short preface on the verso of the title page is written by Poul Reff. He says that the Reverendissimus, etc., had found the manuscripts of the churches *antiquissimi*, written in *desuetis characteribus*; therefore secular priests had adopted Cistercian, Dominican, and Franciscan missals. Now he enjoins Mass to be celebrated in the same way, *uno ore et uno concentu* in the whole ecclesiastical province of Nidaros. To that end he had charged his dean, Olavus Engelberti, and his cantor, Petrus Sigvardi, with producing a corrected and revised manuscript, and me, Poul Reff, with printing it in the best possible way.

Olav Engelbrektsson succeeded Peter Stuth as dean in December 1515, so he could not possibly have started his revision of the Missal before 1516. Yet the Missal was out of press before the Breviary.

When Poul Reff established himself as a printer in Copenhagen, he took over material from Matthæus Brandis, who, in 1510, had printed the Missale Hafniense, his last work after a career of great importance to Danish printing, in his native Lübeck as well as in the Danish dioceses of Ribe and Slesvig. Matthæus Brandis is supposed to have been called to Copenhagen by the chapter for the printing of the Missal. Anyhow, by then he was short of material. He must have intended to introduce each mass by a woodcut initial (43 x 43 mm, see LN p. 177, Init. d), but in the Copenhagen Missal there are only a few such initials on black or red ground; most of the spaces intended for them are left empty. One of these initials reappears in the Nidaros Missal, the initial *S*, used for the introit of Pentecost (p. 251 = e.xxij.).

Poul Reff uses Brandis' Canon- and great and small missal-types for the

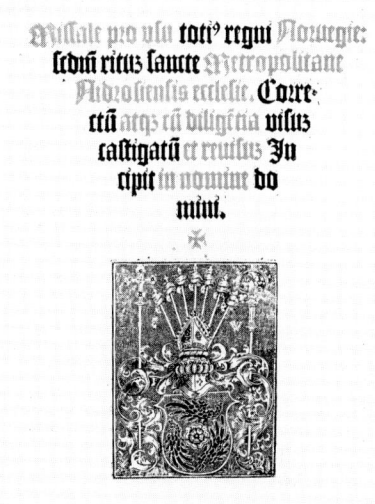

Plate 10. Missale Nidrosiense 1519.
Title page.

Nidaros Missal, and his red Lombard-majuscules, as a rule with perles, and with forms that Lauritz Nielsen found somewhat grotesque.

Poul Reff's own contribution to the Missal are two series of white-on-black woodcut initials, used for the introit, the introductory psalm-verse, of all the masses of the Temporal and of the greater part of the masses of the Sanctoral and the Common. These initials, breaking the monotony of the black and red lettering, are the distinctive feature of the Missal. How much they mean to the general countenance of the Missal can be seen if we put it beside the Hafniense.

There are fifteen initials of the greater size (39 x 37 mm; LN p. 183, Init. f), *B, C, D, E, F, H, I, L, M, O, P, Q, R, S, V*, all with vegetal decoration except *O*, which has a human head in the middle. This *O*, together with *P*, reappear in the work of Hans Barth who settled as a printer in Roskilde in 1534, and who is known to have taken over material formerly belonging to Poul Reff (see LN p. 238 Init. o).

There are sixteen initials of the smaller size (32 x 31 mm; LN p. 183, Init. h); *A, B, D, E, F, G, I, L, M, N, O, P, R, S, T, V*, the *O* again with a human head. The *I* reappears in the work of Hans Barth (LN p. 237, Init. b). These sixteen initials are of the same size as eighteen introit-initials in Christiern Pedersen's Paris-printed Missale Lundense of 1514, and so like them that, though not identical, they must at least be the work of the same craftsman.

A third somewhat smaller (30 x 30 mm) series of initials in the same style is found in the work of Melchior Blumme, who printed in Copenhagen from 1519 to 1520 (see LN p. 189, Init. k), and also in the work of Oluf Ulricksøn, who printed in Malmø from 1528 onwards, and who took over material from Blumme (see LN p. 216, Init. b).

As regards the "new" letters found in the Nidaros Missal, Lauritz Nielsen supposed that they came from Paris (LN p. XXXI). Could Christiern Pedersen have lent a hand in this business? After his return from Paris in 1515 he did not sever his friendly relations with the Paris printers. From Lund he organized the printing of the Lund and the Roskilde breviaries, both executed by Jean Philippe in 1517. Before he left Denmark in 1526, he handed over material to Poul Reff, used by the latter during his third period as a printer, from 1530 to 1533. He may also have had relations with Poul Reff at an earlier stage. Besides, Poul Reff's brother Hans lived in Paris for the years in question, supervising the printing of the Nidaros Breviary.

One of these new letters stands by itself. The great carpet-letter *A* (73 x73 mm) introducing the first Sunday in Advent, with the initials of Erik Valkendorf, his *insignia*, and his coat of arms must also have been ordered especially for the Missal (LN p. 183, Init.g). The same applies to the Crucifixion scene before the Canon, very fine in its simplicity.

The printing of musical notation was still beyond the Copenhagen printers. Note-lines are provided for the Ordinary of the Mass, but not filled in (as they have been in the facsimile edition of 1959). However, the responsibility for the omission of the benediction of the palms on Palm Sunday, of the Adoration of the Cross on Good Friday, of the benediction of the new fire and of the pascal candle with the *Exultet*, as also of the chants of Candlemass, all laid down in the *Ordo*, must rest with the text-editors. One may wonder if a noted gradual-processional, a companion book, had been planned. But the only planned book we hear about was not that. In 1520, April 30, Hans Reff signed a contract with Doen Pieterszon of Amsterdam for the printing of *De stumme Passie*, described as *een bede boeck van die passie ons heren* from an exemplar in his possession. The detailed prescriptions for the decoration of the book would seem to indicate a lavishly illustrated Book of Hours, which, in the circumstances, came to nought (DN VII, no. 552).

The Missal was delivered unbound. In Nidaros there was at that time one

Plate 11. *Missale Nidrosiense 1519, p. 17 = a.j.*

Caspar Bookbinder, likely to have executed the bindings in oaken panels, clothed in goat-skin.[28] Poul Reff's brother Hans administered the stock of the

---

[28] On the bindings of Breviarium and Missale Nidrosiense, see Astrid Schjoldager, *Bokbind og bokbindere i Norge inntil 1850* (Oslo, 1927), pp. 52 sqq., and Plates 4 (the Breviary), and 47-48 (the Missal).

Plate 12. *Missale Nidrosiense 1519, p. 366 = h.vij. verso. Full-page woodcut at the beginning of* Canon Missae.

edition and handed over copies to the parish churches who had paid for them in advance. In 1520, October 31, the Archbishop had a quittance from Hans Reff on behalf of his brother Poul for the remnant of his debts to the latter (DN I, no. 1056).

Erik Valkendorf could not rejoice for long in his new books. By then he had been caught up in the first act of Kristian II's drama. He had done his best to be a loyal servant to the King, negociated his marriage, lent him great sums of money, helped him during his war with Sweden in 1517. But, also a loyal servant of the Old Church, he could not suffer the Archsee's age-old privileges to be stamped out by the King. In 1521 he decided to put his case before the Danish High Council. Before departing, he left his treasury in the hands of the dean, Olav Engelbrektsson, with a list of items available for the continued restoration of the Cathedral. The list includes 120 copies of the Breviary, each valued at three Rheinish gulden (DN VIII, no. 500). Besides, twenty-five copies had been ceded to the newly elected bishop of Skálholt in Iceland, Ögmundur Pálsson.[29]

A storm brought the Archbishop's ship, not to Copenhagen, but to

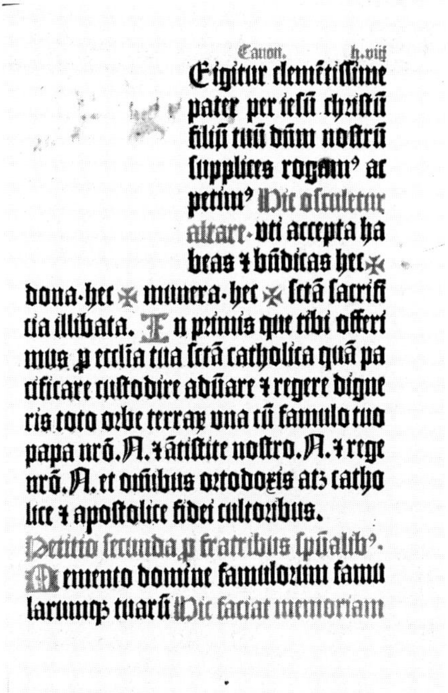

Plate 13. Missale Nidrosiense 1519, p. 367 = h.viij. Beginning of Canon Missae.

Amsterdam, where Kristian II happened to pass on his way to his brother-in-law, the Emperor. After a stormy scene with the King, he decided to appeal to

---

[29] MS AM 680b, 4to is a manuscript of 7 leaves; a stub (with scribbles in Icelandic) adhering to the first leaf may represent the eighth leaf of a regular quaternion. It was written in "missal hand" in the diocese of Skálholt, probably in the 1520s. It contains most of the directions found in the Nidaros Breviary (BN) and Missal (MN). The text ends in mid-page on f. 7r:

> f.1r: *Notata omnium mensium* = MN, p. 15; added separately to the leaves containing the calendar of BN, pp. 341 sqq.
>
> f. 1v: *Nota quod in omnibus festis beate marie uirginis*, etc. = BN, pp. 13-14;
>
> ff. 2r-6r: *De officio diuino et horis canonicis per aduentum annuatim dicendis*, etc. = BN, pp. 7-13, with some additional notes on the feast of St Thorlak, 23 December;
>
> f. 6rv: *Hijs diebus Credo in unum cantatur* = MN, pp. 490-491, except that for *in utroque festo sancti Olaui in ecclesia Nidrosiensi* the Icelandic scribe substitutes *in utroque festo sancti torlaci in ecclesia scaloltensi*;
>
> f. 6v: *Ad alltare* (sic) *beate uirginis Marie hoc mode Credo cantabitur* = MN, p. 491;
>
> ff. 6v-7r: *Taliter ordinetur Officium Ad altare Marie virginis* = MN, pp. 491-492.

Plate 14. *Passionael 1492, fol. 89ᵛ. See p. 67.*

the Pope.[30] He arrived in Rome early in 1522, ill and exhausted, a poor man, with his goods confiscated at home. Letters from the Danish High Council arrived, upbraiding him with having left his diocese. He answered them at length, saying among others: "Nothing could be more contrary to my wishes than that I should not stay with my Cathedral." His letter, his last message, is dated: "Ex Roma communi patria in profesto sancti Valentini martyris," February 13, 1522 (DN I, 1059). He died on 28 November, before the storm broke out at home, and Kristian II, in his turn, became an exile.

---

[30] Before leaving Amsterdam, Erik Valkendorf gave his small, beatifully illuminated Bible, probably written in a workshop of northern France *c*.1300, to his friend and banker Popius Occo. The Bible now belongs to the printing firm Enschede, Stichting Enschede, Haarlem. See J.J. Duin, "Erik Valkendorfs bibel består," in *Norsk Slektshistorisk Tidsskrift*, 29 (Oslo, 1983), pp. 1-12. He gave his Lund Breviary, written on his costs, for the use of poor clerics of Lund, according to a note entered in the manuscript, Lund, Universitetsbiblioteket, cod. 34.

It is unnecessary to insist upon the importance of the printed liturgical books. For one, they were worked out by the most competent churchmen, the members of the cathedral chapters. And they aim at completeness, while the manuscripts, so often copied on old models, tend to leave out the additions to the liturgy made in the course of time.

In Norway, our *Ordo* from the early thirteenth century has survived; we find it embodied in the printed books. But much happened in the course of the three hundred-odd years that separate the *Ordo* from the printed books. Every century has its own climate, reflected in the growth of the liturgical feasts. Manuscript fragments from those centuries are extant, but even if we scrutinized every scrap of fragment, we should never be able to reconstruct more than a fraction of the Nidaros texts. And, it should be remembered, an *Ordo* contains only incipits, so this applies to the contents of the *Ordo* as well. Thus, the Nidaros Missal and Breviary are the unique *summa* of centuries of religious culture.

Erik Valkendorf left his report on the wonders of the North-Norwegian littoral with the Pope.[31] Another illustrious *profuga*, Olauus Magnus Gothus, found it in the Vatican Archives and used it for his *Carta Marina* of 1539, and for his *Historia de gentium septentrionalium conditionibus* of 1555. But Erik Valkendorf's title to perennial glory will always be his rescuing of the Nidaros liturgy, in the nick of time.[32]

---

[31] Arch. Vat., Principi 9, ff. 329-332. Ed. K.H. Karlsson & G. Storm, "Finmarkens Beskrivelse af Erkebiskop Erik Valkendorf," in *Det norske geografiske Selskabs Årbog*, XII (Kristiania, 1900-1901), pp. 1-23, with a facsimile, and with a Norwegian translation and comment.

[32] A second edition of the Breviary was printed for the diocese of Hólar in Iceland at the instigation of its last Catholic bishop, Jón Arason. Its title and colophon are known from a Danish publication of 1740: *Titulus libri*. Breviaria ad usum ritumque Sacrosancte Holensis Ecclesie, jam prius impressa, impensis ac mandatis insignibus, reverendi in Christo patris Domini, Domini Johannis Arneri ejusdem Ecclesie Episcopi felix faustumqve adepta sunt exordium. *Finis libri*. Opus istud impensis ac industria plurimum reverendi in Christo patris Domini Joannis Arneri Sacrosancte Holensis Ecclesie episcopi faustum felicemqve sortitum est exitum finemqve optatum. In residentia sua impressum atqve adauctum Calendas Maji Anno MD.XXX.IIII. It is lost but for two leaves of the Sanctoral from February 10 to 22, which correspond wholly with the Nidaros Breviary, except that for the feast of Cathedra Petri, 22 February, the hymn *Iam bone pastor*, only indicated in the Nidaros Breviary, has been printed in full. See I. Collijn, "Två blad af det förlorade Breviarium Nidrosiense, Hólar 1534", in *NTBB*, I (1914), pp. 11-16; LN no. 26.

(Note added in proof): Seymour de Ricci, *Livres de liturgie imprimés aux XVe et XVIe siècles faisant partie de la Bibliothèque de son Altesse Royale le Duc Robert de Parme* (Paris/Milan 1932), pp. 36-37, no. 73, may be the exemplar of the Nidaros Missal reputed to be privately owned (see above, p. 68) Its present whereabouts are unknown. See further the appendix on p. 168.

Studien zum Wachstum und zur Entwicklung von Bibliotheken in Südostniedersachsen am Ende des 15. und zu Beginn des 16. Jahrhunderts

In memoriam Hermann Herbst
(21.7.1895 – 17.8.1944)

von HELMAR HÄRTEL

Die Zeit zwischen der Mitte des 15. Jahrhunderts und den ersten Jahrzehnten der Reformation im 16. Jahrhundert ist nicht nur für die Geschichte des Buches, sondern auch für die Geschichte der Bibliotheken bewegt und interessant, da in dieser Zeit der Buchdruck seine eigene Wirkungskraft entfaltet. Ich möchte diese Zeit jedoch unter einem *anderen* Gesichtspunkt betrachten. Denn sie ist ohne weiteres als eine gesonderte Epoche mit deutlich markierbaren Charakteristika in der niedersächsischen Bibliotheksgeschichte zu fassen. Ich meine nicht den Humanismus, der Bedeutendes geleistet hat bei der Entdeckung von Handschriften antiker Autoren in den überkommenen Klosterbibliotheken. Man denke an Poggio, der den ahnungslosen Mönchen in Fulda etwa die Germania des Tacitus entführen ließ. Die Tendenzen, die ich meine, sind ganz anderer Art und ihre Initiatoren hatten weder Interesse an noch Verständnis für durch hohes Alter kostbar gewordene Texte, wenn sie nicht ihren unmittelbaren geistigen Bedürfnissen entsprachen. Es fand in dieser Zeit eine Erneuerung bestimmter Klosterbibliotheken statt, die sich aus reformerischen Bewegungen in den Klöstern herleitete. Meine Untersuchung bezieht sich genau genommen auf den ostniedersächsischen Raum Uelzen – Braunschweig – Goslar – Northeim (vgl. Abb. 1). Der Geburtsort des dänischen Erstdruckers Johann Snell Einbeck liegt nur 15 km von Northeim entfernt. Hier in diesem Raum waren es vornehmlich die reformerischen Aktivitäten der Windesheimer und der Bursfelder Kongregation, die auf die Bibliotheksgeschichte Einfluß genommen und die angesichts der sich verbreitenden Buchdruckerkunst sogar zu einer gesteigerten Produktion von Handschriften geführt haben. Interessant ist, daß die Klosterbibliotheken der Franziskaner, obwohl sie der Wirkung dieser Reformen nicht unterliegen, trotzdem im gleichen Zeitraum eine erhebliche Ausweitung erfahren. Eine dritte Gruppe von Bibliotheken kann für diese Periode genannt werden, die ebenfalls starkes Wachstum aufweist: das sind die Bibliotheken der Juristen. Charakteristisch für die hinter den Bibliothekserneuerungen stehenden Initiatoren ist, daß sie keine Trennung in der Aufstellung von Handschriften und Drucken durchführten, daß sie zwischen die Holzdeckeleinbände des 15. Jahrhunderts immer wieder handgeschriebene und gedruckte Einheiten zusammengebunden haben, kurz, daß sie zunächst Buch wie Bibliothek nur als Mittel betrachteten, um Texte verfügbar zu machen.[1] Das hier untersuchte Gebiet selbst verfügte während der Inkunabelzeit über keine Druckerei, sieht man von Lüneburg ab, wo 1493 das bekannte Werk von Thomas a Kempis »De imitatione Christi« bei Johannes Luce gedruckt wurde.[2] Als ein interessanter Aspekt bei diesen Bibliothekserneuerungen wird sich erweisen, daß sie vornehmlich von Einzelpersönlichkeiten initiiert wurden.

Methodisch hat den Gang der Untersuchung die Tatsache beeinflußt, daß nur die Reste der Gandersheimer Stiftsbibliothek und der Lüneburger Franziskanerbibliothek noch an ihrem alten Ort aufbewahrt werden. Alle sonst nachweisbaren finden sich verlagert und verstreut in heutigen Handschriftensammlungen und Altbeständen wieder und müssen mühsam rekonstruiert werden. Methodisch neu ist die bewußte Ausweitung der Betrachtung auf Wiegen- und Frühdrucke. Sie ergibt sich zwingend aus der Beobachtung, daß die zu betrachtende Epoche der Bibliotheksgeschichte ihren Anfang in der Mitte des 15. Jahrhunderts und ihren Endpunkt in der Reformation findet. Frühdrucke und Inkunabeln sind schwerer auffindbar als Handschriften, da sie in der Regel nicht wie diese in Bibliotheken gesondert aufgestellt, sondern häufig über den Gesamtbestand verstreut sind. Auch wenn spätmittelalterliche Handschriften und Wiegendrucke bezüglich ihrer Entstehung und ihrem Schicksal auskunftsfreudiger sind, nicht immer ergeben die Provenienznotizen des jeweiligen Buches ein lückenloses Bild. Oft fehlen sie ganz, für diese Fälle hat der Wolfenbütteler Bibliothekar Hermann Herbst in den Dreißiger Jahren mit Erfolg über den Vergleich von Einbandstempeln weitere Klosterprovenienzen nachgewiesen.

Alle Bibliothekssignaturen, die nicht zusätzlich durch einen Bibliotheksort gekennzeichnet sind, beziehen sich auf Bücher aus der Herzog August Bibliothek Wolfenbüttel. Bei den Handschriften sind nur die Signaturen, nicht Titelkurzfassungen angegeben. Abkürzungen siehe am Schluß der Anmerkungen (S. 105).

[1] Buch und Text im 15. Jahrhundert, Hamburg 1981, S. 8 u. 11. (Wolfenbütteler Abhandlungen zur Renaissanceforschung. Bd. 2).

[2] C.L. Grotefend, Geschichte der Buchdruckerei in den Hannoverschen und Braunschweigischen Landen, Hannover 1840, Tafel I.

Über ausführliche Handschriftenbeschreibungen, weitere Einbandbestimmungen vor allem aus den Beständen der Herzog August Bibliothek Wolfenbüttel habe ich die Zahl von Büchern aus den spätmittelalterlichen Bibliotheken erhöhen können.[3] Auf die Herzog August Bibliothek als besonderes Quellenreservoir sei nicht nur aus Lokalpatriotismus hingewiesen. Angesichts der großen Bücherverluste im norddeutschen Raum während der Reformationszeit hat der Sammelfleiß braunschweigisch-lüneburgischer Herzöge viele niedersächsische Bibliotheksreste des späten Mittelalters aufbewahrt, von denen sonst durch die Säkularisierung von Kirchenbesitz im 16. Jahrhundert und die Wirren des Dreissigjährigen Krieges wohl überhaupt nichts mehr vorhanden wäre. Eine systematische Durchforstung dieser Bestände wäre für die Rekonstruktion spätmittelalterlicher Bibliotheken im norddeutschen Raum sicherlich eine lohnende Aufgabe der Forschung. Ebenfalls noch nicht voll ausgeschöpft sind die entsprechenden Bestände in der Ratsbücherei Lüneburg, den Stadtbibliotheken in Braunschweig und Hildesheim, desgleichen der Hildesheimer Dombibliothek, der Stiftskirchenbibliothek in Gandersheim und der Staats- und Universitätsbibliothek in Göttingen (vgl. Abb. 2).

Wann sprechen wir von einer Bibliothek? Mit ihren etwa 500 Bänden gehört die Franziskanerbibliothek in Braunschweig zu den größten der hier betrachteten Büchersammlungen. Aber auch eine sehr viel geringere Menge von Büchern verdient den Namen einer spätmittelalterlichen Bibliothek, sofern eine Ordnung feststellbar ist, nach der sie aufgestellt, vielleicht sogar katalogisiert bzw. inventarisiert worden ist. Vor allem aber konstitutiv ist ein einheitlicher Erwerbungswille, der für ihre Entstehung oder Weiterentwicklung verantwortlich ist. Dies gilt sowohl für den Typ der institutionalisierten Bibliothek wie etwa

---

[3] Die Ergiebigkeit der Suche nach niedersächsischen Provenienzen sei vorweg belegt. Es fand sich z.B. ein Buch aus dem Kloster Fischbeck an der Weser, über dessen Bibliothek kaum etwas bekannt ist (Yv 528.8° Helmst. = De imitatione Christi HC 9119; BMC II 558 f.), ein Diurnale aus dem Mutterkloster für die Windesheimer Kongregation in Sachsen Wittenburg (S 58d.12° Helmst. = Diurnale canonicorum regularium ordinis sancti Augustini, Paris 1520, nebst angebundenem Handschriftenbruchstück). Für dieses Kloster waren bisher nur drei Handschriften nachgewiesen (Monasticon Windesheimense. Teil 2: Deutsches Sprachgebiet, Brüssel 1977, S. 453.) Für das Franziskanerkloster in Gandersheim war bisher nur eine Handschrift bekannt (Cod. Guelf. 137 Helmst.). Wir wissen nun von vier weiteren Drucken [Ti 67 = Brevier GW 5159, vermutlich erst 1553 dem Konvent zugeschlagen; P 355.2° Helmst. = Johannes de Balbis, Catholicon, Nürnberg 1486; E 115.2° Helmst = Registrum in sermones Jacobi de Voragine C 6545; 82.10 Jur. 2° = Martinus Polonus, Margarita decreti HC 10851 – *pro conventu Gandersheimensi*. Zur Bibliothek s. Hans Goetting: Das Bistum Hildesheim. 2. Das Benediktiner(innen)kloster Brunshausen ... Das Franziskanerkloster Gandersheim ... Berlin, New York 1974, S. 308. (Germania sacra. N.F. 8,2)].

der Klosterbibliothek und sehr viel deutlicher noch für Bibliotheken aus Privatbesitz.

Versuchen wir, diesem Geist auf die Spur zu kommen, so finden wir ihn wirksam vor allem unter den aktiv und bewußt erwerbenden Einzelpersönlichkeiten, gelehrten Juristen und Theologen. Zum Zweck der Ausbildung und Berufsausübung, aus gelehrter Neigung oder wissenschaftlicher Betätigung lassen sie während ihres Lebens Bücher anfertigen und einbinden oder kaufen fertige Bücher. Am Ende ihres Lebens vermachen sie ihre bisweilen stattlichen Bücherschätze gelegentlich städtischen Bibliotheken, vor allem aber Klosterbibliotheken, ganz aus dem mittelalterlichen Bedürfnis heraus, etwa für das Seelenheil zu tun. Zur Multiplizierung der Gebete ergingen häufig Buchschenkungen an mehrere Klöster. Diese Form der Bucherwerbung in Klöstern und bisweilen Ratsbüchereien ist nicht nur leicht zu dokumentieren, sondern wohl fast zum entscheidenden Moment für die kirchliche Bibliotheksbildung im 15. Jahrhundert geworden. Denn die Tätigkeit in der klösterlichen Schreibstube trat dagegen deutlich zurück. Damit ist ein allerdings von außen kommendes Motiv genannt, das den Ausbau dieser Bibliotheken sehr förderte, jedoch ihrer homogenen Gestalt nicht immer dienlich war. Die Privatbibliotheken seien zuerst gleichsam als historisch ältere Bausteine der Kloster- und Kirchenbibliothek betrachtet.

Im weiteren Gang unserer Betrachtung soll dargestellt werden, wie die Privatbibliotheken in die kirchlichen Bibliotheken eingegangen sind. Dabei werden Ratsbüchereien nur gestreift, da für ihren Ausbau nicht wie bei den Klosterbibliotheken besondere Momente wie etwa die kirchlichen Reformbewegungen des 15. Jahrhunderts eine Rolle gespielt haben. Die Ratsbibliotheken waren vom Umfang her wenig bedeutend, sind in ihrer Zusammenstellung eher zufällig und werden deshalb nur der Vollständigkeit halber erwähnt.

Privatbibliotheken

Beginnen wir mit der Bibliothek des Juristen Volcmar von Anderten. Sie ist ein besonders reines Beispiel einer Bibliothek jenes Typs, der ganz für die berufliche Ausübung aufgebaut worden ist. von Anderten war Procurator an der römischen Kurie und Lübecker Kanoniker. Nach seinem Studium in Rostock im Jahr 1444[4] und Erfurt[5] muß er mit dem Bibliotheksaufbau begonnen haben. Mitte der

---

[4] Adolf Hofmeister, Matrikel der Universität Rostock 1 (1889), p. 72 A.
[5] J.C. Hermann Weißenborn, Acten der Erfurter Universität 1 (1881), S. 233, 237.

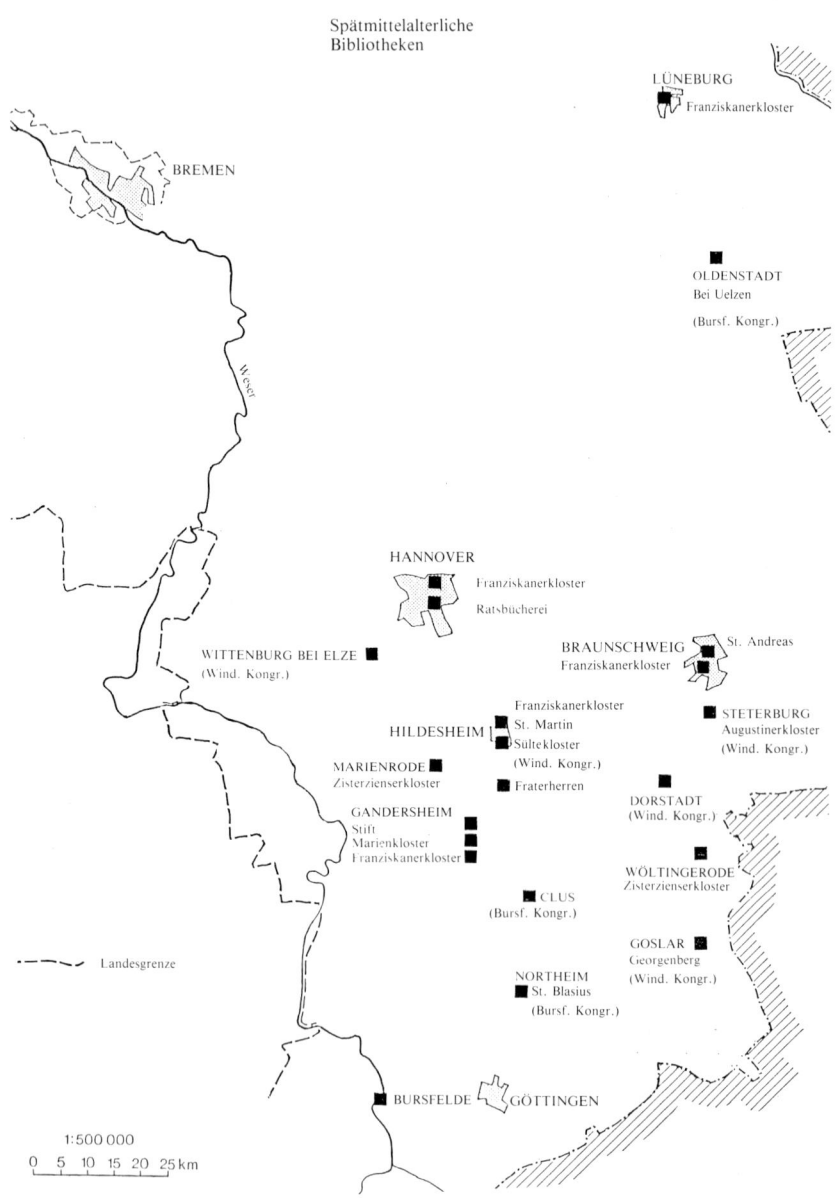

Abbildung 1: Spätmittelalterliche Bibliotheken.

Studien zum Wachstum und zur Entwicklung von Bibliotheken

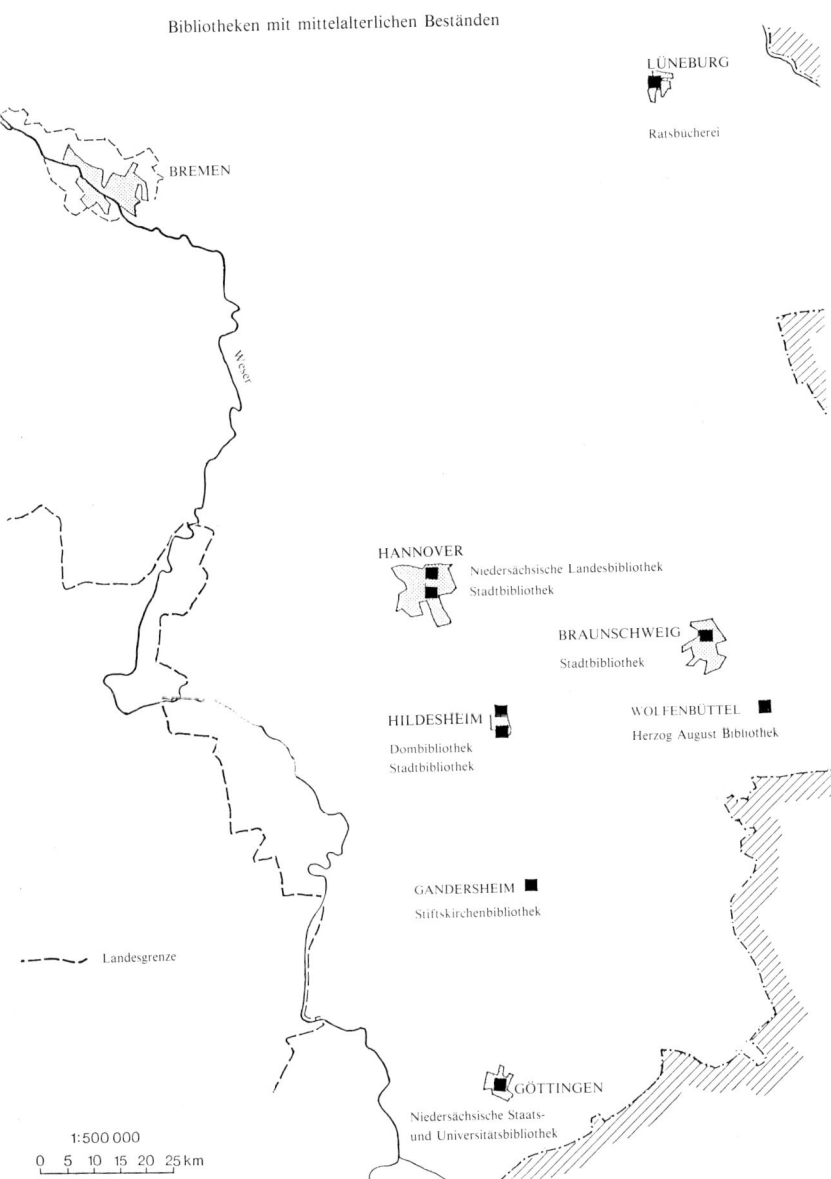

Abbildung 2: Bibliotheken mit mittelalterlichen Beständen.

Sechziger Jahre hat er allein bei dem Kopisten Jacobus Bodeker alias Rothermund de Koningisberch fünf Kodizes über Digestenvorlesungen des Bartoldus de Saxoferrato abschreiben lassen.[6] Der Auftrag wurde auf einmal erteilt und erledigt.[7] Weitere 21 Handschriften aus seinem Besitz enthalten ausschließlich juristische Literatur. Die Ausbreitung des Buchdrucks in den Sechziger und Siebziger Jahren wirkt sich in bemerkenswerter Weise auf das Wachstum der Bibliothek aus. Bis zum Jahr der Schenkung der Bibliothek an den Rat der Stadt Hannover 1479 hat er eine erhebliche Zahl von Drucken erworben, von der noch heute 24 Inkunabeln erhalten sind.[8] Diese jedoch enthalten über das Juristische hinaus auch theologische Materien. Gerade Juristen scheinen kauffreudige Inkunabelliebhaber gewesen zu sein. Die nach Titeln recht gut identifizierte Bibliothek des Braunschweiger Stadtschreibers und kaiserlichen Notars Gerwin von Hameln, also ebenfalls eines Juristen (1415-1496) weist in der Mehrzahl Drucke auf. Sie ist knapp 15 Jahre älter geworden als die Bibliothek Volcmar von Andertens. Den 21 nachgewiesenen Handschriften stehen 91 Drucke gegenüber.[9] Genau ein Drittel der einstmals mit 336 Bänden angegebenen Bibliothek ist also noch vorhanden. Bei den Drucken überwiegen auffälligerweise die Titel der theologischen Disziplin. Es kann beim Bücherkauf also nicht nur um den Erwerb des juristischen Handwerkszeugs gegangen sein, vielmehr galt es, gelehrte Neigungen zu befriedigen, die tatsächlich bestanden. Bemerkungen wie »perlegi« oder »perlegi totum librum« von der Hand Gerwins von Hameln in seinen Büchern[10] beweisen das inhaltliche Interesse ihres Käufers. Beide Bibliotheken sind durch Schenkung in größeren Institutionen aufge-

---

[6] HANNOVER Stadtbibliothek 33 bis 37. Alle Bände ausführlich beschrieben von Emanuele Casamassima, Iter Italicum, Florenz 1971, S. 67-70.

[7] Alle Bände sind auf Papier mit demselben Wasserzeichen Krone PICCARD I 278 (1460-1466) geschrieben worden.

[8] Jürgen Busch, Die Ratsbücherei in Hannover, in: Hannoversche Geschichtsblätter. N.F. 10 (1957), S. 184-185.

[9] Paul Lehmann, Gerwin von Hameln und die Andreasbibliothek in Braunschweig, in: Zentralblatt für Bibliothekswesen 52 (1935), S. 565-586. Hermann Herbst, Die Bibliothek der St. Andreaskirche zu Braunschweig, in: Zentralblatt für Bibliothekswesen 58 (1941), S. 301-338.

[10] Zu den 86 bei Lehmann (s. Anm. 9), S. 581-586 genannten kommen noch zwei von Herbst (ZfB 58 (1941), S. 332, Anm. 1) und drei vom Verfasser ermittelte hinzu (Qu H 23 = 1. Petrus Aureoli, Compendium litteralis sensus totius bibliae GW 3077. 2. Antonius Rampigollis, Biblia aurea HC 13678. 3. Quadragesimale viatoris HC 5001; Li 4° 133 = Johannes Gerson, Collectorium super Magnificat H 7717; 148.29 Theol. = 1. Epistula Pii II papae ad imperatorem Turcorum HC 172. 2. Dialogus Pii II contra Bohemos atque Thaboritas de sacra communione HC 209. 3. Johannes Chrysostomus, Liber dialogorum de dignitate Sacerdotii HC 5048.

gangen, ja haben diese so erheblich erweitert, daß sie durch die Schenkung einen unverwechselbaren Charakter erhielten. Das gilt vor allem für die Bibliothek Gerwins von Hameln. Er hat sie der Andreaskirche in Braunschweig vermacht, die schon über eine ansehnliche Bibliothek verfügte und seit etwa 1422[11] ein eigenes Bibliotheksgebäude besaß, das übrigens noch heute als Sehenswürdigkeit gezeigt wird. Ihre Bücher sind heute verstreut von Braunschweig über Wolfenbüttel, Göttingen bis Karlsruhe.

Diesen Juristenbibliotheken seien drei Theologenbibliotheken gegenübergestellt, deren jede individuell geprägt ist, doch auf Grund der verschiedenartigen Persönlichkeit und Funktion ihrer Schöpfer jeweils einen besonderen Charakter zeigt. Da gibt es die Bibliothek des gebildeten Klerikers, in der sich vornehmlich weit verbreitete theologische Standardwerke fanden wie etwa in der des Seniors des Gandersheimer Kapitels Henricus Coci. Selbst hatte er die Einbände für eine Reihe von Kodizes veranlaßt, selbst Teile einer Handschrift geschrieben.[12] Drucke fanden sich nicht, der Zeitpunkt ihrer Stiftung am 13. 4. 1466 und damit der Abschluß ihres Aufbaues liegt dafür zu früh.[13]

Das gilt auch für die Bibliothek des Guardians im Braunschweiger Franziskanerkloster Ludolfus Sunne. Vor seinem Tode am 11. 9. 1470[14] hatte er die Verfügungsgewalt über seine Bücher dem Franziskanerkloster überlassen, wie es sich aus den Besitzvermerken zu zwölf heute noch bewahrten Handschriften ergibt.[15] Noch deutlicher als bei Henricus Coci läßt sich der Bibliotheksaufbau aus dem Wirken Sunnes erschließen. Sunne schrieb in seiner Funktion als Lector principalis des Klosters selbst Texte ab, veranlaßte zum Zwecke der Ausbildung die studierenden Brüder zu Textabschriften und unterhielt damit gleichsam für die begrenzte Zeit seiner Lehrtätigkeit eine Schreibschule im Braunschweiger Kloster. Jedoch nicht nur für die Textabschriften, sondern auch für das Einbinden der Bücher trug er Sorge. Ganz auf das Engagement des einzelnen

---

[11] Paul Lehmann (s. Anm. 9), S. 571.
[12] Helmar Härtel, Die Handschriften der Stiftsbibliothek zu Gandersheim, Wiesbaden 1978, S. 8. (Mittelalterliche Handschriften in Niedersachsen. H. 2.)
[13] Hans Goetting, Das Bistum Hildesheim. 1: Das reichsunmittelbare Kanonissenstift Gandersheim, Berlin, New York 1973, S. 71 u. 415. (Germania sacra. N.F. 7.)
[14] Stadtbibliothek Braunschweig Ms 74, 33v.
[15] Luitgard Camerer, Die Bibliothek des Franziskanerklosters in Braunschweig, Braunschweig 1982, S. 34-37. (Braunschweiger Werkstücke. Reihe A Bd. 18.)

lehrenden Lektors des Klosters ist das Motiv für die Bibliotheksbildung zurückzuführen.[16]

Die von Hermann Herbst identifizierte Bibliothek des Braunschweiger Stiftsherrn Johannes Schorkop[17] macht uns mit einem Gelehrten bekannt, der nicht nur Teile seiner Bibliothek selbst schrieb, sondern auch verfaßte, denn er nahm als Autor Stellung zu einer Reihe von theologischen Streitfragen seiner Zeit: Reliquienkult und unbefleckte Empfängnis der Jungfrau Maria. Diese Bibliothek verfügte mit Sicherheit über eine Reihe von Drucken. Das legt nicht nur das Datum einer Bücherstiftung aus dieser Bibliothek für das Kloster Clus nahe: das Jahr 1509.[18]

Bei den Juristen steht der Kauf im Vordergrund, woraus sich auch der große Anteil von gedruckten Büchern erklärt. Die Theologen gelangten auf sehr vielfältige Weise in den Besitz ihrer Bestände. Sie ließen Bücher abschreiben, sorgten für den Einband, kopierten eigenhändig, schrieben als gelehrte Autoren ihre eigenen Bücher (Autographen), der Kauf fertiger Bücher ist ebenfalls nachweisbar, gedruckte Bücher fallen dabei allerdings viel weniger ins Gewicht. Nun zu den Bibliotheken des Franziskanerordens, danach zu denen des Benediktinerordens und des Ordens der Augustinerchorherren, die in besonderem Maße von den Reformgedanken des 15. Jahrhunderts beeinflußt worden sind.

Franziskanerbibliotheken

Im 15. Jahrhundert verzeichnen die Bibliotheken des Franziskanerordens im Bereich der sächsischen Minoritenprovinz eine Blütezeit.[19] Beeinflußt von der an der Universität Erfurt getriebenen franziskanischen Theologie erhalten die

---

[16] Helmar Härtel, Studien zu einer Handschrift des Braunschweiger Guardians Ludolfus Sunne OFM, in: Die Diözese Hildesheim in Vergangenheit und Gegenwart 50 (1982), S. 109-118.
[17] Archiv für Kulturgeschichte 29 (1939), S. 78-92.
[18] Archiv für Kulturgeschichte 29 (1939), S. 80 f.
[19] Unsere Kenntnis von einer Reihe spätmittelalterlicher Franziskanerbibliotheken in Niedersachsen ist gerade in den letzten Jahren durch die 1972, 1978 und 1981 veröffentlichten Kataloge zu den Lüneburger und Hildesheimer Franziskanerhandschriften gewachsen. [Irmgard Fischer, Die Handschriften der Ratbücherei Lüneburg. II Die theologischen Handschriften. Folioreihe, Wiesbaden 1972. Doris Fouquet-Plümacher, Die Handschriften des Gymnasium Andreanum im Stadtarchiv zu Hildesheim, Wiesbaden 1978. (Mittelalterliche Handschriften in Niedersachsen. H. 3.) Marlis Stähli, Handschriften der Ratbücherei Lüneburg. III Die theologischen Handschriften, Wiesbaden 1981. (Mittelalterliche Handschriften in Niedersachsen. H. 4.)]. Im letzten Jahr erschien die Arbeit von Luitgard Camerer, in der die Reste der Franziskanerbibliothek der Stadt Braunschweig ermittelt wurden. [Luitgard Camerer (s. Anm. 15)].

Klosterbibliotheken der sächsischen Franziskaner ihren besonderen Charakter. Er findet seinen Ausdruck in selbständigen literarischen Arbeiten der franziskanischen Theologen. Das ungünstige Schicksal der literarischen Zeugen hat lange Zeit der Meinung Vorschub geleistet, als ob der Franziskanerorden mehr auf ein gefühlsmäßig orientiertes Leben in reiner Armut ausgerichtet war. Erst die Arbeiten Ludger Meiers haben hier Licht in die Verhältnisse gebracht.[20] Für den Inhalt dieser Bibliotheken ist es bezeichnend, daß Ludger Meier die Reste der Franziskanerbibliotheken in Hildesheim, Lüneburg, Hannover und Braunschweig in besonderem Maße herangezogen hat, um Schule, Schrifttum und Lehre der Minoritenuniversität zu Erfurt zu erforschen. Denn diese Bibliotheken spiegeln anders als die üblichen Klosterbibliotheken des niedersächsischen Raumes Schwerpunkte der franziskanischen Theologie in Erfurt. Als besonders eindrucksvolles Beispiel dafür mögen die Reste der Hildesheimer Franziskanerbibliothek gelten, unter denen sich eine Reihe von Handschriften aus dem Besitz des gelehrten Franziskaners Hermann Etzen finden. Er ist zugleich als Buchbesitzer, Autor und Schreiber zu nennen. Sein Hildesheimer Büchernachlaß[21] zeichnet sich durch eigenhändig verfaßte und geschriebene Werke aus: etwas überaus Seltenes, denn für das mittelalterliche Handschriftenwesen sind Autographen die Ausnahme. Die für Hildesheim namhaft zu machenden Etzenschen Werke[22] wiederum sind für die Rekonstruktion der franziskanischen Theologie in Erfurt von erheblicher Bedeutung. Meier hat Etzen in seiner Arbeit darüber mehrfach als Gewährsmann herangezogen.[23] An Hand einer Handschrift hat er ihn außerdem als homiletischen Schriftsteller gewürdigt und die besondere Vertrautheit Etzens mit dem Werk Petrarcas herausgearbeitet. Etzens reicher Petrarcacodex, dessen Herstellung er wohl veranlaßt hat (Andreanum 2), läßt auf große Belesenheit und beachtenswerte Textkenntnis schließen.[24] Die Existenz dieser Handschrift stellt zugleich ein

---

[20] Vgl. vor allem Ludger Meier, Die Barfüßerschule zu Erfurt, Münster 1958. (Beiträge zur Geschichte der Philosophie und Theologie des Mittelalters. Bd. 38.)

[21] Dazuzuzählen ist auch die Handschrift des Stadtarchivs HILDESHEIM HA 481 (ehemals X bzw. I A 4), ein Sentenzenkommentar, zu dem HILDESHEIM Andreanum 10 den Ergänzungsband darstellt.

[22] HILDESHEIM Stadtarchiv Andreanum 10 und 13 und HILDESHEIM Stadtarchiv HA 481.

[23] Ludger Meier, Die Barfüßerschule zu Erfurt, Münster 1958, passim. (Beiträge zur Geschichte der Philosophie und Theologie des Mittelalters. Bd. 38.)

[24] Ludger Meier, Das Charakterbild des deutschen Franziskaners Hermann Etzen im Lichte seiner Predigten, in: Franziskanische Studien 24 (1937), S. 145-149.

frühes Zeugnis der humanistischen Bewegung in Norddeutschland dar.

Allgemein besaßen die Franziskaner dieses Raumes nach Sachgebieten aufgestellte, wohlgeordnete und reichhaltige Bibliotheken. Die einstmals wohl bekannteste in Braunschweig enthielt neben theologischer Literatur die für die Seelsorgetätigkeit der Franziskaner so besonders wichtige Predigtliteratur.[25] Neben Nachschlagewerken, Medizin, spielt eine prominente Rolle die juristische Literatur. Die Lüneburger Bibliothek war ähnlich aufgebaut und wies etwa dieselben Schwerpunkte auf.[26]

Die Franziskanerbrüder Ludolfus Sunne und Hermann Etzen hatten der Klosterbibliothek ihre Bücher hinterlassen. Auch die Franziskanerbibliothek begründete also ihren Reichtum mit der Übernahme von Bibliotheken, die einzelne gelehrte Brüder geschaffen hatten. Alle waren in der Regel von der Erfurter Theologie geprägte Franziskaner, so daß auf Dauer diese Bibliotheken einen einheitlichen Charakter erhalten mußten. Die Schenkungsvermerke erwähnen auffällig häufig Lektoren, jene Brüder, die unmittelbar die Buchherstellung förderten. Denn Abschrift und Exzerpt waren wesentliches Element im Lehr- und Studienbetrieb sowohl im Hausstudium wie im Studium generale in Erfurt. Neben dem Braunschweiger Lektor Ludolfus Sunne sei der Lektor Thidericus Struve erwähnt. Er hat während seiner Lektoratsjahre zwischen 1413 und 1415 in Erfurt aus theologischer und mathematischer Literatur zum Teil während seiner vorlesungsfreien Zeit umfangreiche Exzerpte angefertigt.[27] Das Bemühen um Weiterbildung wird besonders deutlich in der autobiographischen Notiz des Franziskaners Hermann Etzen über seine Lektoratsjahre in Prenzlau, Halberstadt, Magdeburg und Erfurt.[28] Wie Lehrbetrieb und Buchherstellung Hand in Hand gingen, lehrt auch eine Lüneburger Handschrift. 1454 schreibt der Bruder Johannes Verwer im Magdeburger Franziskanerkloster die Formalitates des Franciscus de Mayronis ab, ein Jahr später, nun ausdrücklich als Student in Erfurt, einen Sentenzenkommentar des Kilianus Stetzing. Während dieser Zeit macht er die ersten Gehversuche in der selbständigen Durchdringung eines abgeschriebenen Textes. Dem Sentenzenkommentar des Petrus de Aquila fügt er eigene Quaestiones an.[29]

---

[25] Luitgard Camerer (s. Anm. 15), S. 24.
[26] Marlis Stähli (s. Anm. 19), S. 8-10.
[27] Vgl. Pfarramt Bissendorf Hs 20, 178ra, 186ra, 195va u. 197 vb (s. Beschreibung von Helmar Härtel, in: Die Diözese Hildesheim in Vergangenheit und Gegenwart 50 (1982), S. 116-118.
[28] Vgl. HILDESHEIM Stadtarchiv HA 481 (ehemals X bzw. I A 4), 172v.
[29] Vgl. LÜNEBURG Theol. 4° 21.

Vom gedruckten Buch in den Franziskanerbibliotheken war bisher nicht die Rede. Das liegt einmal daran, daß die große Zahl der Inkunabeln aus ursprünglich franziskanischem Besitz in Lüneburg noch nicht abschließend katalogisiert ist, zum anderen in Braunschweig nicht so ohne weiteres als franziskanischer Besitz zu identifizieren ist. Daß diese Bibliotheken eine große Zahl von Inkunabeln besessen haben, ist unstrittig, für Lüneburg sind bis jetzt nachgewiesen 290 Bände,[30] für Braunschweig muß ebenfalls von einer größeren Zahl ausgegangen werden.[31] Für Hildesheim sind allein 65 Titel nachweisbar, eine ebenfalls stattliche Zahl, wenn wir, wie wir noch hören werden, bei anderen Klosterbibliotheken immer nur kleine Druckschriftenbestände nachweisen können. Auch diese Zahl stellt nur noch einen Teil des einmal vorhandenen Bestandes dar. Um ihretwillen wäre sicherlich kein eigener Bibliotheksneubau in Hildesheim nötig gewesen, wie er 1487 begonnen worden ist.[32] Unter den Wiegendrucken finden sich vornehmlich theologische, aber auch eine ganze Reihe juristischer und historischer Titel. Auch Gellius, Juvenal, Ovid, Persius und Terenz sind vertreten, wiederum ein Zeugnis für das Eindringen der humanistischen Bewegung in Norddeutschland. Die große Zahl der Drucke läßt auf weitgespannte gelehrte Interessen schließen, die die Brüder der Franziskanerklöster beherrschten.

Die Reformklöster

Die bisher betrachteten Privatbibliotheken und die Franziskanerbibliotheken lassen sich insofern miteinander verbinden, als in beiden das Motiv zum Ausbau im Streben nach Ausbildung zu suchen ist. Der Aufschwung in anderen Klosterbibliotheken hängt ganz unmittelbar mit der gewaltigen Reformbewegung des 15. Jahrhunderts zusammen, die auch die Orden erfaßte. Er wirkt sich derart stark auf den Ausbau der Bibliotheken aus, daß man in einer Reihe von Fällen von Neugründungen sprechen möchte.

Im niedersächsischen Raum um Braunschweig und Hildesheim treffen zwei Reformbewegungen aufeinander und überlagern sich. Es ist einmal die Windesheimer Kongregation, für die das Kloster Wittenburg bei Elze auf dem Konzil von Basel die Vollmacht erhält,[33] alle Augustinerklöster beiderlei Geschlechts in

---

[30] Diese Zahl verdanke ich Herrn Gerhard Hopf von der Ratsbücherei Lüneburg.
[31] Vgl. Luitgard Camerer (s. Anm. 15). Nur eine Inkunabel wird in der Abhandlung erwähnt.
[32] Urkundenbuch der Stadt Hildesheim 8 (1901), Nr. 145.
[33] Scriptores rerum Brunsvicensium ed. G.W. Leibniz 2 (1710), S. 486 f.

ganz Sachsen zu visitieren und gegebenenfalls zu reformieren. Zum anderen ist es die Bursfelder Kongregation des Benediktinerordens, die seit 1430 von Kloster Clus bei Gandersheim ihren Ausgang nimmt. Beide Bewegungen fördern in ihrem Streben nach Neuordnung des monastischen Lebens auch den Aufbau der Bibliotheken, allerdings steht dabei die Pflege der Wissenschaften im eigentlichen Sinn nicht im Vordergrund. Es geht sowohl bei den selbständigen literarischen Arbeiten wie bei der Vermehrung der Bücher durch das nun wiederum geforderte Abschreiben nicht um literarische Wirksamkeit und Wirkung, sondern um Einhaltung der Ordensregeln.[34]

Im Kloster Windesheim sind es Abschriften von Liturgica für den Gottesdienst, Abfassung der Statuten, des Kalenders und des Ordinarius,[35] in den Reformklöstern der Bursfelder Kongregation Abschrift und Aufbewahrung von Literatur erbaulichen und asketischen Charakters. Die neue Spiritualität war den meditativen und scholastischen Methoden und Fragestellungen nicht gewogen. Nicht Thomas von Aquins große Summen, sondern seine Schrift »De dilectione dei et proximi« wird nun verbreitet.[36]

A. Windesheimer Kongregation und die Brüder vom gemeinsamen Leben

Wie wirkte sich die Reform nun im einzelnen aus? Den Windesheimern eigentümlich war die Hochschätzung der Skriptoriumsarbeit, mit der man die besonders betonte Forderung nach Handarbeit zu erfüllen meinte. Jedoch gerade bei Klöstern, die sich der Kongregation offiziell anschlossen, ist die Zahl der auf uns gekommenen Bücher sehr gering, so daß nicht leicht nachzuvollziehen ist, ob man der Forderung nach dieser speziellen Form der Handarbeit nachgekommen ist. Von dem 1423 als erstem niedersächsischen Augustinerchorherrenkloster gegründeten Wittenburg bei Elze, das eine Zeitlang Ausgangspunkt für

---

[34] Vgl. Iohannes Busch, Chronicon Windeshemense, bearb. von K. Grube, Halle 1886, S. 23. (Geschichtsquellen der Provinz Sachsen. 19.) ... *furtivas sibi horas pro divinis libris in communi conscribendis sollicite captabant et finitis matutinis, quas pro primo legere consueverunt, integram ad horam deputatum habebant.* Vgl. Qu 74 Helmst. = Caerimoniale monachorum ordinis s. Benedicti. Dist. 3, cap. 9: *Opera autem quibus se occupare debent fratres sunt hec: videlicet scribere libros aut rubricare vel ligare...* .H 4883.

[35] Iohannes Busch (s. Anm. 36), S. XVIII u. XIX.

[36] Vgl. Hermann Herbst, Das Benediktinerkloster Clus bei Gandersheim und die Bursfelder Reform, Leipzig und Berlin 1932, S. 65 f. (Beiträge zur Kulturgeschichte des Mittelalters und der Renaissance. 50).

die Reform in Sachsen wird, sind nur noch drei Handschriften bekannt.[37] Eine von ihnen ist zum Teil in Wittenburg entstanden.[38] Teile dieser Handschrift verraten allerdings ihre Herkunft aus einem Reformkloster: es sind Briefe Gerhard Grotes, der die geistige Grundlage der devotio moderna schuf; außerdem Predigten, die in Kloster Wittenburg gehalten wurden. Nur ein Druck des 16. Jahrhunderts aus der Klosterbibliothek ist bisher aufgetaucht, für das Augustinerchorherrenkloster bezeichnenderweise ein Diurnale canonicorum regularium ordinis sancti Augustini.[39]

Die Quellenlage für die Bibliothek des Augustinerchorherrenstiftes St. Bartholomäus auf der Sülte bei Hildesheim ist besser.[40] Wir kennen unterdessen 19 Handschriften und 19 Bände mit Frühdrucken. In den erhaltenen Resten spiegeln sich die Bemühungen um die Kirchenreform im 15. Jahrhundert besonders deutlich.[41]

Hildesheim besaß auch ein Haus der Brüder vom gemeinsamen Leben, jener Nachfolger Gerhard Grotes, die nicht nach der Augustinerregel und einer für alle Mitglieder der Windesheimer Kongregation verbindlichen Regel in einem Kloster leben wollten. Auch sie schufen sich durch Handarbeit die materielle

---

[37] Vgl. Monasticon Windeshemense. Teil 2: Deutsches Sprachgebiet, S. 453.

[38] HANNOVER Ms XIII 859 enthält vornehmlich Exzerpte des Chronisten Theodoricus Engelhus aus historischen Werken. Vgl. Handschriften der Niedersächsischen Landesbibliothek Hannover, Zweiter Teil, Wiesbaden 1982, S. 203 ff. Engelhus war erst zwei Jahre vor seinem Tod dem Kloster Wittenburg als *presbyter donatus* beigetreten. Hermann Herbst (s. Anm. 36), S. 78 Anm. 5 zählt ihn als Beispiel für plötzliche Konversionen auf, die in der Zeit der Reformbewegung zahlreich sind.

[39] S 58d.12° Helmst. = gedruckt Paris 1520. Das Buch war zuletzt im Kloster Steterburg und kam von dort 1572 nach Wolfenbüttel.

[40] Hermann Herbst, Beiträge zur Geschichte der Bibliothek des Sülteklosters zu Hildesheim, in: Alt-Hildesheim, Heft 15 (1936), S. 30 ff.

[41] Hermann Herbst (s. Anm. 40) hat die Charakteristika der Einbände aus dem Sültekloster beschrieben und 10 Handschriften identifiziert, zählt man eine Hannoveraner (Ms I 84) hinzu. Auf Grund erneuter Suche in den Magazinen der Herzog August Bibliothek fanden sich drei weitere bisher nicht identifizierte Kodizes (Cod. Guelf. 1.6 Aug. 2°, 33.2 Aug. 2°, 83.5 Aug. 2°) zusätzlich zu einer unterdessen von Hans Butzmann beschriebenen Handschrift (115 Extravagantes), beschrieben in: Die mittelalterlichen Handschriften der Gruppen Extravagantes ... , Frankfurt a.M. 1972, S. 63 f.; in Hannover ebenfalls noch eine (Ms XXI 1233). Über die üblichen asketischen Traktate und Sermones hinaus finden sich grammatische Schriften (Cod. Guelf. 83.1 Aug. 2°), eine Reihe von Traktaten mit Hinweis auf die Kirchenreform im 15. Jahrhundert (Cod. Guelf. 83.5 Aug. 2°). Der unmittelbare Bezug zur Reform der Windesheimer ist nur in HANNOVER Ms I 84 und Ms XXI 1233 nachweisbar. Bietet die eine den Tractatus de spiritualibus ascensionibus des Gerhard von Zutphen, so die andere eine Hildesheimer Chronik mit einer Reihe von Nachtra-

Grundlage für das fromme Leben. In Hildesheim war 1440 eine Niederlassung der Brüder gegründet worden, für das Jahr 1450 die Einrichtung einer scriptoria gemeldet.[42] Der Neubau des Schreibhauses (domus scriptorum) und ein Anbau an die Buchbinderei[43] zeigen, daß in der Tat die Bücherproduktion in Hildesheim eine größere Rolle spielte. Eine Buchdruckerei ist nicht nachgewiesen, dafür aber eine ganze Reihe von Drucken, die im Besitz des Lüchtenhofes gewesen sein müssen. An Hand der Annalen des Rektors des Lüchtenhofes Peter Dieppurch[44] und eines Inventarisierungsprotokolls vom 14. Dez. 1573 kann auf eine recht große Bibliothek geschlossen werden.[45] Da die Fraterherren mit Aufkommen des Buchdruckes immer weniger über Abschreiben von Büchern ihren Lebensunterhalt verdienen konnten, werden sie sich immer mehr auf das Einbinden von Büchern eingestellt haben. Für ihre eigene Bibliothek haben sie dann immer wieder Titel abgezweigt. Von diesen habe ich eine ganze Reihe noch in der Herzog August Bibliothek auffinden können (25 Bände mit 43 Titeln). Sie zeigen, daß die Bibliothek auch im 16. Jahrhundert weitergewachsen ist.[46] Aber nicht erst dieser Fund läßt etwas von dem Umfang ahnen,

gungen zur Geschichte des Sülteklosters und gehäufte Angaben zur Windesheimer Reform im Hildesheimer Raum. Gibt es nur relativ wenige Nachweise für das Skriptorium des Klosters (nur HANNOVER Ms I 84 und Cod. Guelf. 33.2 Aug. 2°), so sind sie um so zahlreicher für die Buchbinderwerkstatt. Vornehmlich Drucke weisen den charakteristischen Einband des Sülteklosters auf. Über die von Herbst festgestellten Predigtsammlungen (332.3/4 Theol. 2°, 478.2 Theol., 479.2 Theol., 492.1 Theol.), grammatischen Schriften (32.1 Gram. 2°) hinaus konnten weitere festgestellt werden (111.2 Theol. 2°, 879.6 Theol.). Das übrige Schrifttum enthält asketische und Reform-Traktate (130.1 et 2 Quod. 2°, 16.1 Theol. 2°, 479.3 Theol., 493.3 Theol., 111.1 Theol.) und die im Mittelalter beliebten Sammlungen von Wundergeschichten (223.4 Hist. 2°, 153.1 Quod.). Nimmt man die drei von Ernst im Bestand der Hildesheimer Dombibliothek festgestellten Frühdrucke hinzu (Konrad Ernst, Incunabula Hildeshemensia, Fasc. I, Hildesheim 1908, S. 7 Nr. 47, S. 53 Nr. 432 u. S. 25 Nr. 192c), so kennen wir 19 Bände. Die heute in der Dombibliothek Hildesheim aufbewahrten Handschriften Hs 625, 651, 656, 658 erhielten im 15. Jahrhundert neue Einbände, die aus der Werkstatt des Sülteklosters stammen.

[42] Annalen und Akten der Brüder des gemeinsamen Lebens im Lüchtenhofe zu Hildesheim. Hrsg. von Richard Doebner, Hannover 1903, S. XXII (Quellen und Darstellungen zur Geschichte Niedersachsens. IX.)

[43] Doebner (s. Anm. 42), S. XXIV.

[44] Doebner (s. Anm. 42).

[45] Vgl. Die Fraterherren (Brüder des gemeinsamen Lebens) im Lüchtenhof zu Hildesheim, in: Unsere Diözese in Vergangenheit und Gegenwart 13 (1939), S. 101 f.

[46] 680.20 u. 21 Theol. = Haymonis episcopi Halberstattensis Commentarius in cantica canticorum et Commentarius in Apocalypsim beati Johanni libri VII, Köln 1529; 202.17 Quod. = 1. Johann Nider, Manuale confessorum H 11841. 2. Cordiale quattuor novissimorum, Deventer

den die Bibliothek der Fraterherren angenommen hatte, Konrad Ernst weist in seinem Hildesheimer Inkunabelkatalog 128 Titel aus dem Lüchtenhof nach. Zu den Bibliotheksverhältnissen in den Augustinerinnenklöstern Heinin-

1502. 3. F.Jo. Tisserandi Sermones religiosissimi, Paris 1517. 4. Thomas de Aquino, De corpore Christi etc. HC 1370. 5. Konrad Wimpina, De ortu progressu et fructu theologiae H 16211. 6. Doctrinale humanorum a Claudio Peronneo, s.l. et s.a. 7. Aurea opuscula Petri Ravennati Itali, Köln 1508. 8. Johannes Langer, De censibus HC 9892 = H 9893; 62.6 Quod. = 1. Leonardo Bruni, Epistolae familiares GW 5609, HC 1568. 2. Johannes Fabri de Werdea, Carmen de quarundam dictionum recta pronuntiatione GW 9652, H 6851. 3. Orationes legatorum Francorum ad Venetos etc., cum responsionibus HR 12035. 4. Johannes Fabri de Werdea, An licitum sit diebus festivis intendere bonarum artium disciplinis GW 9656, H 6857. 5. Stephanus Gerhardi, Laudationes de domo Saxoniae HR 7617. 6. Raymundus Cardinalis Gurtzensis, Epistolae ad Romani Imperij Senatores, s.l. et s.a. 7. Konrad Wimpina, Oratio habita in Exceptione ..., Leipzig 1503. 8. Victoria ... Henrici Octavi Francie et Anglie regis ..., 1513 (?). 9. Matheolus Perusinus, De Memoria augenda H 10911. 10. Tractatus de arte oratoria, Würzburg 1501. 11. Angebundenes Handschriftenbruchstück: Augustini ... isagogicus libellus ad Andrea ...; 82.19 Quod. = 1. Franciscus Petrarca, De remediis utriusque fortunae HC 12791. 2. Jacobus de Jueterbog, De animabus exutis a corporibus C 3332. 3. Dietrich Gresemund, Lucubratiunculae bonarum septem artium ..., Leipzig 1501. 4. Henricus Aquilonipolensis, Cithara sophialis H 8428. 5. Henning Caldrusius, De vita et passione sanctissime Agnetis, um 1512; 140.18 Theol. = Sermones venerabilis Peregrini ordinis praedicatorum de tempore et sanctis, Köln 1501. 2. Horologium sapientiae C 3171. 3. Petrus Reginaldetus, Speculum finalis retributionis H 13774. 4. Konrad Wimpina, Apologeticus in sacrae theologiae defensionem H 16208; 68.2 Theol. = Nicolaus de Nyse, Gemma praedicantium, Basel 1508; 71.2 Theol. = 1. Nicolaus de Blony, Tractatus sacerdotalis de sacramentis etc. H 3251. 2. Hilarius Litomiricensis, Tractatus contra perfidiam aliquorum Bohemorum HC 8663; 19.6 Gram. = Johannes Melber, Vocabularius Iodoci doctoris et predicatoris sacre scripture H 11030; 71.5 Theol. = Bartholomaeus de Chainis, Confessionale GW 6546; 879.6 Theol. = Cherubinus de Spoleto OFM, Sermones quadragesimales, s.l. et s.a.; 919.133 Theol. = Johannes Reuchlin, de Verbo mirifico, Köln 1532; 236.5 Theol. = 1. Dat werk der apostelen unde de heymelike openbaringe Joannis des apostels, Leyden s.a. 2. Lycht der Selen C 3696. 3. Eingang der Himmel GW 9273, H 9185; 456.1-9 Theol. = Aurelius Augustinus, Opera, Basel 1506; 163.5 Theol. = 1. Enucleamenta Biblie compilata ex Gregorianis codicibus per fratrem Guernerium cenobii victorini apud Parisios ..., Paris 1518. 2. Biblia aurea cum suis historiis necnon exemplis veteris atque novi instrumenti, Straßburg 1509; 193.6 Theol. = 1. Bartholomaeus Sibylla, Speculum peregrinarum quaestionum GW 3460. 2. Legenda sanctissimae matronae Annae, Straßburg 1501; 450.16 Theol. = 1. Homilie divi Gregorij pape super Ezechielem, Paris 1502. 2. Petrus Blesensis, Expositio super librum Iob, Köln 1502 (?). 3. Jacobus Gaudensis, Passio magistralis Iesu Christi, Köln 1505; 149.12 Theol. = 1. Gerhardus Grote, Sermo sinodalis. 2. Directorium concubinariorum, Köln 1508. 3. Defensorium fratrum mendicantium contra curatos. 4. Joannis Pici Mirandulae disputationes adversus astrologos, Deventer 1502. 5. Decreta concilii Basiliensis GW 7284.

gen,[47] Dorstadt[48] und Steterburg[49] bei Wolfenbüttel und dem Augustinerchorherrenkloster Georgenberg bei Goslar sei nur die Beobachtung mitgeteilt, daß die Bibliothek der Frauenklöster sehr einseitig Andachtsliteratur enthielt, während das Männerkloster in Goslar Titel aufweist, die in ein breites Spektrum von Fachdisziplinen einzuordnen sind.[50] Entsprechend reicher sind die Daten zum Bibliotheksaufbau.[50a]

B. Reformierte Zisterzienserklöster

Es waren nicht nur unmittelbar in die Windesheimer Kongregation aufgenommene Augustinerchorherrenklöster, die sich dem Reformgedanken der Windes-

[47] Den 31 bei Heinemann (Die Helmstedter Handschriften Bd 1-3, Wolfenbüttel 1884) nachgewiesenen Handschriften mit vornehmlich asketischer Traktatliteratur stehen fünf in Wolfenbüttel ermittelte Drucke gegenüber: E 320.2° Helmst. = Sermones de tempore Pomerii, Hagenau 1505; S 397.2° Helmst. = Konrad Wimpina sectarum errores, Frankfurt 1528; E 265.2° Helmst. = Sermones Meffret C 3961; Li 4° 56 = Caesarius de Heisterbach, Dialogus miraculorum GW 5881; Li 4° 436 = Rosetum exercitationum et meditationum *H 13995.

[48] Bei Heinemann (s. Anm. 47) werden 16 Handschriften für Dorstadt angegeben. Drei Drucke sind nachweisbar. Bei den Handschriften sind es Breviere, Homilien, Sermones neben der Imitatio Christi des Thomas von Kempen, bei den Drucken Qu H 69 = 1. Marcus Tullius, Cicero de proprietatibus terminorum GW 7028. 2. Guilelmus de Gouda, Expositio officii Missae HC 7831. 3. Nicolaus de Blony, Tractatus sacerdotalis de sacramentis etc. HC 3253; E 31.2° Helmst. = Postilla Guillermi H 8237; Lh 806.2 = Magnus Hund, Expositio Donati H 9036.

[49] Für Steterburg überwiegt die Andachtsliteratur. 23 handgeschriebene und 13 gedruckte Andachtsbücher (Th 305, Th 4° 71, Th 202, S 53.12° Helmst., S 58d.12° Helmst., S 68.12° Helmst., S 339.8° Helmst., S 341.4° Helmst., S 349.8° Helmst., S 378.8° Helmst., S 460.2° Helmst., Yv 420.8° Helmst., Yv 659.8° Helmst.) stehen drei handgeschriebenen und 8 gedruckten Traktaten und religiösen Betrachtungen gegenüber (Ts 502, E 330.2° Helmst., Li 4° 67, E 42.2° Helmst., S 65.12° Helmst., S 69.12° Helmst., S 373.8° Helmst.).

[50] Es gibt nicht nur Sermones wie E 150.2° Helmst. = Sermones peregrini HC 12581; E 249a.2° Helmst. = Aurei Sermones C 4416; E 247.2° Helmst. = Sermones Nider H 11803; E 356.2° Helmst. = Johannes Herolt, Sermones discipuli HC 8503. Es finden sich auch die Werke der großen Kirchenväter: E 90.2° Helmst. u. E 91.2° Helmst. = Bonaventura, Opuscula GW 4648; E 94.2° Helmst. = 1. Perlustratio Sancti Bonaventurae in primum librum Sententiarum. 2. Perlustratio Sancti Bonaventurae in secundum librum Sententiarum H 3541; E 46.2° Helmst. = Secundus liber secundae partis summae operum B. Thomae de Aquino, s.l. et s.a.

Daneben tauchen in Klöstern kaum vertretene historische Werke auf: T 346.2° Helmst. = Rolevinck, Fasciculus temporum HC 6936; T 337-339.2° Helmst. = Antonius Florentinus, Chronicon, Basel 1502; T 330.2° Helmst. = Speculum historiale Vincentii HC 6248.

[50a] Für Dorstadt gab es nur Geschenkhinweise, desgleichen für Heiningen und Steterburg. Bei Georgenberg hingegen werden einzelne Persönlichkeiten faßbar, die den Bibliotheksaufbau förderten wie etwa der Abt Wilhelm von Ahusen. Bei den Drucken findet sich gelegentlich ein Hinweis auf einen Kauf durch den Prior (E 90.2° Helmst. u. E 91.2° Helmst.).

heimer Prägung verbunden fühlten. Der Abt Heinrich Bernthen des Zisterzienserklosters Marienrode bei Hildesheim unterstützte Johannes Busch, den bedeutenden Windesheimer Reformator und Chronisten in der Reform tatkräftig.[51] Heinrich Bernthen hat als Abt ganz im Sinne der Windesheimer die Skriptoriumsarbeit hochgeschätzt. Davon zeugt ein Passus in der von ihm verfaßten Chronik. Danach hat Bernthen im Armarium den Platz für Bücher erweitern lassen, also neben der Braunschweiger Bibliothek St. Andreas und der Hildesheimer Franziskanerbibliothek ein weiterer Hinweis auf eine bauliche Vergrößerung der Bibliothek. Die von ihm gesammelten Bücher werden rechts vom Eingang aufgestellt. Er ließ einige von diesen auf Pergament abschreiben, und veranlaßte die Brüder Albertus und Johannes zur Schreibtätigkeit.[52] Einige Titel werden genannt, unter denen jedoch nicht der heute in der Landesbibliothek Hannover aufbewahrte Marienroder Kodex sich befindet, den Henricus selbst *pro armario ponendum* abgeschrieben hat.[53] Dieser enthält eine Reihe von asketischen Traktaten, er ist ganz dazu bestimmt, den *profectum fratrum suorum* zu fördern, wie es in der Widmungsnotiz Bernthens auf dem vorderen Pergamentspiegel des Kodex heißt. Sein Zweck ist das Exercitatorium hominis religiosi. Der Inhalt entspricht ganz der Reformbewegung. Allein 11 pseudo-bernwardinische Schriften wie der Tractatus de charitate, das Speculum monachorum, die Documenta pie et religiose vivendi, die Formula honestae vitae, reflektieren das fromme Leben der Mönche. Die Grundmotive der Devotio moderna klingen an: die Reinheit des Herzens, das Wachstum der Liebe und die Nachfolge Christi in der Demut. Wie verbreitet diese Traktate waren und daß sie unter den Klöstern dieses Raumes ausgetauscht wurden, zeigen drei Wolfenbütteler Handschriften, in denen ebenfalls zum Teil mit denselben charakteristischen Abweichungen vom Mignetext die pseudo-bernhardinischen Traktate überlie-

[51] Am deutlichsten kommt seine Anerkennung als Reformer zum Ausdruck in seiner Ernennung zu einem der drei generellen Beichtväter für die Gewinnung des Jubiläumablasses in Hildesheim durch Nikolaus von Kues. Scriptores rerum Brunsvicensium ed. G.W. Leibniz 2 (1710), S. 463.

[52] Scriptores rerum Brunsvicensium ed. G.W. Leibniz 2 (1710), S. 453: *Dilataverat insuper locum librorum in armario nostro libros ibidem multiplicando, scribendo et ordinando. Insuper quae ipse propria manu collegerat, simul ad unum locum ad dextram videlicet ingredientium ponendo ibidem. Fecit autem scribi in pargameno de his, quae primo collegerat in paperio, tertium malogranati; nam primum fecit scribi dominus Johannes, secundum dominus Albertus. Idem dominus Johannes procuravit Mammotractum et Mandevillium. Praeterea Abbas Hinricus ingrossari atque scribi constituit Bernhardum super Qui habitat; item Christianismum documentum, similiter Scrutinium scripturarum in duabus partibus, item VIII libros in papiro per ordinem positos in specialibus designatos, in quibus multa per se scripsit, alia autem scribi fecit. Exceptis pluribus aliis voluminibus quibus temporibus suis ditatum esse constat armigerum nostrum, quia duo interstitia superiora de novo fabricata libris fere repleta sunt.*

[53] Vgl. HANNOVER Ms I 251a.

fert worden sind: sie stammen aus den Klöstern Wöltingerode bei Goslar und Marienberg bei Helmstedt.[54]

Daher ist es nicht verwunderlich, wenn die Bibliothek des Zisterziensernonnenklosters Wöltingerode[55] auch sonst ganz ähnliches Schrifttum enthält. Unter den 85 auf uns gekommenen Handschriften und den inzwischen identifizierten 21 Inkunabeln und Postinkunabeln finden sich allein 24 Signaturen mit derartiger Literatur.[56] Dem entsprechen die vielen Andachtsbücher und noch zahlreichere Bücher für den gottesdientlichen Gebrauch.[57] Alle anderen Bücher sind entweder diesen Andachtsbüchern oder den Büchern für den gottesdientlichen Gebrauch zuzuordnen.

[54] Vgl. Handschriften der Niedersächsischen Landesbibliothek Hannover, Wiesbaden 1982, S. 97, zu Ms I 251a, 17r, 43v, 52v, 210v, 222r. Weitere Aussagen über die Klosterbibliothek scheitern am Quellenmangel. Die heute für Marienrode in den Beständen der Niedersächsischen Landesbibliothek Hannover nachweisbaren Handschriften und Inkunabeln sind fast durchweg im 16. und 17. Jahrhundert erworben worden, scheiden also für unsere Betrachtung aus. Es ist für die Quellenlage bezeichnend, daß ein in Deventer veranstalteter Inkunabeldruck von Predigten nach einer hinzugefügten Vorrede angeblich von einem gelehrten Marienroder Bruder erst 1695 von dem Abt Jacobus Lohe von Altenberg an das Kloster Marienrode geschenkt wird (Nr. 207 in Eduard Bodemann, Xylographische und typographische Inkunabeln der Königl. Öffentlichen Bibliothek zu Hannover, Hannover 1866, S. 209. Zu der Verfasserschaft des Druckes vgl. GW 7409 = Conradus de Brundelsheim, Sermones de tempore.)

[55] Wöltingerode bei Goslar war ebenfalls nicht nur der Reform zugetan (Der in Cod. Guelf. 353 Helmst. überlieferte Traktat des Magdeburger Hinricus Token lautet bezeichnenderweise *De virginibus reformatis in Woltingerode apud Goslariam*), sondern auch zur Hilfe in der Reform bereit. 1442 war das Augustinerinnenkloster Derneburg u.a. durch den Visitator des Klosters Henricus Bernthen gewaltsam der Reform zugeführt worden, indem die Nonnen in eine Reihe von Klöstern, darunter auch nach Wöltingerode, abgeführt wurden. Um deren geistliche Förderung war man bemüht. 1444 wird den in Wöltingerode lebenden Derneburger virgines ausdrücklich ein in Goslar geschriebenes Doctrinale virginum gewidmet (Cod. Guelf. 602 Helmst., 4lr: *Virginibus sacris in Woltigerod situatis, perveniant fructus doctrine carmine huius Derneborch missis quoque commendetur ut ipsis.* = »Zu den in Wöltingerode lebenden heiligen Jungfrauen mögen die Früchte der in diesem Gedicht enthaltenen Lehre gelangen, das Gedicht sei auch den aus Derneburg geschickten wie ihnen selbst übereignet«. Bei dem Doctrinale handelt es sich um WALTHER I 7312.). Aus einem Visitationsprotokoll vom Jahre 1483 geht hervor, daß auf die Einhaltung des Breviergebetes, die Lektüre einzelner Schwestern geachtet wurde. Bei Tisch gab es die Sitte der Bibellesung (Adolf Bertram, Geschichte des Bistums Hildesheim 1 (1899), S. 446.).

[56] Cod. Guelf. 384, 602, 610, 667, 708, 804, 1042, 1074, 1078, 1120, 1144, 1163, 1173, 1234, 1235, 1241, 1243, 1251, 1306, 1372, 1393, 1394, 1396, 1399 Helmst.

[57] Sechzehnmal taucht der Titel Liber precum vel orationum auf, noch zahlreicher sind die liturgischen Bücher, es sind 35, davon 12 Breviere (Cod. Guelf. 569, 1111, 1177, 1304, 1328, 1339, 1343, 1351, 1354, 1367, 1369, 1427 Helmst.), 14 Psalterien (Cod. Guelf. 515, 571, 1069, 1072, 1244, 1280, 1285, 1295, 1302, 1309.1, 1317, 1403, 1410, 1418 Helmst.), zwei Lectionarien (Cod. Guelf. 888,

Studien zum Wachstum und zur Entwicklung von Bibliotheken

Ein recht einheitliches Bild also, und dem entspricht Leben und Führung des Klosters im Geiste der Reform. Wie der Abt Henricus Bernthen in Marienrode, so fördert nachweislich für die achtziger Jahre des Jahrhunderts die Äbtissin Elisabeth von Burgdorf in Wöltingerode den Bibliotheksaufbau.[58]

C. Die Bursfelder Reformklöster

Den Reformklöstern Clus bei Gandersheim und St. Blasien in Northeim und ihren Bibliotheken ist seit langem große Aufmerksamkeit zuteil geworden.[59] Entsprechend umfangreich ist die Zahl der für beide Bibliotheken nachweis-

---

1355 Helmst.), eine Agenda (Cod. Guelf. 1355 Helmst.), ein Officium beate Marie virginis (Cod. Guelf. 1301 Helmst.), zwei Evangeliare (Cod. Guelf. 425, 1110 Helmst.), ein Ordo divini officii (Cod. Guelf. 1014 Helmst.), ein Missale (Cod. Guelf. 522 Helmst.), ein Martyrologium (Cod. Guelf. 498 Helmst.). Von welch großer Wichtigkeit die Liturgica für das spirituelle Leben in Wöltingerode waren, bestätigt auch der Blick auf die Inkunabeln. Ich zähle zwei Diurnale Cisterciense (S 57.12° Helmst., S 58.12° Helmst.), fünf Breviere (S 345.8° Helmst. u. S 351.8° Helmst., S 346.8° Helmst., S 348.8° Helmst., Ti 63), drei Psalterien (S 358.8° Helmst., S 359.4° Helmst., S 360.8° Helmst.), wobei eines davon ein Breviarium Halberstadense ist (Tk 31). Die weiteren Drucke enthalten Sermones (E 35.2° Helmst., E 261.2° Helmst., E 358.2° Helmst., E 366.2° Helmst.). Daneben finden sich Johannes de Tambaco, Liber de consolatione (E 162.2° Helmst.), eine Summa de virtutibus des Guilelmus Paraldus (E 43.2° Helmst.), Epistola F. Hieronymi, ein Prologus in Horologium (1504), Ludolphus de Saxonia, Vita Christi. P1 und 2 (S 243.2° Helmst. u. S 244.2° Helmst.).

[58] Auf ihre Veranlassung ist 1481 Cod. Guelf. 166 Helmst. (Speculum conscienciae sive collectura de libro conscienciae) geschrieben worden. Für das Kloster erwarb (comparavit) sie drei weitere Handschriften (Cod. Guelf. 610, 667 u. 708 Helmst.), alle im ersten Teil von derselben Schreiberhand begonnen, desgleichen Cod. Guelf. 166 und 1120 Helmst., von anderen Händen geschrieben (Cod. Guelf. 610, 667 u. 708 Helmst. wie auch Cod. Guelf. 166 Helmst. sind von den Einbandstempeln her eindeutig nach Wöltingerode einzuordnen. Nicht nur die Schrifthände sind dieselben, sondern auch etwa die Lagenzählung. Schunke (s.u.) spricht von der Hauptwerkstatt Wöltingerode.). Bei Cod. Guelf. 1120 Helmst. wird jedoch ausdrücklich gesagt, daß Elisabeth die Abschrift veranlaßt hatte. Auf sie geht auch der Erwerb einer Inkunabel zurück: der vier Jahre vor ihrem Tode gedruckte *Cassianus de institutis cenobiorum* Basel (Joh. Amerbach, nach 24.IX) 1485 GW 6160; Besitzeintrag: *Liber sancte Marie virginis in Woltingerode quem comparavit nobis venerabilis domina Elyzabet de Borchtorpe abbatissa pie memorie. Cuius felix anima...*; die Inkunabel Li 4° 67 weist Stempel der bei Ilse Schunke, Die Schwenke-Sammlung gotischer Stempel- und Einbandabreibungen I, Berlin 1979, mit »Braunschweig Kleinfig.-Meister I« bezeichneten Werkstatt auf. Christkind/Christus Nr. 13 und Nr. 28.

[59] Hermann Herbst, Johann Brakel. Ein Beitrag zur Bibliotheksgeschichte des Benediktinerklosters Clus bei Gandersheim, in: Nunquam retrorsum. Beiträge zur Schrift- und Buchkunde als Ehrengabe für Albert Schramm, Wolfenbüttel 1930, S. 1-16. Ders. s. Anm. 36, ferner Hans Goetting (s. Anm.3).

baren Titel, die Hermann Herbst auf bibliothekshistorische Erkenntnisse untersucht hat.

Das Wachstum der Bibliotheken ist auf Bücherkäufe, Bücherschenkungen und die klostereigene Produktion von Handschriften zurückzuführen. Ist neben dem allerdings in Klöstern seltenen Kauf die Abschreibtätigkeit für die Motive beim Bibliotheksaufbau am aussagekräftigsten, so ist gerade die Zahl der festgestellten Handschriften, die während der Reformzeit ab 1450 im Kloster entstanden sind, relativ klein und die als Geschenke in die Klöster gekommenen um so größer. Schon in den Wöltingeroder Besitzeinträgen hatte es neben comparare sehr viel häufiger conferre geheißen.[60] Die neu eingeschärfte Bursfelder Regel, Bücher zu schreiben, zu rubrizieren und einzubinden hat offenbar das Wachstum der Bibliotheken sehr viel weniger beeinflußt als in den Häusern der von Gerhard Grote beeinflußten Reform.[61] Mit dieser Beobachtung korrespondiert die Tatsache, daß sowohl in Clus wie in Northeim trotz ihrer Größe keine Persönlichkeit in besonderem Maße hervortritt, die dem Aufbau der Bibliotheken ihren Stempel aufgedrückt hätte. Hatte also die dominierende Vermehrung über Schenkungen für den Bibliotheksaufbau reine Zufallsbedeutung? Nicht unbedingt, die Schenker waren darauf bedacht, daß die Bücher pro salute animae suae gelesen wurden. Entsprechend wurde das Buchgeschenk auf die Bedürfnisse des Klosters hin ausgewählt. Hatte der Hildesheimer Vikar Thidericus Roleves für Clus vornehmlich Schriften erbaulichen Charakters vorgesehen,[62] so bedenkt er die Vikare des Domstiftes im urbanen Hildesheim mit Handschriften vornehmlich humanistischen Inhalts.[63] Oder ein Wöltingeroder Beispiel: Das Rationale divinorum des Durandus sollte den Pröpsten des Klosters zur Lesung im Refektorium dienen.[64]

---

[60] Z.B. Cod. Guelf. 1516 Helmst.: *quem contulit nobis fidelis amicus noster Johannes de Swichelte*.

[61] Dem entspricht, daß heute für Clus nur ein Druck nachweisbar ist. 1518 hatte der für die Bursfelder Union im 16. Jahrhundert bedeutende Abt Konrad Hissing ein Missale Benedictinum Bursfeldense gekauft (S 450.2° Helmst.).

[62] Vgl. Hermann Herbst (s. Anm. 36), S. 86 Anm. 2 zu Cod. Guelf. 954 Helmst. und die Inkunabel 432.1 Theol. 2°, woran die Handschrift Cod. Guelf. 315 angebunden war. Die Inkunabel enthält Johannes Gerson, Collectorium super Magnificat H 7717 und Thomas de Aquino, Postilla in Job H 1397.

[63] HILDESHEIM Dombibliothek Hs 624 enthält Petrarcas De remediis utriusque fortunae (vgl. A. Sottili, I codici del Petrarca nella Germania occidentale 1, Padova 1971, 119, Nr. 44); Hs 618 enthält 1. Boetius, De consolatione philosophiae, 2. Satirae und 3. Terenz, Andria; Hs 671 Conclusiones Rotae super dubiis ... per Wilhelm Horborch.

[64] Vgl. Ti 67 = GW 5159 (Anm. 3) ...*ad refectorium precipue deputatum*.

Für Northeim überwiegen jedoch die Gegenbeispiele. Im Kloster St. Blasien in Northeim war das Bibliotheksgebäude im Jahr 1517 erweitert worden, der vierte noch heute nachweisbare Bibliotheksneubau neben St. Andreas in Braunschweig, St. Martin in Hildesheim und Marienrode, und es waren aus »Stiften und Clostern Bücher dahin gegeben« worden.[65] Vor allem sind es zahlreiche Drucke. Noch heute tragen in Wolfenbüttel allein 28 Bände den Vermerk »Liber monasterij sancti Blasij in Northeym anno domini MDxvij«.[66] Diese Vermehrung zeugt sicherlich nicht von einem systematischen Erwerbungswillen, wie wir ihn uns heute vorzustellen gewöhnt sind.

Zusätzlich zu den Geschenken pro salute animarum der Donatoren kommt ab 1521 ein neuer Gesichtspunkt hinzu: Bewahrung der Reste einer Klerikerbibliothek, die 1521 in Erfurt von lutherischen Studenten weitgehend zerstört

---

[65] Vgl. Hermann Herbst, Handschriften aus dem Benediktinerkloster Northeim, in: Studien und Mitteilungen aus dem Benediktinerorden, Jg. 1932, S. 359.

[66] D 85.2° Helmst. = 1. Deflorationes patrum GW 8247; 2. Rethorica divina de Oratione domini Guilermi Parisiensis HC 8303. 3. Ephrem Syrus, Sermones selecti GW 9334. 4. Johannes Andreae, Super arboribus consanguinitatis, affinitatis et cognationis spiritualis et legalis GW 1704; D 412.2° Helmst. = 1. Rabanus Maurus, Liber poenitentialis R 1014. 2. Guido de Monte Rochen s. Rotherii, Manipulus curatorum H 8162. E 32.2° Helmst. = Guillermus, Postilla super evangelia dominicalia et super evangelia de sanctis H 8247; E 87.2° Helmst. = 1. Communiloquium sive summa collationum Johannis Gallensis HC 7444. 2. Albertus Magnus super missus est GW 681. 3. Johannes Nivicellensis, Concordantiae Bibliae et canonum totiusque Juris civilis HC 9417; E 145.2° u. E 146a.2° Helmst. = Reynerus de Pisis, Panthologia s. summa universae theologiae H 13014; E 153.2° Helmst. = Sermones Hugonis de Prato florido de sanctis HC 9009; E 170.2° Helmst. = Thomas de Argentina, scripta super quattuor libros sententiarum HC 603; E 209.2° Helmst. = Vincentius Ferrarius, Sermones de tempore et de sanctis (P.1+2) GW 9838; E 212.2° Helmst. = 1. Vincentius Ferrarius, Sermones de tempore et de sanctis (P.3) GW 9838. 2. Sermones Meffreth alias Ortulus regine de Sanctis (P.3) H 11005; E 214.2°-216.2° Helmst. = Jean Gerson, Opera (3 Bde) H 7624; E 234.2° Helmst. = Johannes Gritsch OFM, Quadragesimale HC 8068; E 263.2° Helmst. = Sermones Meffreth alias Ortulus regine de tempore, pars hyemalis H 11005; E 273.2° Helmst. = Antonius Florentinus, Summa theologica. Mit Beigabe von Franciscus Moneliensis GW 2185; E 286.2° Helmst. = Antonius Florentinus, Tabula zur Summa theologica von Johannes Molitoris GW 2199; E 291.2° Helmst. = Sermones Dormi secure vel Dormi sine cura HC 15959; E 295.2° Helmst. = Sermones Parati de tempore et de sanctis H 12413; E 340.2° Helmst. = Sermones aurei de sanctis fratris Leonardi de Utino sacre theologie doctoris ordinis predicatorum, Nürnberg 1478; E 367.2° Helmst. = 1. Robertus Caracciolus, Sermones de laudibus sanctorum GW 6056. 2. Robertus Caracciolus, Sermones de adventu etc. – Dominicus Bollanus, De conceptione Beatae Virginis Mariae; L 734.2°-738.2° Helmst. (5 Bde) = Panormitanus (Nicolaus) de Tudeschis, Lectura super quinque libros Decretalium HC 12315; S 242.2° Helmst. = Ludolphus de Saxonia, Vita Christi H *10292; T 329.2° Helmst. = Vincentius Bellovacensis, Speculum historiale, [Speculum maius, Teilausg.] HC 6245; T 505.2° Helmst. = Speculum exemplorum HC 14915.

worden war. In diesem Jahr schenkt der Erfurter Dekan des Kollegiatsstiftes St. Marien dem Northeimer Kloster eine Reihe von Handschriften und Drucken, viele mit dem Vermerk:»... eodem tempore ... dominus (scil. Johannes Weidemann) una cum prelatis et dominis spoliatus a luteranis hereticis ibidem in Erffurdia« (der geistliche Herr, nämlich Johannes Weidemann, ist zu dieser Zeit zusammen mit Prälaten und anderen geistlichen Herren von lutherischen Häretikern ebendort in Erfurt ausgeplündert worden).[67] Es waren fast durchgehend Bücher mit juristischem Inhalt, wohl kaum geeignet, ein reformiertes Kloster der Bursfelder Kongregation in seinem geistlichen Zweck zu fördern.

D. Reformkloster und Reformation

Anders ist es bei dem Benediktinerkloster Oldenstadt bei Uelzen, und das liegt wiederum an der eifrigen Tätigkeit eines um die Bibliothek bemühten Abtes. Es gehörte seit 1486 der Bursfelder Kongregation an,[68] ist jedoch nicht nur als Reformkloster dieser Kongregation im 15. und 16. Jahrhundert hervorgetreten, sondern auch ein interessantes Beispiel dafür, daß reformatorisches Gedankengut bei um strenge Einhaltung der monastischen Lebensform bemühten Klosterinsassen einen besonders gut bereiteten Boden vorfand. Damit läßt sich über das Uelzener Kloster der Bogen von den Reformbewegungen des 15. Jahrhunderts zur Reformation des 16. Jahrhunderts schlagen. Die wenigen für das Kloster überlieferten Handschriften stammen aus dem 16. Jahrhundert und sind durchweg Abschriften der Werke Jakobs des Karthäusers.[69] Es liegt nun nahe zu vermuten, daß der letzte Abt des Klosters Heyno Gottschalk die Abschrift veranlaßt hat. Nicht nur, weil eine Reihe von Marginalien in den Handschriften sicher von seiner Hand stammt,[70] sondern auch, weil er bis 1516 ein eifriger

---

[67] Vgl. Hermann Herbst, Dr. Johannes Weidemann und seine Bibliothek, in: Sachsen und Anhalt 7 (1931), S. 341-359.

[68] Germania Benedictina 6 (1979), S. 393.

[69] Cod. Guelf. 691, 703, 870 Helmst. GÖTTINGEN UB Cod. theol. 129; Cod. theol. 130; Cod. theol. 131; Cod. theol. 132 (von 1514). In dem »Verzeichnis der Bücher so zur Oldenstadt gewesen vnd gehn Vlzen gethan worden. 1535« (Zeitschrift des historischen Vereins für Niedersachsen 1855, S. 122 f) werden »Opera Jacobi Carthusiensis, octo libri scripti« (S. 123) aufgeführt; die in Wolfenbüttel und Göttingen bewahrten sind mit ihnen sicherlich identisch, weisen diese doch eine Uelzener Eigenart auf: sie sind im Schnitt signiert: G 6, G 8 und G 9 etc. Sie haben das gleiche Format, sind zum Teil von denselben Händen etwa in den Jahren zwischen 1511 und 1514 geschrieben worden.

[70] Diese Hand ist identisch mit der, in der eine Reihe von Besitzvermerken in den Uelzener Drucken geschrieben ist.

Studien zum Wachstum und zur Entwicklung von Bibliotheken 101

Besucher der Generalkapitel der Bursfelder Kongregation war. Denn die Abschrift der Werke Jakobs des Karthäusers und eine strenge reformerische Gesinnung im Sinne der Bursfelder Kongregation bedingen einander. Schon 1455 hatte Jakob selbst auf einem Generalkapitel der Bursfelder in Erfurt die Mönchsreform erläutert. Später wurden seine Werke studiert als Hilfen zur Bewahrung des kontemplativen Möchtums und zur Förderung der »kontemplativen Spiritualität«.[71] Ganz in diesem Sinne ließ Heyno Gottschalk die Werke Jakobs abschreiben und machte damit Oldenstadt noch einmal kurzzeitig am Anfang des 16. Jahrhunderts zu einem Zentrum der Rezeption Jakobscher Werke.

Mit derselben Intensität, mit der Heyno Gottschalk die Werke des Jacobus Carthusiensis abschreiben ließ, muß er die Ereignisse um Luther und die sich anbahnende Reformation der kirchlichen Verhältnisse verfolgt haben. Bis zur Durchforstung der Herzog August Bibliothek auf die Uelzener Bände war von der alten Klosterbibliothek nur noch ein Buch bekannt.[72] In Wolfenbüttel fanden sich nun 52 Bände aus dieser Bibliothek mit 272 Titeln,[73] auffälligerwei-

---

[71] Vgl. Dieter Mertens, Iacobus Carthusiensis, Göttingen 1976, S. 97 u. 99. (Veröffentlichungen des Max-Planck-Instituts für Geschichte. 50.) (Studien zur Germania sacra. 13.).

[72] Franciscus Irenicus, Germaniae exegeseos volumina duodecim, Hagenau 1518. Vgl. Günter Bismark, Die Oldenstädter Klosterbibliothek, in: Der Heidewanderer. Niedersächsische Heimatzeitung der Allgemeinen Zeitung der Lüneburger Heide 54 (1979), S. 162.

[73] Die Kenntnis eines großen Teils der folgenden Signaturen verdanke ich Ulrich Kopp: C 85b.4° Helmst (= Oekolampad mit einem und Luther mit zwei Titeln aus d.J. 1525-30 vertreten); C 198.4° Helmst. (alte Sign. D1) (= Melanchthon mit drei, Huldreich Mutius mit drei, Andreas Rudolf Bodenstein, Oekolampad, Johann Wessel, Ulrich Zwingli, Lorenzo Valla mit je einem Titel aus d.J. 1521-23 vertreten); C 201.4° Helmst. (Johann Brenz, 1526); C 235.8° Helmst. (ein Titel von Martin Bucer, zwei von Oekolampad, einer von Zwingli aus d.J. 1526-28); C 251b.8° Helmst. (alte Sign. L 12) (= ein Titel von Erasmus, dazu Samuel Maroccanus, Epistola contra Judaeos aus d.J. 1523); C 283.8° Helmst. (alte Sign. D 3) (= drei Titel von Melanchthon aus d.J. 1523); C 289.8° Helmst. (Bucer, 1527); C 290.8° Helmst. (Bucer, 1528); C 374a.8° Helmst. (alte Sign. L 10) (= Erasmus, 1521); C 374b.8° Helmst. (alte Sign. L 9) (= drei Titel des Erasmus aus d.J. 1520 u. 1521); C 391.8° Helmst. (= ein Titel von Bugenhagen, zwei von Euricius Cordus aus d.J. 1525); C 425.8° Helmst. (= je ein Titel von Oekolampad, François Lambert u. Erasmus aus d.J. 1524 u. 1525); C 478a.8° Helmst. (= vier Titel von Melanchthon, zwei von Bucer, einer von Andreas Althamer aus d.J. 1525-27); G 85.4° Helmst. (ein Titel von Martin Luther a.d.J. 1519); H 4.2° Helmst. (=Johann Fabri, Malleus, 1529); H 54.4° Helmst. (= drei Titel von Hutten, zwei von Erasmus, je einer von Franciscus Faber, Huldreich Mutius, Johann Jaeger, Johann Montanus, Johann Callerius, Oekolampad, Udelo Cymber, Raphael Musaius, Wilhelm Nesen, Eobanus Hessus, Jacobus von Hoogstraten, Melanchton, Augustin Alveldt, Johann Lonicer aus d.J. 1519-21); H 56d.4° Helmst. (alte Sign. L 9) (= zwei Titel von John Fischer, je einer von Erasmus u. Luther aus d.J. 1521-25); H 60.4°

se nur zeitgenössische, und das heißt Literatur von Reformatoren und Humanisten. Viele Namen neben bekannten wie Erasmus, Thomas Morus, Bugen-

Helmst. (alte Sign. F 6) (= je zwei Titel von Hutten, Johann Römer, Karsthans, Pamphilius Gengenbach, je einer von Michael Stifel, Urbanus Rhegius, Kunz von Oberndorff, Joachim von Walt, Bucer, Johann Eberlin, Johann Schweblin aus d.J. 1519-22); H 72.4° Helmst. (=vier Titel von Zwingli, zwei von Oekolampad, je einer von Capito u. Wolf Cyclop aus d.J. 1525 u. 1526); H 102.4° Helmst. (alte Sign. C 18) (= je ein Titel von Justus Jonas, Andreas Althamer, Andreas Osiander, Sebastian Franck, Dominicus Burgauer aus d.J. 1531-34); H 460.4° Helmst. (= drei Titel von Kaspar Schatzgeyer, zwei von Johannes Cochlaeus, je einer von Thomas Radinus Todischus, Hieronymus Emser, Johann Eck aus d.J. 1519-23); J 150.8° Helmst. (alte Sign. D 12) (= je zwei Titel von Antonius Corvinus, einer von Urbanus Rhegius aus d.J. 1537 u. 1538); K 149.8° Helmst. (= zwei Titel von Bugenhagen aus d.J. 1528); Li 5530 (2,18) (= Luther aus d.J. 1522); Li 5530 (6,100) (= Luther a.d.J. 1532); Li 5530 (7,104) (= Luther, 1533); Li 5530 (38,662) (= Insignium theologorum..., Paris um 1520); Li 5530 (63,1292a) (= Luther, 1534); P 521.4° Helmst. (alte Sign. F 7) (= je zwei Titel von Erasmus u. Christophorus Hegendorff, je einer von Thomas Morus, Johannes Frobenius, Basilius magnus, Pomponius Laetus, Melanchton, Johannes Gertophius, Johann Pupper van Goch aus d.J. 1516-21); P 585.4° Helmst. (alte Sign. L 7) (= zwei Titel von Erasmus, je einer von Dionysius Cato, William Lily, Jacobus Wimpheling, Peter Schade aus d.J. 1517-19); P 2156.8° Helmst. (alte Sign. L 15) (= zwei Titel von Erasmus, einer von Rupertus Tuicensis aus d.J. 1524); Qu H 161.31 8° (= 5 Titel von Luther, je einer von Justus Jonas, Nicolaus von Amsdorff u. Melanchthon a.d.J. 1532-1536); S 188.4° Helmst. (= je zwei Titel von Jodocus Clichtoveus u. Johannes Cochlaeus, einer von Jacobus von Hoogstraten aus d.J. 1525); S 287.4° Helmst. (alte Sign. B 16) (= je zwei Titel von Antonius Corvinus, Melanchthon u. Luther, je einer von Hieronymus Emser, Hermann von Mengersen, Urbanus Rhegius, Heinrich Dorpius, Nicolaus von Amsdorff, Johann Fritzhans, Juan Luis Vives u.a. Schriften über Münsteraner Widertäufer aus d.J. 1524, 1532-36); Tf 43 (= Confessio fidei nebst Apologia confessionis, 1531); Yf 1.4° Helmst. (alte Sign. C 3) (= je ein Titel von John Fischer u. Erasmus aus d.J. 1525 u. 1526); Yk 16.8° Helmst. (alte Sign. A 22) (= je zwei Titel von Luther u. Melanchthon aus d.J. 1538 u. 1539); Yk 78.8° Helmst. (= drei Titel von Erasmus aus d.J. 1525 u. 1529); Yv 482.8° Helmst. (alte Sign. A 18) (= je ein Titel von Luther u. Brenz aus d.J. 1532); Yv 677.8° Helmst. (alte Sign. D 4) (= Bugenhagen, 1524); Yv 688.8° Helmst. (alte Sign. D 5) (Bugenhagen, 1524); Yv 1104.8° Helmst. (= Bugenhagen, 1530); Yv 1271.8° Helmst. (alte Sign. E 19) (= zwei Titel von Oekolampad, einer von Jacobus Lathomus aus d.J. 1525); 96.19 Theol. (alte Sign. C 10) (= fünf Titel von Nikolaus Amsdorff, zwei von Melanchton, einer von Bugenhagen aus d.J. 1526-29); 96.20 Theol. (= u.a. drei Titel von Michael Stifel, je einer von Hartmut von Cronenberg, Johannes Briesman, Johannes Schwan, Nikolaus Amsdorff, Johann Eberlin, Eckhart zum Drübel, Zwingli, Thobias Fabri, Bartholomeus Usingen aus d.J. 1522 u. 1523); 155.7 Theol. (= u.a. ein Titel von Jacob Schorre, Karsthans, Johann Langen, Caspar Hedion, je zwei von Eberhard Widense aus d.J. 1525-26); 181.16 Theol. (alte Sign. C 12) (=u.a. zwei Titel von Urbanus Rhegius, einer von Martin Undermarck, Nikolaus Krumpach aus d.J. 1529); 194.4.1 Theol. 4° (alte Sign. A 10) (= Mattheus Zell, 1523); 478.3 Theol. 2° (= ein Titel von Trithemius u. Thomas v. Aquin 1516, 1508); 990.54 Theol. (alte Sign. G 15) (= zwei Titel von Luther a.d.J. 1538 u. 1540); 990.78 Theol. (alte Sign. A 21) (= Luther, 1535).

hagen, Melanchthon, Bucer, Luther und Zwingli tauchen als Autoren auf. Alle Bände sind gemäß dem eigenhändig von Gottschalk geschriebenen Besitzvermerk unmittelbar nach der Veröffentlichung in Uelzen eingetroffen und offenbar von Gottschalk intensiv studiert worden, wie die vielen Notabene in den Werken beweisen. In vielen Fällen ist das Datum im Impressum des Buches mit dem von Heyno Gottschalk regelmäßig verzeichneten Zugangsdatum identisch. Die Lektüre zeigte auch bald ihre Wirkung. Denn 1528 fragt Heyno Gottschalk bei keinem Geringeren als Luther selbst an, ob es zu vertreten sei, weiter im Kloster zu verbleiben. Luther bejaht diese Frage, solange im Kloster die Freiheit des Geistes herrsche.[74] Am 10. Juli 1529 verzichtete Heyno Gottschalk auf das Amt des Abtes und übergab Herzog Ernst von Braunschweig und Lüneburg die Verwaltung des Klosters. Für sein Verbleiben im Kloster und sein leibliches Wohl sorgte der Herzog. Bis zu seinem Tod am 9. 11. 1541 kaufte und las er weiter Bücher, änderte den Besitzeintrag allerdings auf bezeichnende Weise: es hieß nicht mehr »Liber monasterij sancti Johannis baptiste in veteri Ultzen«, sondern »Liber Heynonis olim abbatis in veteri Ultzen«. Kurz vor seinem Tode kaufte er noch die 1538 in Wittenberg erschienenen *Annotationes Doctoris Martini Lutheri in aliquot capitulos Matthaei*.[75] Alle in Wolfenbüttel bewahrten Bände besitzen nicht nur charakteristische Merkmale, die sie einer Buchbinderwerkstatt, vermutlich der des Klosters, zuweisen. Auffällig ist auch der reichliche Gebrauch von Pergamentvorsatzblättern aus früh- und hochmittelalterlichen Handschriften, vielleicht aus der Uelzener Klosterbibliothek.[76] Der Umfang der Klosterbibliothek ist aus dem im Jahre 1535 bei der Überführung in die Stadt Uelzen verfaßten Verzeichnis noch zu ermitteln: 274 Bände werden aufgeführt, 1545 folgen 91 weitere, die man dem Abt und den Brüdern zur Benutzung gelassen hatte.[77] Auffällig ist nun, daß die 44 in Wolfenbüttel festgestellten Bände mit ihren Titeln in diesen Übersichten nicht auftauchen. Hatte Abt Heyno diese Titel mit eindeutig reformatorischen Inhalten zusätzlich separiert? Denn sie sind nicht unter denen zu finden, die laut Übergabeprotokoll aus dem Jahr 1545 in der unmittelbaren Benutzung von Heyno Gottschalk sich befanden.[78]

Mit dem Brand der Uelzener Marienkirche im Jahr 1646 ging die vor den

---

[74] Martin Luthers Werke. Briefwechsel Bd. 4, Weimar 1933, S. 390-391.
[75] Yk 16.8° Helmst. Besitzeintrag: Liber Heynonis olim abbatis in veteri Ultzen 1540.
[76] Z.B. P 585.4° Helmst.; Yv 1104.8° Helmst.
[77] Zeitschrift des historischen Vereins für Niedersachsen 1856, S. 129-131.
[78] Zeitschrift des historischen Vereins für Niedersachsen 1856, S. 130 f.

Wirren der Reformation gerettete Bibliothek zugrunde. Nur Reste wie die in Wolfenbüttel festgestellten überdauerten die Zeit. Ähnlich ging es den meisten Bibliotheken in den ca. 250 Klöstern des heutigen Territoriums in Niedersachsen.[79] Die Reformation ließ die klösterlichen Reformbewegungen abreißen, ihre geistige Hinterlassenschaft wurde zerstört, da sie nicht mehr von Bedeutung schien. Die Reformation hatte die Epoche der spätmittelalterlichen Reformen abgelöst, wie auch diese wiederum eine ältere Phase der klösterlichen Bibliotheksgeschichte zu einem Ende gebracht hatte. Die vielen Pergamentreste in den von Heyno Gottschalk eingebundenen Büchern machen das deutlich. So spiegeln die Oldenstädter Bücher- und Bibliotheksreste die verschiedenen Epochen der Bibliotheksentwicklung vom 14. bis zum 16. Jahrhundert deutlich wieder.

Damit komme ich zum Schluß und fasse die wichtigsten Ergebnisse unserer Untersuchung in einigen Thesen zusammen:

1. Für den südostniedersächsischen Raum ist eine etwa um die Mitte des 15. Jahrhunderts einsetzende und mit der Einführung der Reformation in den einzelnen Klöstern endende Epoche der Bibliotheksgeschichte auszumachen.

2. Zur Identifikation der in der Regel untergegangenen Bibliotheken dieser Epoche sind nicht nur Handschriften, sondern Inkunabeln und Drucke des 16. Jahrhunderts hinzuzuziehen, da diesen Bibliotheken in unterschiedlichem Umfang Drucke inkorporiert worden sind.

3. In Zukunft sind daher bei der Katalogisierung alter Drucke alle Provenienznotizen festzuhalten, um die Quellenlage für diese Epoche der Bibliotheksgeschichte zu verbreitern.

4. Treibende Kraft beim Bibliotheksauf- und ausbau ist die bewußt erwerbende Einzelpersönlichkeit, der Theologe oder Jurist, im Studium, Beruf und bei gelehrten Neigungen.

5. Ein weiteres den Bibliotheksaufbau vor allem im klösterlichen Bereich beeinflussendes Moment ist die kirchliche Reformbewegung des 15. Jahrhunderts.

---

[79] Vgl. Doris Fouquet, Mittelalterliche Handschriften in Niedersachsen, in: Wolfenbütteler Beiträge 1 (1970), S. 234, Anm. 36.

6. Ein intensiver Ausbau der Klosterbibliothek ist jedoch nur zu konstatieren, wenn individuelles Engagement und reformerisches Bemühen in der Gestalt eines Abtes zusammen wirksam werden.

7. Institutionalisierte Bibliotheken in Rathäusern und Klöstern profitieren von Buchschenkungen individueller Sammler. Privatbibliotheken sind daher gleichsam als historisch ältere Bausteine von kirchlichen, aber auch weltlichen Bibliotheken zu betrachten.

8. Bleibt die Bibliothek der Reformklöster im wesentlichen auf Andachtsliteratur beschränkt, so spiegeln die Bibliotheken des Franziskanerordens in besonderem Maße die theologischen Fragen der Zeit. Nicht so sehr Andacht, sondern vielmehr wissenschaftliches Fragen beherrscht das franziskanische Kloster. Dem entspricht die Erwerbung zahlreicher Drucke für die Franziskanerbibliothek.

9. Die Kräfte der kirchlichen Reform im 15. und der Reformation im 16. Jahrhundert wirken gleichermaßen beflügelnd auf den Ausbau von Bibliotheken. Es verdient festgehalten zu werden, daß die Reformation, die später zur Zerstörung vieler Klosterbibliotheken führte, in ihren Anfängen einen weiteren Impuls in Richtung auf den Ausbau und die Bereicherung von Klosterbibliotheken auslöste.

Abgekürzt zitierte Literatur

BMC
Catalogue of books printed in the XVth century now in the British Museum. (1-8: Lithographic reprint.) 1-9 nebst Facs. London 1962-63.

GW
Gesamtkatalog der Wiegendrucke. 1-, Leipzig 1925-.

H
Repertorium bibliographicum... opera Ludovici Hain. 1-2, Stuttgart 1826-1838.

HC
Supplement to Hain's Repertorium bibliographicum. By Walther Arthur Copinger. 1-2, London 1895-1902.

HR
Dietrich Reichling, Appendices ad Hainii-Copingeri Repertorium bibliographicum. 1-6 nebst Ind. u. Suppl. Monachii 1905-14.

PICCARD
Gerhard Piccard, Die Kronenwasserzeichen, Stuttgart 1961.

WALTHER I
Initia carminum ac versuum medii aevi posterioris Latinorum. Bearbeitet von Hans Walther, Göttingen 1959. (Carmina medii aevi posterioris Latina. 1.)

ZfB
Zentralblatt für Bibliothekswesen. 1-, Leipzig 1884-.

William Caxton: a review

by N.F. BLAKE

William Caxton remains a somewhat shadowy figure outside England and the Low Countries, and so it is desirable to begin this review by briefly surveying his life if only because it provides a convenient lead into the scholarship which has developed around the introduction of printing into England. Nothing is known of his parents or early life before he became apprenticed to William Large, a mercer in London, who was later to become Lord Mayor. It is reasonable to suppose that his parents were themselves merchants or officials of one kind or another. His enrolment as an apprentice by Large which took place by 1438 was the most important event in his life for it shaped the pattern of his future career. The mercers constituted one of the most influential guilds in London in the fifteenth century and they dominated the trade between England and the Low Countries. This was technically in the hands of the Merchant Adventurers Company, a loose conglomeration of merchants engaged in the overseas trade. The Merchant Adventurers had little formal organisation and, as they used the Mercers' Hall in London as their administrative centre, the mercers formed the controlling group in the Merchant Adventurers Company. Inevitably a boy who enrolled as an apprentice with the mercers would drift into the overseas trade with the Merchant Adventurers. This trade was less regulated than that within England. Whereas the mercers in England were restricted to handling items of 'mercery' which included haberdashery, cloth and silks, those engaged in the overseas trade could deal in almost any item they chose except wool. At a later period, for example, we find Caxton involved in transactions in pewter. It was also in the overseas trade that the largest fortunes were made.

By joining Large, Caxton became associated with a powerful man in an important guild which dominated the trade with the Low Countries. He naturally acquired influential and rich friends among the merchant class; he learned how to handle money, how to float a loan, and how to arrange complicated financial transactions; and he became involved in some of the political and diplomatic events of the time. The merchants traded with the Low Counttries and with France, where some of them lived. They were naturally involved in negotiations with the local authorities there in an effort to improve their trading conditions. Because of this expertise, merchants were frequently used by the crown to conduct negotiations at a national level. One of England's major exports at this time was wool, which was in great demand in the Low Countries by the many weaving establishments. The Low Countries were part of the Duchy of Burgundy, a large conglomeration of possessions acquired through dynastic succession and marriage which stretched from Switzerland through north-eastern France to embrace much of modern Holland and Belgium. For his French possessions the Duke owed feudal allegiance to the French crown, and the dukes were princes of royal French blood with pretensions to the French throne. Their Low Countries territories were outside French royal authority and encouraged the dukes to pursue a more independent political policy, which included the possible creation of a kingdom of Burgundy. These possessions were also among the most lucrative and made the dukes perhaps the richest and most powerful rulers in Northern Europe. In their efforts to achieve independence from France and in an attempt to protect the supply of English wool, the dukes were often encouraged to form an alliance with the English against the French. The political realities of the time led to the constant re-grouping of alliances among the English, French and Burgundians.

It was this political situation which operated when Caxton first went to Flanders, probably in the late 1440s. English merchants were attracted to Flanders and the Low Countries in general by the international markets held there, particularly the one at Bruges. There they were able to buy many exotic items to import into England. In addition, Flanders was at the centre of the production of de luxe manuscripts which were sought after both inside the Low Countries and beyond. Important libraries were owned by the dukes themselves and by Louis de Gruuthuse, who was made Earl of Winchester by Edward IV. Edward was said to be very impressed by Louis's library which he saw during his exile in the Low Countries in 1471. Many Flemish manuscripts now form part of the Royal collection of manuscripts in the British Library; and no doubt some joined the collection in the fifteenth century. One of these, Royal 19 A ix, has been identified as the copy used by Caxton to make his translation, *Mirror of the World*, which he subsequently printed. The mercers were involved in the import of such manuscripts into England, and although definite proof is lacking in Caxton's case there seems little doubt that he also took part in this business. Certainly many manuscripts passed through his hands and he had sold some to important clients in England, such as the manuscript containing the French version of *Blanchardin and Eglantine*. After he returned to England to establish his press in Westminster, he imported many books, printed and manuscript, into England, and it is reasonable to assume that this was a continuation of what he had been doing for a long time. It is even possible that he gave commissions to Flemish scriveners for texts which he wished to sell in England. Shortly after acquiring a press and setting up in Bruges, he entered into a publishing association with a former scrivener, Colard Mansion, which may reflect previous business contacts between the two.

According to his own account in the prologue to *History of Troy*, the first book published in English, Caxton started to translate this work in 1469 and after completing a few quires gave up the project. There is no evidence that Caxton had made any translations before this time, and the question naturally arises as to why he should have started translating then. The most acceptable hypothesis is that he did so with a view to publishing, presumably through printing, the finished translation. If this were so, it would have important implications for our understanding of the man. By 1469 printing had spread as far as Cologne, but it had not yet reached the Low Countries. Yet Caxton foresaw its possibilities and had already made plans to capitalise upon them. Furthermore, it would imply that he had also thought out a publishing policy long before he had acquired the means of printing. If so, this implies a man who did not enter printing accidentally through some fortunate coincidence, but who went out of his way to acquire a press. This point we may return to later. In 1471 he took up the translation again and went to Cologne where, as we know from Wynkyn de Worde, he was involved in the printing of a Latin version of the *De proprietatibus rerum* by Bartholomaeus Anglicus. The only edition that was printed in the early 1470s in Cologne is attributed to the printer of the *Flores Sancti Augustini*, now identified through typographical and other evidence as Johannes Veldener, who subsequently practised as printer and typecutter at Louvain. It is from Veldener that Caxton acquired his press and presumably the workmen to operate it. What is of particular importance is that *De proprietatibus* is the largest work printed by Veldener in Cologne and indeed the biggest book produced in Cologne by that date, where small quartos rather than large folios were the order of the day. It is clear that Veldener had an additional source of capital to finance the volume, and the most likely source for that money is Caxton. As a merchant he could have financed the project out of his own resources or he would have known how to borrow the necessary capital.

When he left Cologne at the end of 1472 he returned to Bruges where first he printed *History of Troy*, the book he had translated from French. This work was written in French by Raoul Lefèvre, a secretary at the Burgundian ducal court, and had been dedicated to Duke Philip. Caxton's version was dedicated to Margaret, the sister of Edward IV and now the wife of Charles Duke of Burgundy. From typographical investigations into this edition, it has been shown that four compositors worked on it. One of these who worked on the start of the first two books of *History of Troy* has been identified as Johannes Veldener because of the printing in red found only there which is elsewhere such a characteristic feature of Veldener's work. It seems probable that Veldener assisted in the setting up of the press, lent a hand in the early compositorial work to get it off to a good start, and then went off to re-establish his own business elsewhere, presumably Louvain. Caxton meanwhile continued at Bruges where he issued another of his translations, *Game of Chess*, which was dedicated to George Duke of Clarence. Then he issued four editions in French. In 1476 he returned to England where he established his printing press in the precincts of Westminster Abbey. There he continued with his publication work, issuing perhaps a further hundred editions of different texts, many of which were his own translations. Many of these editions were dedicated to various members of the nobility and some to merchants and officials. He continued as a printer, publisher and translator till his death. According to Wynkyn de Worde, Caxton completed his translation of the *Lives of the Fathers (Vitas patrum)* only just before he died. It was printed by de Worde after Caxton's death, which took place in 1492.

The following points emerge from this resumé of his career and have been at the centre of some of the controversies in Caxton studies. Caxton was a successful printer and publisher; he did not go bankrupt as so many early printers did. If we include his Cologne period, he was in the printing and publishing business for twenty years and issued over a hundred editions. He clearly had sufficient commercial acumen to survive where so many others foundered; and the question that has been asked is in what precisely the secret of his success lay. Most attention has been focussed on his choice of texts to print, for in such a long career there are sufficient texts to make analysis worthwhile. To many of his editions Caxton added a prologue and/or epilogue. These often provide his reasons for printing a particular text and his remarks have been accepted as accurate accounts of what happened. They have also been admired as writings in their own right, and therefore he has come to be accepted by some as a literary figure rather than as just a printer. He lived off and on in Bruges for well over twenty years and Bruges was in the dominions of the Dukes of Burgundy. He translated works written for the dukes and dedicated his first printed book to the then duchess. Scholarship has naturally focussed on the influence exerted on him by Burgundian literary taste and to what extent he was trying to capitalise on the fashion for things Burgundian in England. The problem with this view has been to fit his publication of English works, such as the poems by Chaucer, into such a theory. When he includes a prologue and/or epilogue he often introduces the name of a patron who is made to seem responsible for the volume in question. The many patrons mentioned have provoked dispute as to how far Caxton was responsible for the choice of the works he printed or whether he was following the whims of individual patrons. In other words, did he lead or follow public taste? Finally, there is the question of the sort of man he was: printer, merchant, scholar, diplomat and politician have all been put forward. They are not necessarily mutually incompatible, though individual scholars have emphasised one aspect to the exclusion of others. Many of these points are interrelated and I shall not attempt to keep them separate in what follows.

In England Caxton is generally honoured as the man who introduced printing into England – indeed, to many he still remains (erroneously) the man who invented printing. Although he is remembered as a printer, most of the scholarly argument about him has been over his role as publisher. He is not usually criticised for the quality of his printing, his use of particular type, his choice of woodcuts, or the layout of his page, though in all these points his record is poor. He is generally criticised or praised for the choice of texts he chose to print, though occasionally it is his command of English which is brought into question. An anonymous writer of 1766 complained that he »was but an illiterate man, and of small judgement, by which means he printed nothing but mean and frivolous things«.[1] Gibbon a little later noted that »In the choice of his authors, that liberal and industrious artist was reduced to comply with the vicious taste of his readers; to gratify the nobles with treatises on heraldry, hawking, and the game of chess, and to amuse the popular credulity with romances of fabulous knights and legends of more fabulous saints«.[2] Caxton had not produced any classical or humanist texts. Although nineteenth-century scholars tried to salvage his reputation from the attacks of their predecessors, they did so by excusing or explaining his choice of material to print. It is regarded as a mark of his good taste that he should have printed so much English poetry. Naturally to modern ages like our own which do not read the

---

[1] *Anonymiana* (London, 1809), p.136.
[2] *The Miscellaneous Works of Edward Gibbon, Esq.*, edited by John, Lord Sheffield (London, 1814), III, 563-4.

classics in the original language, it may not seem too reprehensible that a printer should have omitted classical texts from his list.

The problem of this dispute has been establishing the data which can form the basis of the discussion. Most scholars work from modern bibliographical lists of Caxton's output, though these can differ as to what they include. This arises not so much because it is uncertain whether a particular edition was printed by Caxton as from the differing premisses of such lists. For example, should the *De rerum proprietatibus* printed in Cologne about 1472, which I referred to earlier, be included in a list of Caxton's printed books? The problem is that in the fifteenth century specialisation in the production of books to which we are accustomed today had not yet arisen. This specialisation has since affected almost all products: goods are not made and sold on the same premises. For example, now when you buy a loaf of bread you would not expect that it had been baked in the shop where you purchased it. Similarly today a publisher chooses books to print, edits them and markets the finished product. The actual printing is entrusted to a printer, who simply sells his services to the publisher. The printer will expect to be reimbursed for his labour fairly promptly, but the publisher will only see a return on his capital investment as the books are sold. For publishers the problem of cash-flow is important, for investments may be of a long-term nature. The financial demands of the two occupations are very different. A printer will have made a capital investment in his equipment and he will employ staff to help him carry out the diverse tasks of the printing process. He will need to keep his equipment and staff busy by acquiring a constant stream of work. A publisher can publish as many books as he wants to: it can be a few or it may be a large number. He need not employ staff if he can handle the volume of business himself. But each edition that he publishes is a financial gamble: he may lose heavily or he may make a fortune. In any event he is not likely to get his money back quickly, and he can easily be beaten to the post by another publisher and find he has a stock of unsaleable books on his hands.

It is important to bear this distinction in mind, because it is clear that Caxton was both a printer and a publisher. He printed at least seven indulgences while he was at Westminster. In producing these he was acting only as printer, for he must have printed them for whoever was going to sell and distribute them. Caxton had no right to sell indulgences, which were issued by some ecclesiastical authority with a view to raising money for a particular clerical purpose. We may assume that Caxton was paid for these indulgences in much the same way as any printer is paid today. On the other hand, he acted on some occasions as publisher. Guillaume Maynial, a Paris printer, printed a Sarum *Missal* and

Legenda for Caxton in 1487-88. Apparently after these books arrived at Westminster Caxton added his mark, which here does duty as a publisher's sign. Caxton presumably paid Maynial for the printing of these volumes and he took the financial risk involved in distributing (i.e. publishing) them.

Bibliographers are concerned with the printed book, because it is something tangible which can be described: a book has type, paper and watermarks, which can be objectively analysed and catalogued. They therefore group books under the printer rather than under a publisher. A publisher is too shadowy a concept for most bibliographers. In most lists of Caxton's books, therefore, the indulgences are included, but not the two books printed by Maynial. Yet if Caxton is being criticised for his choice of books to print and publish, then the indulgences should be discounted because he did not choose to publish them; he simply printed them. However, the Sarum *Missal* and *Legenda* ought to be taken into account because Caxton made the decision that these books should be printed and published, even though he farmed out the actual printing to someone else. Inevitably there are books for which it will be more difficult to decide how far Caxton's involvement extended. Thus if one wished to refute Gibbon's claim that Caxton had published no classical or humanist texts, one might point to three works in particular: the *Nova rhetorica* and its *Epitome* by Lorenzo Guglielmo Traversagni and the *Sex epistolae* or letters sent between Pope Sixtus IV and Venice, provided of course that these works were *published* by Caxton.

The *Nova rhetorica* and the *Epitome* were printed in 1479 and 1480 respectively, and *Sex epistolae* appeared in 1483. The first of these texts is of particular interest for it has now been shown that it was set up from Vatican Library MS Latin 11441: the compositor's marks are clearly visible and correspond to the pages in the printed edition. This manuscript was Traversagni's personal copy. Traversagni was an Italian who had come to England to teach rhetoric and had established himself in Cambridge. That Traversagni should have known there was a printer working in Westminster is more probable than that Caxton should have known there was an Italian rhetorician teaching in Cambridge who had written a new book. The *Nova rhetorica* would itself be used as a text book, and it is likely that its author, a teacher, would want to provide his pupils with copies. Since the copytext was his personal copy, the conclusion seems inescapable that it was Traversagni who asked Caxton to print the text. Whether Traversagni or some of his friends in Cambridge distributed the text and so acted as publishers is less easy to determine, though it is quite probable. In other words for this text we may assume Caxton was acting more in the role of printer than of publisher. The *Epitome* was not set up from Latin 11441, though a copy of it is in that manuscript. Traversagni left England after *Nova rhetorica* was printed and before *Epitome* went to press. He may well have allowed a copy of the *Epitome* to be made from his own manuscript to act as the printer's copytext. Again we should probably conclude that Caxton's part in the edition was that of printer. This text, like *Nova rhetorica*, was probably going to be distributed in Cambridge and other university towns where Traversagni taught. Their distribution is likely to have been in the hands of the author and his friends, who to that extent were acting as publishers. *Sex epistolae* contains letters between Sixtus IV and Venice, and since few Englishmen were likely to be very interested in the subject matter the interest of the edition probably lay in its style. Presumably the edition was used as a teaching aid to provide models of epistolary rhetoric. In the colophon to the edition it is stated that the letters were *diligenter emendate* by Pietro Carmeliano, another Italian who had come to teach in England though he had settled in Oxford. This phrase can only mean that Carmeliano corrected the proofs of the letters as they were going through the press, and therefore he had some special interest in the edition. Presumably his interest sprang from the fact that he had asked Caxton to print the volume and may also have contributed financially to the printing. He may also have distributed the printed copies. For this text as well Caxton probably acted as printer rather than as publisher. Consequently it is insufficient to work from a list of books attributed to the printer Caxton by bibliographers if we want to consider his work as a publisher. As we have seen the three books which have the best reason to be labelled as humanist texts among his printed editions were probably not chosen by him and he may not even have published or distributed them. Caxton the printer needed a constant flow of material to keep his presses busy; if he had no material of his own, he would have to take work in from outside. But the financial dictates of the printing business should not influence our understanding of what was going on in the publishing business.

On the other hand, Caxton dedicated many of his books to patrons, who in some cases had asked (according to Caxton) for the work in question to be printed. This point has been seized on by defenders of Caxton. Gibbon and the eighteenth century attacked him for the trivial nature of the books he published. But Caxton the man was excused because he was, in Gibbon's words, "reduced to comply with the vicious taste of his readers". Many have followed this lead to suggest that he had to print what members of the aristocracy demanded. If this were so, it would reduce his role as publisher since the choice of texts would be taken out of his hands and even his financial involvement may have been reduced. It should be emphasised that this defence accepts that the books were bad ones; it simply shifts the blame for publishing them on to different shoulders. However, the most recent scholarship has tended to increase the part played by Caxton in the choice of these texts at the expense of his patrons.

This may seem a surprising trend for there is much to support the general idea of patronage and specifically in England. Patronage seems to have been an important feature in early printing and there is frequent reference to patrons of early printers in almost all countries. Literature, especially poetry, is associated with the court in the period immediately before and during the first age of printing, and court poetry is often a patronised poetry. In English this is apparently substantiated by such facts as the picture of Chaucer reading his poetry to the assembled court in Corpus College Christi Cambridge MS 61 of *Troilus and Criseyde*. Lydgate also mentions many aristocrats who had commissioned poems from him. The patronage of printers would follow on naturally from the patronage of poets, and there are presentation pictures of books (printed or manuscript) being offered to patrons. In Caxton studies the most famous is the woodcut in the Huntington copy of *History of Troy* showing the presentation of the volume to Margaret of Burgundy. A manuscript copy of the printed version of *Dicts or Sayings* in Lambeth Palace Library MS 265 contains a frontispiece illustrating the presentation of the book to Edward IV. Caxton for his part frequently refers to his patrons and claims that they had requested individual volumes. Finally, he was employed on diplomatic missions by the crown and it is thought he may have been in more permanent employment with Margaret of Burgundy. If this were so, it is natural to assume that his employers were his patrons as well.

These arguments are, however, far from conclusive. That many early printers had patrons is hardly surprising since they were artisans who lacked financial expertise and often had little literary sophistication. Caxton was a different kind of person – a publisher rather than a printer, a merchant rather than an artisan. He did not work in the printing shop himself; he employed others to do it. The role which patrons played for other early printers was filled by Caxton himself. He had the capital and literary knowledge to direct a publishing house; and it was others who did the work of printing. How far the poetry of the hundred years before Caxton was a court poetry is difficult to decide for England. For example, Chaucer did not dedicate any of his poems to a member of the aristocracy, though one might assume the *Book of the Duchess* was written for John of Gaunt since it is a consolatory poem for the death of his wife Blanche. The picture in Corpus MS 61 dates from after Chaucer's death and is based on iconographical models depicting preachers; it may therefore have little basis in reality. Although Lydgate mentions patrons in his works, he was not a courtier since he was a monk at the Abbey of Bury St Edmunds. What the relation between Lydgate and these patrons was is difficult to decide, though we have been too quick to decide that it was the patrons who took the initiative in deciding what poem Lydgate should write. Since many of his poems were translations from Latin and French, and since Lydgate is more likely to have had access to the originals than his patrons, the primary impetus for the translations is likely to have come from the poet. That Caxton acted for the crown in various negotiations is no more proof that he was employed permanently by the crown than it would be today if a university professor, for example, served on a government commission. Caxton was employed, just as a professor would be employed, on a temporary basis because of the particular expertise he had. It has, however, been frequently claimed that he was in the employment of Margaret of Burgundy and went to Cologne on her behalf to acquire a printing press. The reasons given for this are that in the prologue to the *History of Troy* he described himself as her 'servant', he said he has often received a fee from her, and she had commanded him to complete the translation which he had put aside when it was barely started. In the fifteenth century the word 'servant' was used by the member of one class to express deference to a member of a higher class and does not signify an employer-employee relationship. It was still used like this till the nineteenth century, and even today this usage is reflected in those letters which end 'Your obedient servant'. Caxton used the word to express his deference to several 'patrons', and no one has dared to claim he was an employee of all these other people. The fee is equally without value as evidence. Caxton received fees from other patrons. A fee was a payment for services rendered, although it could also be given to those who occupied influential positions as a mark of favour. Caxton had been Governor of the English Nation, in which position he had received many fees, and it is likely that the Duchess of Burgundy would wish to show particular favours to a countryman in such an important job. In addition, the duchess dabbled in the overseas trade herself and she is likely to have sought advice about her financial ventures from such people as Caxton. A fee would be a natural reward for such advice, though it need not have been paid in cash. The fee he received from the Earl of Arundel consisted of a buck in summer and a doe in winter. Although it is true that he said Margaret had ordered him to complete the translation, she clearly knew nothing about the project at its inception. Caxton started to translate the text in 1469 and then put it to one side for two years after completing a few quires. If he showed the incomplete translation to Margaret, it can have been only in 1471. Margaret can have had nothing to do with the choice of text, or presumably, with the underlying project of setting the finished translation up in type. This point, however, needs to be considered in relation to why Caxton wrote his prologues and what he included in them.

Not all of Caxton's editions have a prologue or epilogue. All his translations from the French contain one, as does his edition of Malory's *Morte Darthur* which had been written only fifteen years before it was printed. In addition some reprints, such as the second edition of the *Canterbury Tales*, contain a prologue. A few other texts also have one. From this it seems likely that a prologue or epilogue was included when a text was less well known or where it might be in competition with another text such as the first edition. The inclusion of a prologue or epilogue was designed, in part at least, to introduce a new text or new edition to the potential purchasers to encourage them to buy it. It is likely that the use of the names of patrons was designed to accomplish this end. However, individual patrons are not named in all prologues. In addition to the prologues or epilogues which name individual patrons, there are those which refer to anonymous patrons. These latter may be generalised in such references as 'diverce gentlemen' or 'all noble ladies and gentlemen' or they may be specific as the 'noble lady' who is referred to as the patron of the *Knight of the Tower* (1484). These types of reference are not mutually exclusive. The *History of Troy* was completed at the request of Margaret of Burgundy, though in the epilogue Caxton wrote that he had asked for copies by *dyverce gentilmen* (p.100).[3] The *Order of Chivalry* (c.1484) had been requested by an anonymous *gentyl and noble esquyer* (p.126) who provided Caxton with the French original to translate, though the edition is presented to Richard III. Malory's *Morte Darthur* (1485) was printed after a *copye unto me delyverd* (p.108-9), but the book was presented *unto alle noble prynces, lordes and ladyes, gentylmen or gentylwymmen* (p.109). This mixing of categories is significant, for it suggests that in trying to increase the appeal of his editions Caxton felt a single patron (whether named or not) was insufficient. It was important for him to make as general an appeal as possible; the patrons were only part of a wider policy. He was using them to sell his books. This does not necessarily mean that what he wrote about his patrons was fictitious, though it should alert us to that possibility.

Let us consider the *Game of Chess*. This text was translated from French by Caxton and printed twice: once in Bruges on 31 March 1474 and once in West-

---

[3] References in brackets after quotations from the prologues and epilogues are to N.F. Blake, *Caxton's Own Prose* (London, 1973).

minster about 1483. The second edition contains woodcuts, but is otherwise reprinted from the first. Both editions contain a prologue, though each one is different. The prologue to the first edition commences with an elaborate dedication to George Duke of Clarence by his *most humble servant* (p. 85), William Caxton. Clarence is devoted to promoting English interests and therefore Caxton has translated a book which came into his hands recently. "Whiche booke, right puyssant and redoubtid Lord, I have made in the name and under the shadewe of your noble protection not presumyng to correcte or enpoigne onythynge ayenst your noblesse" (p. 85). Caxton asks Clarence not to scorn this book from his *humble and unknowen servant* (p. 85). Evidently it was Caxton who had chosen the book which he had published without Clarence knowing anything of it. What is more Caxton was unknown to Clarence, who presumably knew nothing of the edition until he received a copy. Caxton had chosen an English nobleman to act as dedicatee and patron of his edition without that person's knowledge or even his acquaintance. He was quite prepared to exploit other people's positions for his own commercial ends. Presumably he thought the introduction of any noble name would help to make his edition better known.

Clarence was the brother of Margaret of Burgundy and of Edward IV, and it was doubtless for this reason he was chosen. However, after the first edition was printed Clarence was beheaded for treason in 1478, and so his name became a liability. When Caxton issued the second edition of *Game of Chess*, he composed a completely new prologue. In this second prologue he extols all writing as moral, and among the moral books available there was one written by a Hospitaller of St John's in France. Caxton then adds that he had come across a copy of this book when he was living in Bruges and he had decided to translate it into English. The translation had been printed and then sold. Because it contains such wholesome wisdom he has reprinted it, including in the reprint pictures of the people who appear in the game of chess. He concludes by asking the reader for his indulgence as regards the translation. There is no patron to this edition, which is recommended because of its moral value and of its woodcut illustrations. These two attributes perform the same function as Clarence's name. Caxton was evidently sensitive to local developments and wrote his prologues with care and attention. He may have felt another patron's name would not be apposite at this time, and so relied on more general recommendations. He was prepared to use a name and to drop it again as circumstances warranted. The second prologue contains genuine information which could have been used earlier, whereas the first edition has a prologue which is pure propaganda. The patron had nothing to do with the book and his name was introduced to increase the book's sales. Caxton was quite unscrupulous in his use of such names. He alone was responsible for the edition.

By the same token when he refers to anonymous patrons it seems likely that was often inventing little stories to make his edition more attractive. When the second edition of the *Canterbury Tales* was printed he claimed he had been asked by an unnamed gentleman to print a better text from a manuscript in his father's possesion. This was probably a way of suggesting that those who had bought the first edition should also buy the second since it had a better text, and that was a more important recommendation than a noble name would have been since the second edition was in direct competition with the first. Similarly when Caxton refers directly to a named patron, we cannot always trust his word that the patron had asked for the edition. In the prologue to *Charles the Great* (1485) he wrote "for to satisfye the desyre and requeste of my good synguler lordes and specyal maysters and frends, I have enprysed and concluded in myself to reduce this sayd bood into our Englysshe" (p.67). Yet in the epilogue he wrote "I Wylliam Caxton was desyred and requyred by a good and synguler frende of myn, Maister Wylliam Daubeney, ... to reduce al these sayd hystoryes into our Englysshe tongue" (p.68). Here we have two contradictory statements: one that Caxton decided to make the translation, and the other that he was asked by Daubeney to do so. Perhaps we may assume that Caxton actually hit upon the text and decided to translate it, and then at some state he asked Daubeney to be its patron, or perhaps just as likely, he used Daubeney's name without permission. The introduction of a patron's name is no evidence that the patron took any initiative in getting a text into print or even that he knew anything about it. We must be cautious in accepting anything that Caxton wrote in these prologues and epilogues as genuine. He needed names to recommend his books, but that does not imply that the patrons had formally given permission for their names to be used or even that they knew their names were being used in this way. It is only when fairly precise details of the commission are given, as in the case of his formal audience with Henry VII to receive a commission to translate *Feats of Arms*, that we may give credence to what he writes.

If we return to the *History of Troy* I think we might reasonably conclude that Margaret's part in it was much less than is at first implied. Caxton thought of the translation, completed it, acquired a press, and printed the finished translation. Margaret may at best have encouraged him in his venture and she may have made recommendations as to his style. The volume was dedicated to her, but her involvement was otherwise very limited. If the humanist texts were commissioned and perhaps published by others, the translations from French were very much Caxton's own initiative. He is responsible for their choice and marketing.

This conclusion leads naturally to a consideration of whether in his publishing policy which these translations from French represent Caxton was trying to promote Burgundian culture in England. Ever since Huizinga's *The Waning of the Middle Ages* we have been fascinated by Burgundian culture and sensible of its influence elsewhere. More recent studies have built on his foundations to fill in the debt that England owed to Burgundy. It was natural therefore that it should be supposed that Caxton himself shared with his countrymen a respect for Burgundian literary and chivalric taste. His association with Margaret of Burgundy and his translation of books by secretaries to the dukes were taken as proff of this thesis. Furthermore, the contents of the Burgundian ducal library were catalogued on the deaths of each duke, and two of these catalogues from the fifteenth century have survived and been printed. It was therefore relatively easy to compare Caxton's output with the contents of that library. One important feature of the ducal library was that the majority of its holdings were in French rather than Latin; it was a vernacular library devoted to didactic and romance works rather than a scholarly library devoted to scholastic learning and intellectual dispute. The duke's secretaries made translations of Latin works for them. It was one of these that Caxton began translating in 1469, his first attempt at translation.

That Caxton should have made translations from French does not in itself prove that he was directly influenced by Burgundian taste as represented in the ducal library. Now that his link with Margaret has been shown to be rather tenuous, his knowledge of its contents would have been limited. He may have known scriveners like Colard Mansion who produced de luxe manuscripts for the library, including those of texts made by the ducal secretaries, but this would provide him with a restricted idea of the contents. Furthermore, some studies have revealed that many of the books Caxton translated were also found in many other libraries in the Low Countries, and it is equally true that others were not to be found in the ducal library at all if we can trust the extant inventories. While Caxton was in Bruges it was natural that he should translate texts that were readily accessible there and which had recently become available. Translations by Raoul Lefèvre fall into this category, and his position as ducal secretary can only have increased the attraction of the works he translated. Yet when Caxton returned to England, he did not continue to produce works which had a close connection with Burgundy. He was on the look out for works in

French that had recently appeared. Since the majority of works in French appeared in France, it is naturally to France that he looked to satisfy his demand. Many vernacular texts were printed in Lyons and the trade links between England and France were so well developed that books printed there could be published in an English translation within a couple of years. Lyons editions lie behind Caxton's versions of *Paris and Vienne* (Westminster 1485, Lyons 1480), *Four Sons of Aymon* (Westminster c.1489, Lyons 1480), and *Eneydos* (Westminster c.1490, Lyons 1488). This may also apply to other texts like *Book of Good Manners*, *Doctrinal of Sapience* and *Feats of Arms*. From this it would seem as though he chose French texts which were readily available rather than those which had a particular link with Burgundy. Furthermore when he returned to England he did not continue referring to Burgundian ideas or people in his prologues and epilogues. *History of Troy* is dedicated to Margaret of Burgundy, and *Jason* which is a continuation of it and which appeared shortly after his return to England refers to Duke Philip's castle at Hesdin, though the book is dedicated to the Prince of Wales. References to France and French people are frequent in the later books, usually because they are translations of books written there. For example, the *Royal Book* refers to Philip the Bold, King of France, for whom the French original had been written. Finally, we may note that even in his project to *History of Troy*, which might be considered a Burgundian text, he mentions that he was not sophisticated because he had never been to France. It was France that was the true home of French language and culture.

If Caxton was not directly motivated by the wish to introduce Burgundian texts to his English readers, what were the principles he was following? Where did he get his inspiration? Undoubtedly he did look for foreign texts to translate into English and for the most part these were French texts because they were among the foreign texts most readily accessible in England. Yet in acting thus Caxton was not behaving very differently from his predecessors in English cultural life. We have ignored the continuity that exists between the manuscript culture of the fifteenth century and the incunable period. After all many of the texts Caxton translated had been available in earlier translations. The *Royal Book* was available in six pre-Caxton English translations, though clearly many of them had only a local circulation since these earlier translations were unknown to him. The *Knight of the Tower* is the second translation of this work into English; the first one, made at the beginning of the fifteenth century, is now considered not to have been used by Caxton. However, for his translation of the *Golden Legend* Caxton used the Latin and French versions as well as the earlier English translation, now referred to as *Gilte Legende* to distinguish it from his own translation. Caxton also knew that translations had been a staple part of literary life in England before his time, for he refers to many translators and translations. It is probable that he knew many more than those he mentioned, for he tends to refer only to courtly translations by name. Among earlier translations he printed one may pick out Chaucer's version of Boethius's *De consolatione*. Since he praised Chaucer so highly as a stylist, he must have approved of translation in general and this translation in particular. Lydgate made a poetic version of the Troy story, which Caxton describes in his *History of Troy* as a translation. Here is another famous poet making a translation. In his prologue to the *Polychronicon* he refers to John Trevisa, chaplain to Thomas Lord Berkeley, who translated (according to Caxton) the Bible, *De proprietatibus rerum* and *Polychronicon* into English. Caxton printed Cicero's *De amicitia* translated by John Tiptoft Earl of Worcester and his *De senectute* in a translation made for Sir John Fastolf of Norfolk, though he does not give the name of the translator. It does not follow, of course, that Caxton knew of the existence of all these translations before he commenced his own first translation in 1469, though it is likely that he knew of some of them such as Lydgate's *Troy-Book* which is referred to in that work. English literary life in the Middle Ages thrived on translation, and there had been a great spate of translation from French since at least the early fourteenth century. These translations were made by nobles and great poets as well as by obscure clerics. For the most part they consisted of romances, in poetry or prose, and of moral and didactic tracts, usually in prose. There was a well developed literary tradition with which Caxton was surely familiar, since his choice of material to translate is similar to that which was being translated by others in the fifteenth century. If he differs from his predecessors it is only in having greater access to French originals through his links with the Continental booktrade. Translation is only one aspect of English literary life; the other is the composition of courtly poetry by Chaucer, Gower and Lydgate. If we accept that Caxton was responding to the English tradition in his publishing policy, there is no need to question why he published both English poetry and translations of French prose works.

It is evident that Caxton knew quite a lot about the literary scene in England. Equally he seems to have had connections with scribes and booksellers. He imported many books and manuscripts which he must have passed on to others. More important perhaps are his links with the producers of Malory's *Morte Darthur*. Only one manuscript of this work survives. It was discovered at Winchester in 1934 and is now British Library MS Additional 59678; its date is uncertain. Malory completed his work in 1469/70 and Caxton printed it in 1485.

Editors of the text have claimed, convincingly I feel, that Caxton's edition was not set up from Additional 59678, but from a manuscript which is no longer extant. However, it has recently been shown that Additional 59678 was in Caxton's workshop because it contains offsets of Caxton's type on some folios. It may have been in the workshop form about 1480 until 1489, which of course covers the time when Caxton printed his version of *Morte Darthur*. It has usually been argued that Additional 59678 and Caxton's copytext were closely related copies of the same original. In other words it is posited that there were at least three manuscripts of this work, the original, Caxton's copytext and Additional 59678; and now it might be claimed that of those three at least two were in Caxton's workshop at the same time. Why this should be so we cannot tell, though it has been accepted for some time that Caxton ran a bookshop as well as a publishing business. It is possible, therefore, that Caxton had an association with the scriptorium that produced two copies of the *Morte Darthur* – a sign that he had very close links with other providers of fashionable reading matter. Such links would provide him with material to print as well as giving him some insight into the sort of material which it would be worth his while to translate.

These conclusions have an important bearing on the question of patronage and on the sort of man Caxton was. Here was a man who ran a printing and publishing business as well as a bookshop. He imported books and disposed of these as well as his own output. He had links with other producers of literature and could acquire manuscripts produced in England, though he cannot have known all that was being produced on literature. He was familiar with the main lines of literary development in England and he directed his business in a traditional way, that is he produced English courtly literature and translations of romances or moral and didactic texts just as many before him had done. He had a publishing policy and he was uniquely placed to chart literary developments in England and abroad. It would therefore be natural to suppose that it was Caxton who was responsible for the choice of texts coming off his press rather than the nobles or merchants who are mentioned in them. The continuity in his choice of books can be explained only on the basis of a single controlling mind; it is not reasonable to assume that he was responding to the whims of many various patrons.

There is also the question of the sort of man Caxton was. The important features of his career are his period as a merchant, his success as a printer, and his knowledge of the publishing business. For many years he was thought to have been a kind of hack who responded to the poor taste of his patrons and initiated little himself. Then it was proposed he was a scholar. Neither of these views now seems tenable. There is nothing to support the idea that he took an academic interest in the texts he printed and we have just seen that patronage was part of the method of book promotion and had little to do with the publishing policy. It has also been suggested that he was a political person who entered into publishing in order to promote particular political views. This also seems unlikely, although it is true that he moved on the fringes of political circles for many years and had considerable diplomatic experience. It is difficult to see what political message is encapsulated in his prologues and epilogues or even in the actual books he printed which fall in so easily with what was being read in the fifteenth century. Political advocacy demands a little more clarity than is found in his books. It still seems most acceptable to regard Caxton as a merchant, as a man that was interested in buying and selling. Early in his life he dealt in many goods, but later in his life he confined his entrepreneurial activities to books and manuscripts. He probably acquired a press because it enabled him to control the means of production and so to impose his own policy on the material he sold. It was his mercantile experience that enabled him to survive both by planning a policy in his buying and selling operations and by obtaining the necessary credit and loans. Naturally a rich man who had control of one means of communication might well have been drawn into political and other activities, but these should be regarded as secondary to the main purpose of his life and work.

Naturally over the recent past research has also been carried out into the typographical aspects of Caxton's production, and important new discoveries have been made in dating and related matters. Yet these discoveries have followed traditional paths of investigation and perhaps hold less interest in methodology to the delegates at this conference. What is important about Caxton's career is what it can tell us about the relation between producer and buyer, about the processes involved in the choice of texts – in a word about those details which we today associate with publishing rather than with printing. But discussion about publishing is always bedevilled by the presentation of the extant material in a manner which suits the bibliographer, who catalogues the actual books. Yet it is in the publishing aspects of incunables that the greatest controversies are likely to continue.

Bibliography

Armstrong, E. "English Purchases of Printed Books from the Continent 1465-1526," *English Historical Review*, XCIV (1979), 268-90.
Bennett, H.S. *Chaucer and the Fifteenth Century*. Oxford: Clarendon, 1947.
Blades, W. *Life and Typography of William Caxton*. 2 vols. London & Strassburg: Trübner, 1861-3.
Blake, N.F. "William Caxton: His Choice of Texts," *Anglia*, LXXXIII (1965), 289-307.
— *Caxton and his World*. London: Deutsch, 1969.
— *Caxton's Own Prose*. London: Deutsch, 1973.
— *Caxton: England's First Publisher*. London: Osprey, 1976.
— "A New Approach to William Caxton," *Book Collector*, XXVI (1977), 380-5.
— "Dating the First Books Published in English," *Gutenberg Jahrbuch* (1978), 43-50.
— *William Caxton after Five Hundred Years*. Davis, Calif.: Library Associates, 1980.
— "William Caxton again in the Light of Recent Scholarship," *Dutch Quarterly Review*, XII (1982-3), 162-82.
Bornstein, D. "William Caxton's Chivalric Romances and the Burgundian Renaissance in England," *English Studies*, LVII (1976), 1-10.
de Ricci, S. *A Census of Caxtons*. London: Bibliographical Society, 1909.
"Eight Papers Presented to the Caxton International Congress 1976," *Journal of the Printing Historical Society*, XI (1976-7), 1-133.
Gallick, S. "The Continuity of the Rhetorical Tradition: Manuscript to Incunabulum," *Manuscripta*, XXIII (1979), 31-47.
Goldschmidt, E.P. *Medieval Texts and their First Appearance in Print*. London: Bibliographical Society, 1943.
Heilbronner, W.L. *Printing and the Book in Fifteenth-Century England*. Charlottesville, Va: University Press of Virginia, 1967.
Hellinga, L. "Caxton and the Bibliophiles," *Actes du XIe Congrès International de Bibliographie Bruxelles 1979*, (Brussels, 1981), 11-38.
— *Caxton in Focus. The Beginning of Printing in England*. London: British Library, 1982.
Huizinga, J. *The Waning of the Middle Ages*. London: Arnold, 1924.
Kekewich, M. "Edward IV, William Caxton, and Literary Patronage in Yorkist England," *Modern Language Review*, LXVI (1971), 481-7.
Kerling, N.J.M. "Caxton and the Trade in Printed Books," *Book Collector*, IV (1955), 190-9.
Kipling, G. *The Triumph of Honour: Burgundian Origins of the Elizabethan Renaissance*. Leiden: Leiden University Press, 1977.
Lucas, P.J. "The Growth and Development of English Literary Patronage in the Later Middle Ages and Early Renaissance," *The Library*, 6th ser., IV (1982), 219-48.
Needham, P. "Bibliographical Evidence from the Paper Stocks of English Incunabula,"*Book and Text in the Fifteenth Century*, Ed. L. Hellinga and H. Härtel (Hamburg: Hauswedell, 1981), 79-87.
Nixon, H.M. "Caxton, his Contemporaries and Successors in the Booktrade from Westminster Documents," *The Library*, 5th ser., XXXI (1976), 305-26.
Noguchi, S. "Caxton's Malory," *Poetica* (Tokyo), VIII (1976), 72-84.
Painter, G. *William Caxton. A Quincentenary Biography of England's First Printer*. London: Chatto and Windus, 1976.
Penninger, F.E. *William Caxton*. Boston, Mass.: Twayne, 1979.

Pickford, C.E. "Fiction and the Reading Public in the Fifteenth Century," *Bulletin of the John Rylands Library*, XLV (1962-3), 423-38.

Ruysschaert, J. "Les manuscrits autographes de deux ouvrages de Lorenzo Guglielmo Traversagni imprimés chez Caxton," *Bulletin of the John Rylands Library*, XXXVI (1953-4), 191-7.

Takamiya, T. and D. Brewer (edd.) *Aspects of Malory*. Cambridge: D.S. Brewer, 1981.

Thielemans, M.R. *Bourgogne et Angleterre. Relations politiques et économiques entre les Pays-Bas bourguignons et l'Angleterre 1435-1467*. Brussels: Presses Universitaires, 1966.

Thompson, S.O. (ed.) *Caxton: An American Contribution to the Quincentenary Celebrations*. New York: Typophiles, 1976.

Vanderjagt, A.J. *Qui sa vertu anoblist. The Concepts of noblesse and chose publicque in Burgundian Political Thought*. Groningen: Miélot, 1981.

Typologie du livre et de la lecture dans l'Italie de la renaissance : De Petrarque à Politien

par Armando Petrucci

Au cours du XIVe siècle l'expérience culturelle de Pétrarque fut décisive pour changer le cours de la production du livre italien et européen et de l'évolution de l'écriture latine. Son extrême sensibilité aux questions du livre et de l'écriture avait été rendue plus vive avec le temps, soit par la comparaison directe avec des expériences qui n'étaient pas italiennes, mais surtout françaises, soit par son activité de collectionneur et de bibliophile de plus en plus attentive. On sait que Pétrarque critique plusieurs fois l'écriture textuelle de son temps, c'est-à-dire l'écriture gothique, en en caractérisant efficacement les éléments les plus négatifs: l'aspect excessivement artificiel du dessin, la compacité des lettres pressées les unes contre les autres, l'exiguité des signes; et il lui oppose les qualités de clarté, de sobriété et d'élégance de l'ancienne minuscule caroline proposée comme le modèle même d'un nouveau style graphique que lui-même essaya de réaliser dans sa «semigothique» textuelle. Mais Pétrarque ne se bornait pas seulement à contester, d'un point de vue purement esthétique ou graphique, l'écriture dominante de son temps; dans sa pleine maturité et dans sa vieillesse il parvint même à renverser la hiérarchie des typologies du livre qui dominaient le monde de la production d'alors, en mettant en oeuvre un nouveau modèle: celui du «libretto de mano», maniable d'une seule main qu'il nomma dans une lettre (Sen. XV,7) de l'année même de sa mort, adressée à Luigi Marsili, et dont il laissa au moins deux mémorables exemples de sa main: l'autographe du *Bucolicum Carmen* du 1357 (Vat. lat. 3358) et le premier des deux autographes du *De sui ipsius et multorum ignorantia* (Hamilton 493 de Berlin) de 1368: tous les deux hauts de 16 mm. environ et larges d'onze mm. à peine.

Même dans ce cas, il faut préciser tout de suite que la proposition avancée par Pétrarque d'un petit livre de lecture facile à manier d'une seule main, soigneusement mais clairement écrit, dépassait considérablement les aspects extérieurs d'une contestation uniquement formelle de la hiérarchie des types du livre propre à la culture officielle de son temps. En effet, cette proposition était seulement un des éléments de la polémique que Pétrarque, soit dans sa pratique presque quotidienne de copiste, soit dans ses déclarations publiques, conduisit contre les fondements mêmes du système contemporain de production du livre, en en contestant la pratique rigide de division du travail et l'image-clef du scribe-ouvrier.

Les raisons de la position critique de Pétrarque sont énoncées très clairement soit dans le chap. XLII, *De librorum copia*, du traité *De remediis utriusque fortune*, auquel il travaillait à Milan en 1353, soit dans une lettre à son frère Gherardo d'un an après (Fam. XVIII, 5). Dans le traité, P. accuse directement toute la societé de son temps, des autorités publiques à chaque savant, de n'avoir aucune sensibilité pour les problèmes culturels et de ne pas soigner la préparation technique des scribes comme il aurait également fallu le faire. Ceux-ci, en effet, «ne sont contenus par ancune loi, ne réussissent aucun examen, ne sont pas choisis par jugement»; de sorte que, conclut-il «quiconque aura appris à peindre quelque chose sur le parchemin ou à tenir la plume en main, sera considéré comme copiste.» Cette situation déterminait, selon l'opinion de P., non seulement un état d'incertitude et de confusion dans la transmission et dans la diffusion des textes, mais des graves dangers aussi pour leur intégrité; à tel point qu'on ne pourrait - affirme-t-il, «reconnaître les écrits mêmes qu'on a composé». D'autre part dans la lettre à Gherardo il critique la pratique de la division du travail, responsable, à son avis, de l'incorrection des textes; «chez nous, affirme-t-il, certains préparent le parchemin, les uns écrivent les livres, d'autres les corrigent, les uns les illustrent et d'autres enfin les relient et en ornent la surface extérieure.»

À ce point il ne restait rien du système de production du livre et de la hiérarchie typologique qui en était le soutien idéologique; par conséquent il fallait rétablir le processus de production du livre manuscrit en revenant à l'origine: c'est à dire qu'il fallait résoudre avant tout le problème fondamental, celui du rapport entre l'auteur et son texte, et seulement après et par voie de conséquence celui du rapport entre le texte et le public.

Le mécanisme de production industrielle du livre propre aux grandes villes de l'Europe gothique ignorait pratiquement les auteur et en excluait toute participation au processus de reproduction et de diffusion des textes; c'est un autre aspect dont P. se plaint, en dénonçant l'indifférence des savants envers leurs oeuvres, confiées aux mains de copistes ignorants: «l'esprit généreux -remarque-t-il, aspire aux choses les plus hautes, négligeant les humbles; de sorte que les livres des savants, comme les champs des riches, semblent souvent plus incultes que ceux des autres».

La solution du problème proposée par P. est contenue dans le produit qu'on peut définir le «livre d'auteur», c'est-à-dire le manuscrit autographe que le créateur du texte écrit de sa main et qui était destiné à une circulation très limitée et à une reproduction garantie par d'autres collègues-auteurs, par d'autres intellectuels, si on peut définir ainsi les amis et les disciples qui constituaient son premier public d'élection. Il représentait le point culminant d'un long processus d'élaboration du texte entièrement contrôlé par l'auteur même au moyen d'une totale autographie, de la première ébauche sur le papier jusqu'à la dernière page du manuscrit définitif; lequel, par après, redevenait souvent «code-archives», oeuvre ouverte, recevant lui aussi corrections, adjonctions, remaniements. Un processus que P. lui-même a réalisé pour chacune de ses oeuvres, des plus complexes, poursuivies pendant de nombreuses années et jamais terminées, jusqu'aux lettres; il en a laissé un témoignage directe et éloquent dans plusieurs manuscrits de sa main et surtout dans les deux du *Canzoniere*, celui des brouillons de papier (Vat. lat. 3196) et celui sur parchemin (Vat. lat. 3195), qu'on a l'habitude d'appeler l'«original».

Dans la pensée et la pratique d'écriture de P. le «livre d'auteur» ne pouvait qu'être aussi le meilleur livre de lecture, car sa parfaite textualité, émanation directe de l'auteur et garantie par son autographie, était, et restait toujours une garantie de lisibilité absolue pour le lecteur. De cetta façon le cercle se fermait et le problème samblait résolu; mais il l'était seulement pour une élite très restreinte d'humanistes.

La reforme de la production et de la typologie du livre que arrivée des textes en langue vulgaire n'avait pas réussi à provoquer, causant seulement une réorganisation au plan inférieur des catégories existantes, fut donc proposée par P.; mais uniquement pour les haut niveaux du système, c'est-à-dire pour la production savante (et pour personnes cultivées) en langue latine: le *Canzoniere* original, le seul, grand livre d'auteur en langue vulgaire de P., se distingue de tous les autres. Malgré cela la réforme proposée par P. s'imposa seulement dans le domaine de l'écriture, avec le succès de la stylisation graphique qu'on appelle «semigothique», et non par rapport au livre comme marchandise; c'est pourquoi la production continua à suivre lex vieux modèles et les vieux systèmes. Pourtant, les modèles proposés par P., difficiles à appliquer dans la société culturelle du XIVe siècle, demeurèrent à titre de proposition et avertissement pour le futur; dans une certaine mesure ils seraient repris, même si ce devait être beaucoup plus tard, par les intellectuels italiens de la fin du XVe siècle. En réatlité P. avait déjà saisi très clairement une des raisons de la crise qui minait la production du livre à son époque; celle-ci, à cause de son impersonalité mécanique et répétitive et de l'étroitesse de son répertoire, ne répondait plus aux exigences d'un public qui allait changer; un public composé d'hommes socialement importants et d'une culture raffinée; un public représenté par P., par ses amis, ses disciples et correspondants, par les savants ecclésiastiques et laïques, les maîtres, les notaires, les juges et les fonctionnaires répandus en peu partout en Italie, et aussi en Europe.

Ce nouveau public réclamait un nouveau répertoire; et ce nouveau répertoire présentait à son tour l'exigence d'une identification précise et d'une fonction différente du livre et de la lecture, et par conséquent d'une nouvelle typologie du livre; et cette nouvelle typologie demandait aussi de nouveaux moyens et systèmes de production. Tout cela se réalisa graduellement dans l'Italie du centre et du Nord pendant les dernières années du XIVe siècle et d'abord dans des milieux très limités; mais un changement capital se produisit à Florence au tournant des siècles grâce à Niccolò Niccoli, qui, de marchand, devint humaniste, et à Poggio Bracciolini, qui, très jeune (il n'avait pas encore vingt ans) était déjà un scribe de grande valeur.

Il semble que dans l'histoire de la culture écrite il n'existe pas de changements ou d'innovations, même radicales, qui ne s'inspirent de modèles éventuellement antérieurs de plusieurs siècles. Cela se vérifia aussi a propos du type de livre tout-à-fait nouveau, d'aspect et d'écriture, que Niccoli et Poggio, aidés par Coluccio Salutati, élaborèrent et produisirent pour leur compte à Florence dans les dernières années du XIVe siècle et les premières du XVe; un livre qui voulait être, et était pour une bonne part, une reproduction exacte des manuscrits d'étude produits en Italie du XIe au début du XIIe siècle; on en reproduisait d'une façon mécanique le format, le système de réglure, la mise en page, l'ornamentation (les célèbres initiales à «bianchi girari») et enfin, ou avant tout, l'écriture, la minuscule caroline, «castigata et clara» portée aux nues déjà par P., qui fut reproduite d'une façon presque photographique et qui fut appelée «antiqua» avec un certain orgueil; une écriture pour tout dire, à la fois ancienne et nouvelle, une exhumation qui affirma en peu de temps sa très grande vitalité et qui se répandit dans presque toute l'Italie en vingt ou trente ans.

Dans le processus entamé par les deux réformateurs florentins, l'un en sa qualité de bibliophile, l'autre en celle de scribe-amateur, deux éléments, qu'on peut qualifier de structuraux, mettaient en cause le système productif existant. Le premier était constitué par la radicale révolution dans la technique d'écrire imposée par les modèles de la minuscule caroline: c'est ainsi que furent rejetées et la plume biseautée à gauche, et l'écriture brisé qui en derivait, au profit respectivement de la plume taillée centralement et d'une écriture librement dessinée, liée moins que l'autre au travail répétitif du scribe-ouvrier. Le deuxième élément consistait dans la différente répartition, par rapport au passé, des centres de la nouvelle production du livre, formés par des libraires-papatiers specialisés ou même par des scribes qui ne s'etablissaient plus à côté des universités, mais plutôt dans les capitales de la nouvelle écriture, Florence dans la première moitié du siècle, et ensuite Rome, ou du près des cours des grands princes mécènes et leurs bibliothèques; ils se déplaçaient d'un endroit à l'autre d'Italie, là ou tantôt l'avantage économique, tantôt la création d'une nouvelle bibliothèque, tantôt l'appel d'un mécène pouvaient les pousser.

Les nouveaux livres, de format moyen, parfois presque carré, avec le texte disposé sur une seule colonne, à peu près dépourvu d'abréviations, d'une écriture et d'une ornamentation tout-à-fait nouvelles, contenaient presque exclusivement des textes en latin, surtout des auteurs classiques, des traductions du grec et des textes d'humanistes; très rarement, au moins dans les dix ou vingt premières années, quelque chose de différent; aussi bien, les produits différents etaient démandés et achetés en passant par les vieux intermédiaires et en respectant les vieux modèles.

Le livre vulgaire continuait en effet à être produit suivant les schémas formels du XIVe siècle; et il en allait de même pour les livres liturgiques et pour ceux qui étaient liés à la culture universitaire, dont personne n'avait modifié le système de production, notamment parce qu'aucune demande d'innovation n'était partie du public d'ecclésiastiques, de professeurs et d'écoliers qui en faisaient toujours usage. Cependant même si le nouveau modèle du livre, au début pratiquement en dehors du champ de la littérature vulgaire, il en influença négativement le diffusion en contribuant à une élimination graduelle de ses véhicules et de ses intermédiaires naturels.

Cette éviction se produisit automatiquement lorsque, en vertu de la conversion à la culture humaniste des plus importants réprésentants de la grande bourgeoisie mercantile d'un côté et de l'introduction du nouveau répertoire dans les bibliothèques princières de l'Italie du Nord de l'autre, vint à manquer aux vieux modèles de livre de lecture et de prestige en langue vulgaire leur public naturel; si bien qué après le milieu du XVe siècle le livre humaniste remplissait pratiquement dans toute l'Italie la double fonction de livre de luxe pour les hommes cultivés et de livre courtois pour et dans les bibliothèques princières.

La chute de la production organisée, qui, même dans le passé, reposait seulement sur l'initiative des scribes et d'un nombre très limité d'ateliers, fut probablement immédiate. En 1429 déjà Ambrogio Traversari n'arrivait pas à trouver à Florence de manuscrits en langue vulgaire et il s'en plaignait en écrivant à Leonardo Giustiniani, qui les lui avait démandés. Il semble évident que le commerce de ces textes, négligé par les entrepreneurs plus importants, était confié à de modestes ateliers, comme celui du libraire-papetier florentin Giovanni di Michele Baldini, mort en 1425, dont l'inventaire révèle l'existence, à côté de petits livres scolaires, d'un Marco Polo, de légendaires et «Cantari», du Philostrate de Boccaccio et ainsi de suite.

Pourtant ces textes avaient encore leur public, que la diffusion toujours croissante de l'alphabétisme rendait même progressivement plus vaste, surtout dans les villes les plus peuplées.

Il s'agissait d'un public à la culture presque exclusivement vulgaire, pratiquement obligé à écrire lui-même lex textes qu'il voulait lire et conserver à cause de la crise de la production artisanale organisée; et à les écrire surtout dans cette écriture cursive, la «mercantesca», qui était devenue habituelle pour les exclus de l'école de *grammatica*. En effet, c'est justement au cours du XVe siècle que se manifeste de la façon la plus évidente et la plus crue une espèce de bipolarisation graphique qui divisa l'Italie alphabétisée, et en vertu de la quelle ceux qui étudiaient et connaissaient le latin employaient la nouvelle écriture humanistique ou ses variantes cursives, tandis que les autres, confinés dans la seule connaissance du vulgaire, écrivaient en cursive mercantesca. Cette bipolarisation était très bien connue des contemporains, puisque en 1454 Enea Silvio Piccolomini pouvait réprimander un de ses correspondants, coupable de lui avoir écrit dans une graphie indéchiffrable, en lui rappelant qu'il avait appris «latinas litteras, non uncinos mercatorios». Les «crochets» des marchands, c'est-à-dire la cursive «mercantesca», allaient donc acquérir une connotation non seulement graphique ou culturelle, mais aussi sociale, de diversité et d'émargination, en tant que signe visible d'une culture inférieure et unilingue.

Et cependant precisément à cette époque continuait et augmentait quantitativement dans chaque région d'Italie la production de livres vulgaires, confiée aux humbles faiseurs de livres sur papier en écriture «mercantesca», aux religieux et aux religieuses qui employaient encore une écriture gothique déformée, aux copistes isolés qui utilisaient de plus élégantes cursives bâtardes ou semigothiques. À propos de la survivance de textes en langue «franco-veneta» dans des copies du XVe siècle, Gianfranco Folena écrivait: «Ces copies présentent les signes d'une dégradation, d'un déclin culturel, mais aussi d'un élargissement social, et en outre d'un tenace amour pour la littérature vulgaire»; et il postulait l'existence de nouveaux marchés et d'un vaste commerce de détail.

Voyons maintenant de plus près qui pouvait alimenter ce commerce et élargir les nouveaux marchés du livre vulgaire au cours d'un siècle dominé par le livre latin de type humaniste. Un recensement sommaire des copistes en langue vulgaire du XVe siècle a révélé l'éxistence de 230 copistes environ qui écrivaient des livres contenant des textes en Italien, dont dix-sept seulement semblent être des professionnels; deux d'entre eux sont des notaires, un est un maître d'école; certains écrivent surtout des textes en latin, comme les celèbres copistes humanistes Cinico ou Veterano; parmi tous les autres, copistes par passion ou par goût, on peut identifier dix-huit réligieux et treize notaires; les autres – l'immense majorité – ne sont pas des professionels de l'écriture; beaucoup d'entre eux écrivent pour eux-mêmes et pour leurs bibliothèques familiales en declarant de le faire «par divertissement», «pour s'amuser», «pour se consoler», ou «pour vaincre l'oisivité».

Copier pour lire, plus qu'un plaisir, etait donc une nécessité et il n'etait pas question de trop se préoccuper de l'aspect extérieur du produit, dont les copistes eux-mêmes déploraient parfois l'incorrection et la négligence; mais jamais ils ne se plaignaient de leur fatigue physique, comme le faisaient les scribes-ouvriers du moyen-âge, dont les lamentations ou les expressions de soulagement pour avoir achevé l'oeuvre caractérisent tant de souscriptions. Il nous semble que l'écriture comme divertissement est un aspect à relever de cette «liberté d'écrire» qui avait été conquise au XIIIe siècle par un cercle toujours plus large de laïes alphabetisés et qui, au XVe siècle, n'était pas encore menacée dans sa créativité par l'avènement de l'imprimerie et par l'organisation de l'enseignement primaire.

Au cours des trente dernières années du XVe siècle, le monde de la culture écrite italienne fut dominé par un événement d'une énorme portée culturelle aussi bien que sociale: l'introduction dans la Péninsule de de l'imprimerie en caractères mobiles et sa première diffusion dans les villes les plus grandes et les plus petites; mais cet événement, même s'il élargit énormément le public des lecteurs et fit de livre un produit de prix relativement modeste, ne provoqua pas, au moins au XVe siècle, de profondes modifications dans la typologie du livre. Les prototypographes, en effet, se bornèrent à transférer dans les nouveaux livres les formats, les mises en page, les caractères, les ornements typiques et propres des manuscrits, en faisant vivre ainsi dans de nouvelles formes les mêmes types de livre qui vers le milieu du siècle environ étaient dans le commerce en Italie, même si ce fut à travers un procès ni immédiat, ni linéaire, mais contradictoire, parfois incertain, souvent tourmenté.

Le premier type de livre que l'imprimerie reproduisit fut, comme on l'avait déjà vu en Allemagne, le livre solennel de la tradition ecclésiastique et de la culture officielle et universitaire, le grand livre «da banco» en caractères gothiques ou semigothiques; suivit le livre de lecture humanistique, plus petit, et avec des caracteristiques graphiques et typographiques differentes; et enfin ce fut le tour aussi du livre en langue vulgaire, du livre «da bisaccia», qui, avec une production de plus en plus vaste, connut le dernier après les années soixantedix, la consacration de l'imprimerie.

En 1479, Vespasiano da Bisticci, le papetier-libraire florentin qui avait été le plus grand pourvoyeur de livres humanistes de luxe pour les bibliothèques nobiliaires et princières d'Italie et d'Europe, avait fermé son atelier; l'année suivante Antonio Sinibaldi, le plus habile des copistes florentins de son temps, accusait explicitement le nouvel art typographique d'avoir détruit l'art de l'écriture à la main et de l'avoir personnellement ruiné: «Et lo exercitio mio è solo di scrivere a prezo, quale è riducto per mezo della stampa, in modo che apena ne trago il vestito, et è exercitio infermissimo...». Et cependant la production de manuscrits se poursuivra pendant tout le XVe siècle et encore an XVIe; mais dans la masse deux catégories prennent un relief tout particulier, celles qui se situent aux limites extrêmes et opposées de l'échelle typologique; c'est d'un côté celle des livres «courtois» en parchemin, d'un niveau toujours plus raffiné, et de l'autre celle des livres vulgaires en papier d'un niveau toujours plus bas, tant au point de vue du texte, que de l'aspect matériel.

Au cours des vingt dernières années du siècle les manuscrits courtois de luxe adoptent de plus en plus un format réduit il s'agit, en général, de livres en parchemin éxécutés avec le plus grand soin, habilement écrits en écriture humanistique posée ou en italique et généreusement ornés ou enluminés. Pour une bonne part, ces manuscrits contiennent des textes d'auteurs classiques latins (ou grec en traduction), sans commentaires ni annotations; ils sont produits dans les plus grands centres de la culture et de la production italienne du livre du temps: à Florence, à Milan, en Vénétie, à Naples. Il s'agit évidemment d'exemplaires de luxe, destinés à l'usage privé de personnages cultivés et socialement éminents et à la conservation dans des bibliothèques nobiliaires ou princières.

Parfois ces petits manuscrits, très richement enluminés, contiennent aussi des textes vulgaires poétiques; mais, quand cela arrive, il s'agit toujours d'un type particulier, ou mieux unique de texte: il s'agit, à savoir, des *Rime* et/ou des *Trionfi* de P. Exemplaire de ce point de vue apparaît en Italie la production de deux des plus grands calligraphes de la Renaissance: le florentin Antonio Sinibaldi, qu'on a déjà mentionné, et le vénitien Bartolomeo Sanvito. Tous deux copient beaucoup de manuscrits qui contiennent des textes classiques, dont plusieurs dans un très petit format; Sanvito, en particulier, copie aussi des délicieux recueils épigraphiques. Tous les deux copient également de petits livres d'heures; cela a beaucoup d'importance, car le livre d'heures représenta longtemps dans l'Europe de la fin du Moyen Age et de la Renaissance le premier et le seul exemple de livre manuscrit de petit format. L'un et l'autre, enfin, écrivent un seul type de texte

vulgaire: les oeuvres poétiques de P. et toujours en manuscrits de petit format.
Si on étendait les recherches aux manuscrits de luxe des oeuvres de P. produits en Italie à la fin du XVe siècle, on s'apercevrait tout de suite que le phenomène n'intéressa pas seulement les deux copistes qu'on vient de mentionner. En effet, entre les années '60 du XVe siècle et la fatidique année séculaire de 1500, il y a beaucoup de «petrarchini» de luxe produits par des copistes anonymes dans les plus importantes villes d'Italie, et tous se ressemblent: même format, même mise en page, mêmes ornements. Qu'est-ce-qu'il y a derrière ce phénomène? De nombreux facteurs d'origine différente; peut-être l'influence, lointaine sans doute, mais toujours vivante, des autographes vénérables de P. lui-même; certainement l'influence du livre quotidien de lecture le plus répandu parmi les laïes à savoir le livre d'heures; mais aussi la naissance d'une nouvelle façon de lire, favorisée par la diffusione du livre imprimé, et qui transférait l'operation de lecture de ses peu nombreux et solennels lieux-obligés d'autrefois (l'atelier, la bibliothèque, la cellule), aux lieux et aux habitudes plus communs et fréquents de la vie quotidienne; une façon de lire typique d'une société cultivée, mais non pas professionnellement littéraire, qui aurait appris tout de suite à aimer le texte libre à commentaires, l'élégance et la lisibilité immédiate des caractères, le format miniable: une société en même temps bourgeoise et bilingue.

Dans l'espace d'un peu d'un mois et demi, entre la fin de septembre et le mois de novembre 1494 mouraient à Florence Angelo Poliziano et Pico della Mirandola et commençaient à être dispersées leurs deux collections de livres, qui, pour des raisons opposées, avaient admirablement représenté la phase de transformation de la bibliothèque privée du modèle du Moyen Age au modèle moderne, du trésor de manuscrits à la collection de livres imprimés. La bibliothèque de Giovanni Pico della Mirandola était une des plus importantes de son époque, parmi les privées; à sa mort elle comptait 1190 volumes, dont 500 environ imprimés; mais sa caractéristique ne consistait pas tant dans la quantité des livres, que dans la grande variété d'intérets qui y etaient représentés, reflétés aussi dans la pluralité des langues et des cultures. Si les volumes en latin constituaient la grosse majorité (900 numéros environ), remarquable était aussi la présence de textes en grec (160 environ) et significative celle de 70 manuscrits hébreux, de 7 manuscrits arabes, de quelques manuscrits araméens; en comparaison les volumes avec des textes en langue italienne (parmi lequels on remarque Dante, Cecco d'Ascoli, Giacomo da Varazze) ou en langue française sont très peu nombreux. L'intérêts particulier du possesseur pour la philosophie et les sciences occultes et naturelles mis a part, l'ensemble des textes en latin donnait un tableau suffisamment complet non seulement du répertoire litteraire classique et humaniste du temps, mais aussi de la grande tradition scolaire de la fin du Moyen Age.

L'aspiration de Pico était évidemment de posséder une bibliothèque totale, un «thesaurus» de la culture écrite dans les limites de l'univers qui lui était connu; et certainement ce n'est pas par hasard qu'on trouve parmi ses livres une copie de l'inventaire de la bibliothèque de Sixte IV et une copie de celui d'Urbino, c'est-à-dire de deux de plus importantes «bibliothèque d'Etat» de l'Italie contemporaine. A en croire une anecdote racontée par Pietro Crinito, Pico, loué un jour pour son talent par Politien et d'autres, soutint qu'il ne fallait pas tant exalter ses qualités naturelles que plutôt l'étude intensive et ce qu'il appelait «supellectilem nostram», c'est-à-dire les livres de sa bibliothèque; une bibliothèque que Crinito définissait riche, remarquablement fournie et où il y avait un grand nombre de livres de tous les genres.

Il semble donc que Pico, par sa part, pensait que l'étude pouvait se réaliser à travers un seul moyen, le livre, et une seule méthode, la lecture; et que par conséquent il écartait du processus formatif l'élément oral, qui avait pourtant joué un rôle important dans l'éducation cultivée du Moyen Age, et la pratique d'écrire aussi, qui avait été partie intégrant de cette éducation. La conception générale de la culture écrite que Pico s'était formée dans le rapport obsédant avec sa bibliothèque finissait par proposer en termes nouveaux les modes mêmes de la lecture et le rapport entre le livre et le lecteur; et c'étaient des modes et des rapports bien plus libres et plus complexes que ceux qui étaient supposés par le schéma, ancien mais encore trè vivant dans la réalité contemporaine, de la bibliothèque publique avec les livres enchaînés; des modes et des rapports typiques d'une nouvelle réalité culturelle modifié rapidement et profondément par l'irruption du livre imprimé, sa diffusion rapide, son envahissante réalité quantitative.

Angelo Poliziano n'était pas seulement un admirateur et un ami fidèle de Giovanni Pico, mais aussi un usager assidu de sa bibliothèque; et il lui était étroitement lié, même si Pico avait une conscience très vive du professionalisme philologique et littéraire de Poliziano et l'opposait, dans un élan de fausse modestie, à un certain dilettantisme qui lui était propre. Mais, tandis que la bibliothèque de Pico pouvait paraître dans son imposant caractère organique comme la bibliothèque d'un professionel des études philosophiques, celle de Poliziano avait une toute autre consistance et un tout autre aspect. Il s'agissait, en effet, d'une «petite et pauvre bibliothèque», dont, après l'immédiate dispersion, survivent aujourd'hui moins de 60 pièces, parmi manuscrits, incunables, autographes et mélanges littéraires.

D'autant plus fort apparaît donc à la posterité la disparité entre la petite collection de livres du génial lettré et l'énorme quantité des lectures dont, avec une discipline assidue, s'était nourrie son «eruditio interior atque politior», d'après une expression de Filippo Beroaldo. Il s'agissait d'une disparité comblée par la pratique du travail exercé non pas au dedans d'un cabinet confortable, mais dans les bibliothèques publiques de Florence, dans les collections privées des Médicis et de son ami Pico, dans le bibliothèques de Rome et d'autres villes d'Italie; et grâce aussi à des prêts qu'on lui accordait généreusement. Il s'agissait d'une disparité et d'une pratique de travail qui trouvaient un point de rencontre et de médiation dans la philologie entièrement formelle de Politiano, qui l'amenait à privilégier naturellement le rapport verbal avec le texte, plutôt que le rapport physique avec le livre, et à mettre sur le même plan l'usage d'un manuscrit ou celui d'un livre imprimé. Il s'agissait encore d'une disparité et de pratiques qui sont toujours typiques des habitudes de travail des savants pauvres, mais qui, dans l'expérience de Politiano, devaient prendre l'aspect d'un refus personnel des éléments rituels de la fonction professorale, dont la possession de beaucoup de livres était partie essentielle; disparité et pratique marquées également par ce sens de tragique précarité qui exerça son influence à tous les moments de sa brève existence en conditionnant aussi sa façon d'étudier et de lire.

Celle-ci était certainement conçue par le philologue des Médicis dans une perspective totalement hédoniste des faits de la vie, où la lecture se plaçait simplement à côté d'autres et différentes attitudes de corps e de l'esprit, presque comme une conséquence et une prémisse; comme lui-même l'expliquait dans une lettre en langue vulgaire adressée à Clarice de Médicis: «Iersera giunti a San Miniato cominciamo a leggere un poco di Santo Agostino. E questa lezione risolvessi in fine nel musicare e in iscorgere e dirozare un certo modello di ballerino che è qua». Si on compare une de ces citations avec les éléments et les impressions tirés des vicissitudes humaines et culturelles de Politiano, encore vivantes dans ses autographes, ses lettres, ses oeuvres, on peut dire qu'avec son expérience de lecture globale, affranchie des limites idéologiques, des contraintes rituelles et des règles fixés, il allait dépasser les vieilles expressions de l'acculturation du livre; en effet, en inventant de nouveaux et plus libres rapports avec les textes écrits et un nouveau statut de la lecture savante, il niait dans les faits la valeur symbolique de la possession des livres.

En réalité, à la fin du XVe siècle, des facteurs plus généraux de renouvellement convergaient pour conférer à des textes nouveaux, parmi lesquels ceux en langue vulgaire, le droit à la conservation de longue durée et la consécration bibliothécaire, qu'on leur avait niée jusqu' alors; à côté de l'expérience «livresque» d'un Pico et d'un Poliziano qui devançait les développements et les progrès futurs, ce furent aussi voire, d'un côté, la pression d'une industrie du livre naissante et à la recherche de nouveaux marchés, et de l'autre le commencement d'un processus ininterrompu de canonisation de la langue écrite italienne. On s'aperçut beaucoup plus tard de l'effet de ces tendances dans la pratique et aussi dans la théorie de la conservation des livres, mais on ne peut nier que le début de la transformation qui rendit les bibliothèques de la seconde moitié du XVIe siècle très différentes de celles du siècle précédent se situe dans le bref espace de temps compris entre les expériences de Pico et de Poliziano, qui vit changer le livre même, avant les lieux de sa conservation.

Comme on l'a vu, ce fut précisément à la fin du XVe siècle que, grâce à des scribes et des artisans du livre parmi les plus géniaux et raffinés que l'Europe ait jamais connu, naquit le petit livre à tenir en main, nouveau quant au format, à la mise en page, à l'emploi du texte (à lire, non pas à étudier) et en conséquence quant au rôle, mais qui resta simplement «courtois» et d'élite, tant qu'il fut manuscrit; c'est à dire jusqu'au moment où, au début du XVIe siècle (1501) 'Alde Manuce eut l'intuition qu'il avait une valeur potentielle de marchandise de masse et en fit un produit de grande diffusion: ses «libelli portatiles in formam enchiridii».

La collection de petits livres de poche inaugurée par Alde en 1501 sous la direction de Pietro Bembo contenait et des livres latins, et des livres grecs, et des livres italiens. Il faut donc dire qu'exactement au moment où il allait céder la place à l'imprimerie le livre manuscrit se révéla encore capable de renouveler types, expressions et fonctions de la production et de la jouissance intellectuelles, et de garder et de transmettre au processus industriel naissant un rapport fécond avec le public.

Bibliographie sommaire

Pour la culture écrite de la Renaissance italienne, A. Petrucci (éd.). *Libri, scrittura e pubblico nel Rinascimento*, Bari 1979. Pour le Pétrarque, A. Petrucci, *La scrittura di Francesco Petrarca*, Città del Vaticano 1967 (Studi e Testi, 248). Pour la lettre de Traversari, B. Migliorini, *Storia della lingua italiana*, Firenze 1961, p. 250. Pour le «cartolaio» Baldini, A. de la Mare, *The Shop of a florentine «cartolaio» in 1426*, in *Studi offerti a Roberto Ridolfi*, Firenze 1973, pp. 237-48. Pour la lettre de E.S.Piccolomini, S. Rizzo, *Il lessico filologico degli umanisti*, Roma 1973, p. 143. La déclaration de A. Sinibaldi dans T. de Marinis, *La biblioteca napoletana dei re d'Aragona*, II, Firenze 1947, pp. 311-2. Pour le Politien, C. Mutini, *Interpreta-*

zione del Poliziano, Roma 1972; pour sa bibliothèque, A. Campana, *Contributi alla biblioteca del Poliziano*, in *Il Poliziano e il suo tempo*, Firenze 1957, pp. 175-229: I. Maier, *Les manuscrits d'Ange Politien. Catalogue descriptif*, Genève 1965. Pour la bibliothèque de Pico, P. Kibre, *The library of Pico della Mirandola*, New York 1936.

Je désire remercier très vivement mon ami le mons. prof. Paul Canart, qui a révisé la traduction française de mon texte.

The copying of printed books for humanistic bibliophiles in the fifteenth century

by ALBERT DEROLEZ

The copying by hand of printed books was quite a common practice in the second half of the fifteenth century and was done probably at a much larger scale than is generally estimated. This contribution will deal successively with some earlier studies on this seemingly strange practice, and with a few well-known examples, especially in Quattrocento Italy, where bibliophiles had incunabula copied fairly often; thirdly I shall deal more circumstantially with a Flemish ecclesiastic bibliophile from about 1500, whose library consisted of de luxe manuscripts of which a great majority appear to have been copied from printed editions; and in a final section I shall try to give an historical explanation for this phenomenon.

Obviously late fifteenth-century manuscripts – with the exception of the well-known and so often exhibited and reproduced Books of Hours – have not attracted much attention till now. For the philologists they are generally quite too late and without any interest for establishing the text. Art historical research, on the other hand, has been focused on Livres d'Heures and fine illuminated vernacular manuscripts, e.g. those executed for the Dukes of Burgundy, the Kings of England and of France and for the princes and noble collectors in those countries. As for the mass of Latin manuscripts produced in that half century, it has generally been considered worthless, anachronistic remnants from a period which saw the invention, the spread and the triumph of the printed book. Still now in many eyes the printed book is the only real book, as is suggested by the title of Fèbvre and Martin's well-known book *L'apparition du livre*.[1] This is a false idea in two respects: the manuscript is a book as well as the printed copy, it has only been made non-mechanically and could never attain the same public as the printed book could do; and for the historian there is no reason why a manuscript copy would loose at once its cultural value just because it was written after the invention of printing. Fortunately, meetings like the Wolfenbüttel Arbeits-

---

[1] L. Fèbvre & H.J. Martin, *L'apparition du livre* (Paris, 1958; *L'évolution de l'humanité*).

gespräch of 1978[2] and the present symposium have been organised to fill the gap existing between the manuscript and the printed book and to remove the barrier between their respective scholars, the codicologists and the bibliographers.[3]

But till now it is easily understandable why studies on late fifteenth-century manuscripts copied from printed books are extremely scanty. In fact, the best-known authority in this field remains Curt Bühler, who deals with the phenomenon in the first chapter of his *The Fifteenth-Century Book*.[4] He, and all the other scholars who have occasionaly been writing on the subject, have quoted the famous sentence of the Florentine bookseller and biographer Vespasiano da Bisticci about his illustrious client Federico da Montefeltro, Duke of Urbino, who had an insurmountable aversion to printed books and refused to have one in his library in the Ducal Palace.[5]

At once it is suggested that the phenomenon of copying printed books is due to a more or less misplaced sense of grandeur of the rich bibliophile, who desires to stand supreme, high above the poor book-collectors who content themselves with plain printed books. This élitist attitude has no doubt been the principal reason why so often printed books have been copied by hand: first the price of the manuscript was a multiple of the price of the printed book, secondly the manuscript enabled the collector to dispose of large-sized books on vellum instead of paper, and thus fit to be decorated and illuminated by artists and to be given an individuality and uniqueness which the printed book had not by definition. But there have been other reasons too to copy printed books, as will be demonstrated further on.

It is well known that the great majority of books printed in the fifteenth century were Latin books. Culture, and especially scientific culture, was still mainly a business of the clergy, and even at the end of the century private book-collections were chiefly to be found in the houses of priests and canons.[6] In England, in France, in Germany, in the Low Countries, the secular bibliophiles, kings, princes, noblemen confined themselves to vernacular books. In Italy, however, there were lots of rich secular libraries consisting exclusively or

---

[2] *Buch und Text im 15. Jahrhundert. Book and Text in the fifteenth Century. Arbeitsgespräch in der Herzog August Bibliothek Wolfenbüttel vom 1. bis 3. März 1978. Vorträge* herausg. von L. Hellinga & H. Härtel. Proceedings ... (Hamburg, 1981; *Wolfenbütteler Abhandlungen zur Renaissanceforschung*, II).

[3] Cf. a plea for a more integrated study of manuscripts and incunabula by D. Coq, *L'incunable, un bâtard du manuscrit?* (*Gazette du Livre médiéval*, 1, 1982, pp. 10-11).

[4] Philadelphia, 1960.

[5] Bühler, *op. cit.*, p. 62.

[6] As is clearly demonstrated by fifteenth-century library catalogues, wills and inventories.

mainly of Latin books. In general the great Italian bibliophiles read – or pretended to read – only Latin books: the Duke of Urbino just referred to, the Medici in Florence and, in a lesser degree, the Sforza in Milan and the Kings of Aragon in Naples. Just like the great ecclesiastic bibliophiles of the second half of the Quattrocento, they all had a strong predilection for the manuscript book, which cost so much more than the printed copy.[7] But for making a manuscript copy a model is needed, which traditionally was another manuscript, but could be a printed edition as well now. And as printed texts were already spread all over Italy in the seventies and eighties, why should the copyist or his employer have searched for a manuscript model, when abundant printed models were available close at hands? No wonder then, that a great deal of all the Latin de luxe manuscripts produced in Italy in the latter half of the fifteenth century should be copied from incunabula. In fact, this may be supposed principally in all cases where a printed edition of the text copied existed. Of course, normally only a closer investigation may permit to decide whether in each individual case this is true or not. Where such closer investigation has not been carried out – i.e. in nearly all cases – only particular circumstances may give a clue. The copyist may have transcribed the full printer's colophon or other texts peculiar to the printed book, as prefaces by the editor, laudatory poems on the art of printing, poems in praise of the printer etc. Although of course only unattentive or unschooled scribes commit such "Schönheitfehler", they occur from time to time and constitute our major source of information on the subject under discussion. I have the impression that Italian copyists did not often copy the colophons of printed books in their manuscripts just because they used to write their own colophon formulas much more often than their colleagues in the more Northern parts of Europe did.[8] Everybody who has been working with the *Colophons de manuscrits occidentaux* by the Benedictines of Le Bouveret knows what an immense part in this work is played by Italian scribes. I think Italian humanistic individualism could not be more properly demonstrated than by the extraordinary number of signed manuscripts produced in that country in the fifteenth century. But when the scribes had the habit of writing their proper colophon formulas,

---

[7] On this class of Italian manuscripts see: A. Derolez, *Codicologie des manuscrits en écriture humanistique sur parchemin* (Turnhout, 1984; Bibliologia, 5-6).

[8] A. Derolez, *Observations on the Colophons of Humanistic Scribes in Fifteenth-Century Italy*, in: *Paläographie 1981. Colloquium des Comité International de Paléographie, München, 15.-18 September 1981*, herausg. von G. Silagi (München, 1982; *Münchener Beiträge zur Mediävistik und Renaissance-Forschung*, 32), pp. 249-261.

subscribed with their own names, they could not easily be induced to copy at the same time the formula of their printed model. Nevertheless a number of examples could be given: a Florentine manuscript of Bessarion's *In calumniatorem Platonis* is obviously copied from the Sweynheym and Pannartz edition of 1469,[9] and a scribe called Salvatus Calliensis, who copied Themistius, *Paraphrases in libros Aristotelis*, for Pope Sixt IV, admits in his colophon that he copied a printed edition (obviously the Treviso edition of 1481) and adds that he spoiled his eyes in trying to read the badly printed pages of this exemplar.[10]

If such colophons are generally missing in late fifteenth-century manuscripts, there is sometimes internal evidence for the existence of a printed exemplar for a given manuscript: a manuscript containing a series of different texts derives probably from a printed edition, if the latter contains the same texts in an identical sequence; probability is likewise great when a manuscript offers additions to the text proper in the form of editor's prefaces, notes by translators etc. which are known to have been made for and to have been included in one or more printed editions, as has been said earlier. Unfortunately, the existing bibliographies of the early printed book are really insufficient for this kind of research. The *Gesamtkatalog der Wiegendrucke* is a splendid piece of scholarship and helps a lot in the confrontation of texts in manuscripts and in incunabula, but it was not designed for that, so that one often needs to recur to the actual fifteenth-century printed editions for purposes of collation. And this is only practicable in the world's greatest libraries, which offer large collections of incunabula. The *British Museum Catalogue*, on the other hand, has the advantage of being complete and containing authors and titles from A to Z, but of course a lot of editions are missing in it and its descriptions are shorter than those of the *Gesamtkatalog*. As for the early sixteenth-century impressions, the historian is totally unarmed and most of his assertions have to be followed by question-marks: it is nearly impossible to affirm with certainty that a manuscript has been copied from a definite sixteenth-century edition unless a copy of the edition is close at hands. A final difficulty is in the fact that not all fifteenth-century editions are recorded in the bibliographies of incunabula, but only the editions of which at least one copy survives. But there are manuscripts which seem to derive from unrecorded

---

[9] Vatican Library, MS Urb. lat. 196; the model is GKW 4183.
[10] Vatican Library, MS Vat. lat. 2142, f. 280v: *Salvatus Calliensis (...) se commendat adeo ut lucem quam exemplaris impressure vicio pene amisit se non amisisse penitus cognoscat*. The model is probably the Themistius edition BMC, vol. VI, p. 894.

editions, as is the case in the library of a great Flemish bibliophile, who will be dealt with in the main part of this paper.

The bibliophile under discussion is Raphael de Marcatellis (or Mercatellis), born in 1437, deceased in 1508. A couple of years ago I devoted a book to the library of this Flemish ecclesiastic of Italian origin, one of the natural children of Philip the Good, Duke of Burgundy, himself one of the foremost book-collectors of the fifteenth-century.[11] Raphael's mother's husband (we don't know whether she married him before or after Raphael's birth) was obviously a member of the Italian colony in Bruges. Marcatellis himself entered the Church in which, thanks to his father's almighty protection, he rose rapidly to high posts, ensuring him a considerable income: as abbot of St Bavon's abbey in Ghent, one of the richest abbeys in Flanders, and as bishop *in partibus* of the Eastern diocese of Rhosus, he missed no opportunity to augment his fortune, generally neglecting his ecclesiastical duties and spending the better part of his life in Bruges with his Italian relatives. Years after his death he was still referred to as *homo Italus*, which in his case can hardly have been a compliment. Through his Italian acquaintances, however, he came into contact with Italian Humanism, so that in setting up a book-collection he could continue and combine two different and till that time separate traditions: the tradition of Burgundian bibliophily, of which his father was the most brilliant representative, and the tradition of humanistic book-collecting as practised on a large scale by his Italian contemporaries. Add to this a highly developed megalomania and consider again his immense wealth, and it will be possible to imagine what his private library looked like. It consisted only of large-sized manuscripts, the smallest ones being 30 cms., the largest ones 54 cms. high, heavy volumes carefully written on the whitest vellum, abundantly illuminated and illustrated, and bound in *de luxe* bindings with oak boards covered with leather and precious textiles in various colours, such as silk and camlet, and protected by magnificent gilt brass bosses and corner-pieces. Script and decoration of these massive volumes are gothic in style (although in some manuscripts the handwriting proves to be under humanistic influence),[12] but the texts in them are clearly of a humanistic nature, in such a degree that Marcatellis is to be considered the most important humanistic-

---

[11] A. Derolez, The Library of Raphael de Marcatellis, Abbot of St. Bavon's, Ghent 1437-1508 (Ghent, 1979).

[12] Derolez, *The Library*, pl. 1.

minded book-collector of about 1500 in the Low Countries.[13] He had a strong predilection for classical authors (the Greeks in Latin translations), writings of the Italian Humanists, Platonic and Neo-Platonic philosophy, ethics and education, history and geography (with a special interest in Eastern Europe and the Near East), astronomy, astrology, natural science, medicine and music.

Like Burgundian manuscripts in general and in contrast again with Italian manuscripts a great deal of his manuscripts were illustrated with lots of large-scale miniatures. Up to this day 58 manuscripts are known to have survived from Marcatellis's library, which according to a late sixteenth-century catalogue originally consisted of 80 manuscripts. So 22 manuscripts seem to have gone lost, although this number may be smaller: two unrecorded Marcatellis manuscripts have been discovered only in recent years: one in the de Rothschild collection in Great Britain,[14] and one very recently in the library of Yale University.[15] The manuscripts are now scattered all over the world, but there are still important collections to be found in Ghent (University Library and Cathedral Library), Haarlem, Holkham Hall and elsewhere. It is important to notice that all surviving manuscripts have been written by order of Marcatellis himself – he obviously disliked second-hand books – and that, although the major part of them does not bear a date, they may be dated between c.1475 and 1505. As far as we know they were written in two centres – the two principal centres of manuscript production in Flanders at the time: Ghent and Bruges, but information is scanty on which manuscripts were produced in Ghent and which in Bruges.[16] In

---

[13] Earlier in the fifteenth century Flemish humanistic-minded bibliophiles assembled interesting libraries, e.g. Antoine Haneron and Jan Crabbe, but these were obviously much smaller than Marcatellis's one. See G.I. Lieftinck, *Antoine Haneron introduisant l'écriture humanistique dans les Pays-Bas*, in *Classical, Mediaeval and Renaissance Studies in Honor of B.L. Ullman*, vol. II (Rome, 1964), pp. 283-4; N. Huyghebaert, *Trois manuscrits de Jean Crabbe, abbé des Dunes* (*Scriptorium*, XXIII, 1969, pp. 232-42); N. Geirnaert, *De bibliotheek van de Duineabt Jan Crabbe (1457/59-1488)*, in *Vlaamse Kunst op Perkament. Handschriften en Miniaturen te Brugge van de 12de tot de 16de Eeuw* (Exhibition catalogue, Bruges, 1981), pp. 176 ff.

[14] Derolez, *The Library*, pp. 138 ff.

[15] Yale University, Beinecke Library, Mellon Alchemical MS 25, an astrological miscellany, discovered in november 1979 by Professor James Marrow, whom I wish to thank most sincerely for the description and photographs he has generously provided me with. For a description of the manuscript, see my forthcoming article: "Nieuwe gegevens in verbrand met de ateliers van Rafhael de Mercatellis" [New Evidence concerning the Mercatel Workshops], in *Feestbundel Jan Deschamps*.

[16] No. 21 in Derolez, *The Library*, was written in Bruges in 1488, No. 33 in the same city in 1496, No. 42 in Ghent in 1503-4.

fact, by their script, their decoration and their illustration they are a unity, clearly distinguishable from the manuscripts made for other Flemish bibliophiles of the second half of the fifteenth century. As to the illumination, we must admit that to the Ghent abbot quantity seems to have been more important than quality. If, however, the artistic level is not very high, the hundreds of miniatures in these manuscripts are of exceptional iconographic importance.

Finally, to understand rightly the significance of Marcatellis's library, one must know that the majority of all surviving manuscripts are composed of different sections, each one containing one or more different texts, so that the relatively small number of eighty books represents in fact a collection of several hundreds of texts.

Now, of all 58 surviving manuscripts, only 10 seem to be totally independent of printed sources, the remaining 48 being, in their entirety or partially (sometimes only for very small sections of text), copied from printed books. The models came principally from Italian printing houses (mainly from Venice), as will be easily understood; but also products of French, German and Flemish printers have sometimes been copied for Marcatellis. It would take too much time to discuss one after the other all the manuscripts in the Marcatellis collection and their possible exemplars. I shall therefore limit myself to some obvious cases of dependence and begin with the earliest manuscripts.

The second section of MS Cambridge, Peterhouse 269 contains the *Historia Alexandri Magni* by Quintus Curtius.[17] The scribe did his work so conscientiously that at the end of his text he even copied a laudatory poem on the famous Venetian printer Vindelinus de Spira, under the heading *Loquitur lector ad Vindelinum Spirensem artificem qui Quintum Curtium reddit in lucem*. This proves that his model was the *editio princeps*, published in Venice by Vindelinus of Speyer, probably in 1471.[18] But it would be a mistake to reject this manuscript simply for that reason (which in fact one should do with no manuscript at all). Indeed, the Venetian edition starts with Book III of Quintus Curtius, the first two books being lost. In our manuscript, on the contrary, Books I and II have been supplied in an anonymous version which is known through four manuscripts only. This confers to our manuscript an unexpected importance.

In the same manuscript Cicero's *Tusculanae quaestiones* occur, probably copied from an uncommented edition,[19] but the text has afterwards been thoroughly

---

[17] Derolez, *The Library*, p. 43.
[18] BMC, vol. V, p. 163.
[19] GKW, 6888-93; as the manuscript dates from before the year 1487 (the date of Marcatellis's

corrected, by Marcatellis himself apparently, as is mentioned in the ownership-inscription at the end of the book: *Hoc volumen comparavit Raphael de Marcatellis, (...) et quoad potuit correxit anno Domini 1495* (the date is certainly wrong).[20]

MS Haarlem 187 C 15, an extensive *corpus Platonicum*, contains among many other texts Cardinal Bessarion's *In calumniatorem Platonis*, copied from Sweynheym and Pannartz's *editio princeps* of 1469, but here an extensive Table of Contents of 22 pages has been added.[21]

Marcatellis's magnificent Ptolemy copy is dated 1482 and 1485.[22] Although the script is obviously a *gothica textualis formata*, the inscriptions on the maps, by the same scribe, are in humanistic capitals. Originally there were 28 maps, as in the earlier printed editions,[23] but in the same year 1482 a new edition appeared, by Donnus Nicolaus Germanus, which contains five additional maps.[24] These maps were copied in Marcatellis's manuscript afterwards, most probably in 1485, in a workshop different from that where the first series of maps were made, perhaps the Jan van Kriekenborch workshop in Ghent. Van Kriekenborch's atelier made a similar Ptolemy atlas for Marcatellis's illustrious contemporary, townsman and friend Louis of Gruuthuse, likewise in 1485.[25] In Marcatellis's copy we see that the manuscript is obviously based on two consecutive Ptolemy editions; if the maps could be copied from the woodcuts in the original books, the miniaturists had only to add the colours.[26]

Copying printed books was probably not so easy as one would think at first sight. At least Marcatellis's splendid manuscript containing Plutarch's *Vitae parallelae*[27] presents a number of textual anomalies: extensive corrections, portions of text added in the margins, some leaves being partially blank etc. As

episcopal consecration), GKW 6894, dated 1499, cannot have been the model.

[20] About the poor value of the 'acquisition'-dates in the Marcatellis manuscripts, see Derolez, *The Library*, p. 23.

[21] Derolez, *The Library*, p. 47; the edition is GKW 4183.

[22] Brussels, Koninklijke Bibliotheek, MS 14887; cf. Derolez, *The Library*, pp. 48 ff.

[23] First edition with maps: Bologna, Dominicus de Lapis, 1477 (BMC, vol. VI, p. 814).

[24] C. Lemaire in *Le cinquième centenaire de l'imprimerie dans les anciens Pays-Bas* (Exhibition catalogue, Brussels, 1973), No. 24.

[25] Paris, Bibliothèque Nationale, MS lat. 4804; cf. the article by Mrs Lemaire quoted in note 24. The handwriting of this manuscript is, however, totally different from the handwriting in the Marcatellis manuscript.

[26] But the additional map of Gaul in the Marcatellis manuscript presents a lot of Flemish towns with their names in Dutch. C. Lemaire (article quoted in note 24) thinks the main part of the manuscript cannot have been copied from the 1477 edition.

[27] Ghent, University Library, MS 109; cf. Derolez, *The Library*, pp. 74 ff.

we don't know the *Vorlage* of this manuscript, it is difficult to explain these anomalies (which occur also in several other Marcatellis manuscripts).[28] Anyhow, there existed no models for the illustrations, as well the full-page as the half-page ones, and here we see a strange phenomenon in the Marcatellis collection: the manuscript has not been finished: the text ends abruptly and the illumination, which started so sumptuously, is not continued up to the end. This is not the only example of an unfinished *de luxe* manuscript in this library, and I do not know whether it is explained by shortage of funds (this looks rather improbable) or to a trait of character of the Ghent abbot, which made him lose his interest in a book before it was finished and turn to new projects.[29]

To give oneself an idea of the size of a Marcatellis manuscript one has only to look at a manuscript in the Staatsbibliothek Preussischer Kulturbesitz in Berlin,[30] which contains two texts, each of which normally fills a large volume by itself: Martianus Capella's *De nuptiis Philologiae et Mercurii* and Boethius' *De consolatione philosophiae*, each being accompanied by an extensive commentary. Moreover the Boethius section is illustrated with large full-page miniatures. Its text is a copy of the edition Nuremberg, Anton Koberger, 1483,[31] as appears from the colophon copied with the text. The manuscript was written two years later, in 1485, as is likewise mentioned in the colophon. For the miniatures there did not exist printed models, but we know that about that time there was a close interest in Flanders in Boethius illustration: one has only to mention the Bruges edition of 1477 by Colard Mansion[32] and the Ghent edition by Arend de Keysere, of the same year as our manuscript, 1485,[33] in both of which space was provided for hand-painted miniatures, which have been executed in several copies.[34] Marcatellis's books often keep a surprise in reserve: here it is the gloss to Martianus Capella, dated 1483, which proves to be unrecorded: so we find side by side, in one binding, simple copies of printed books and unique texts.

Marcatellis's copy of Boccaccio's *De casibus virorum illustrium* and *De claris mulie-*

---

[28] See also the Boccaccio manuscript discussed below.
[29] Derolez, *The Library*, p. 306.
[30] Berlin (West), Staatsbibliothek Preussischer Kulturbesitz, MS lat. fol. 25; cf. Derolez, *The Library*, pp. 95 ff.
[31] GKW 4533.
[32] GKW 4579.
[33] GKW 4574.
[34] S. Hindman & J.D.Farquhar, *Pen to Press: Illustrated Manuscripts and Printed Books in the First Century of Printing* (University of Maryland, 1977), pp. 126 ff.

ribus[35] derives from two editions by the Strasbourg printer Georg Husner, published about 1474-75.[36] Here too copying did not succeed without difficulties; e.g. one page was obviously missing in the model and a corresponding (but too large) space has been reserved in the manuscript. It was filled in later by another scribe, after another model had been found (Pls. 1-2). For the rest the text of the *De casibus virorum illustrium* has been so thoroughly changed, corrected and extended, that it is no longer to be considered a simple copy of an incunabulum, but a text established on the basis of two or more sources.

One of the finest manuscripts in Marcatellis's collection is his copy of the complete works of the Roman poet Virgil, with the commentary by Servius.[37] It contains numerous splendid miniatures framed in gold. The book was written, and probably also illuminated, in Bruges in 1488. It again has a most remarkable colophon: *Omnia hec volumina que Virgilius Maro vates eminentissimus composuit, una cum Servii Honorati gramatici commentariis ac eiusdem poete vita mira quadam arte ac diligentia scripta Brugis anno 1488*: except the words *scripta Brugis* etc., which were skilfully substituted by the scribe, this colophon is identical with the colophon of the edition Venice, Jacobus Rubeus, 1475.[38] Again, the manuscript is no plain copy of the incunabulum, as the order of the texts has been inverted: at first the manuscript did not contain the *opera minora*, which were afterwards added and placed in front of the Bucolics, Georgics and Aeneid. As a matter of course the illustration is highly interesting.

A collection of rhetorical treatises[39] contains the two best known of all Marcatellis pictures: the workshop of the Greek painter Zeuxis (in fact one of the very rare representations of a late mediaeval painter's atelier), and an image of Cicero in the vestment of a university professor in a library room containing books which bear a striking resemblance to the Marcatellis manuscripts themselves.[40] The texts depend on four different incunabula, among which a pamphlet by Ermolao Barbaro, printed in the small Belgian town of Alost in 1486.[41]

In some cases the scribe was really absent-minded and copied again and

---

[35] Ghent, University Library, MS 134; cf. Derolez, *The Library*, pp. 119 ff.
[36] GKW 4430 and 4484.
[37] Ghent, Cathedral Library, MS 9; cf. Derolez, *The Library*, pp. 128 ff.
[38] BMC, vol. V, p. 214 (Virgil).
[39] Ghent, University Library, MS 10; cf. Derolez, *The Library*, pp. 141 ff.
[40] Reproduced in Derolez, *The Library*, pls. 19 and 58.
[41] GKW 3343.

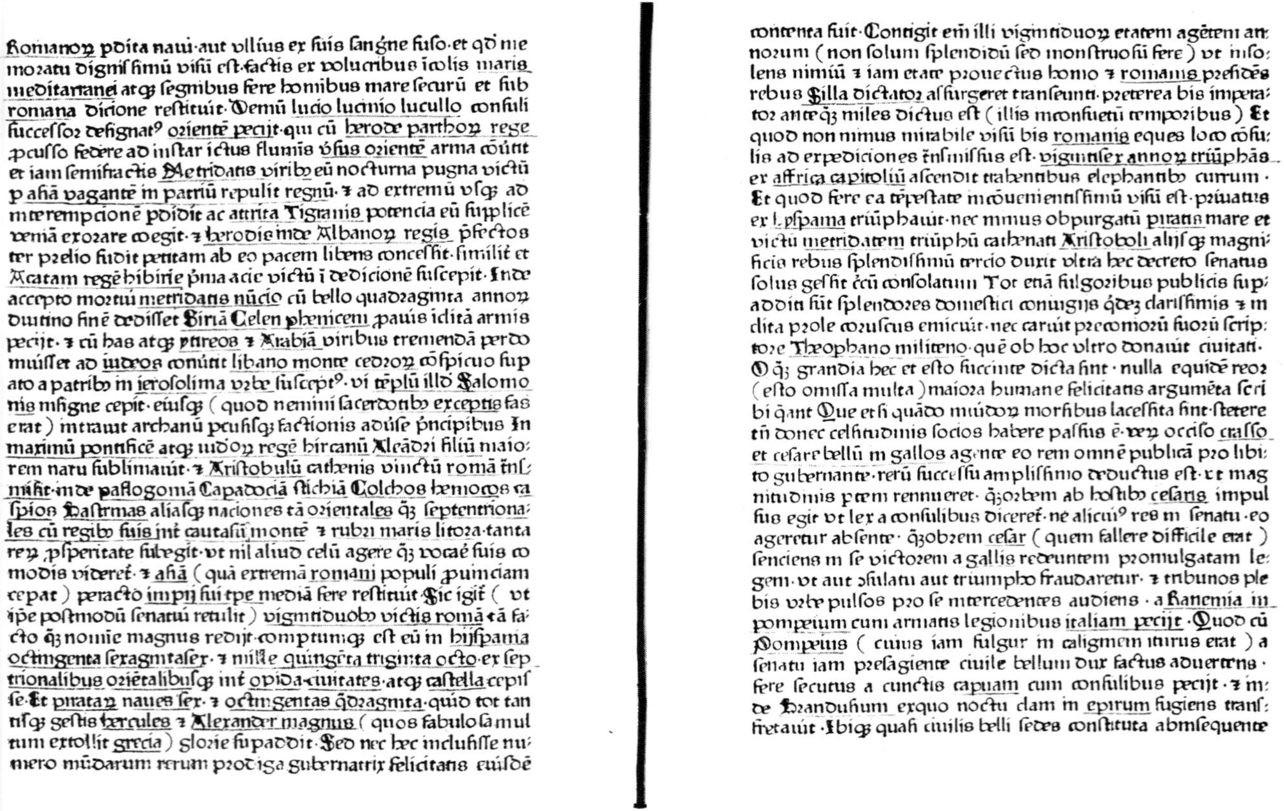

Plate 1. Boccacio, De casibus virorum illustrium (Strasbourg, Georg Husner, c. 1474-75), ff. [85]v°-[86]r°.

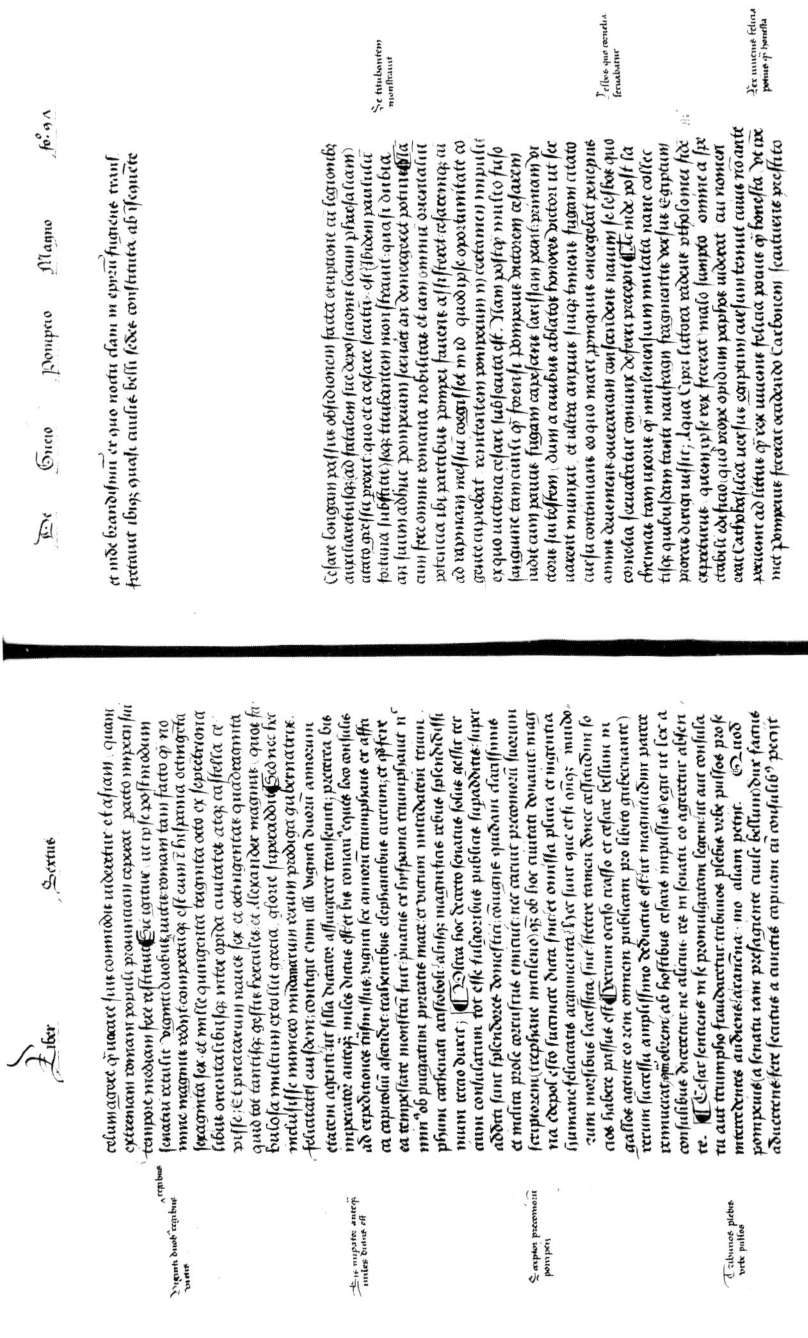

Plate 2. Ghent, University Library, MS 134, ff. 96v–97r.

again the full printer's colophon, as in a collection of treatises on letter-writing and poetics, now in the University Library in Ghent[42]: Franciscus Niger's *Grammatica* ends with the words *Anno salutis MCCCCLXXX, XII cal. April. impressum est hoc opus Venetiis duce virtute et comite fortuna*[43]; the same was done in the copy of a Parisian edition of 1480 and another one of 1487, all in the same manuscript.[44]

A counterpart to the Virgil is the collection of mythological texts by Ovid and Hyginus, lavishly illustrated and copied form three Italian incunabula.[45] For the Hyginus illustrations only the illuminator could rely on the wood-cuts occurring in the incunabulum which furnished also the text: a Venetian edition by Jacobus Sentinus and Johannes Lucilius Santritter.[46] In general the artistic level of the paintings in this manuscript, as in many of the later Marcatellis manuscripts, is not very high.

An interesting example of texts copied from fifteenth and early sixteenth-century impressions is a large collection of astronomical and mathematical texts, now in the Cathedral Library in Ghent.[47] It contains no less than six different sections with texts by Alfraganus, Johannes de Sacrobosco, Regiomontanus, Peuerbach and others. The four primary sections are copies from at least five different editions printed in Ferrara, Venice, Zwolle (in the Netherlands) and Paris; the last two sections, on the contrary, contain three unrecorded astronomical texts by obscure authors as Perscrutator and Bartholomaeus Marien Slesita. Again we see that combination, in one single volume, of copies of editions and *rariora* or even *unica*.

I would like to end this series of examples with a large illustrated encyclopaedia entirely copied from a printed edition of the first years of the sixteenth century: the *Margarita philosophica* by ghe German author Gregorius Reisch, dated 1505, the latest one of all dated Marcatellis manuscripts.[48] The *editio princeps* was printed in Freiburg im Breisgau in 1503 and a second edition was issued in 1504. Both were illustrated with numerous woodcuts and one of them has been the model for text and illustration of the Marcatellis manuscript. This is easily seen when comparing manuscript and printed book: both are very close to each other, except where the size is concerned: the printed book is of modest

---

[42] Ghent, University Library, MS 112; cf. Derolez, *The Library*, pp. 154 ff.
[43] BMC, vol. V, p. 281.
[44] Robertus Gaguinus, BMC, vol. VIII, p. 26, and Theodulus, Polain (Belgium) 3682.
[45] Ghent, Cathedral Library, MS 12; cf. Derolez, *The Library*, pp. 161 ff.
[46] In fact one of the editions dated 1482, 1485 and 1488.
[47] Ghent, Cathedral Library, MS 11; cf. Derolez, *The Library*, pp. 199 ff.
[48] Ghent, University Library, MS 7; cf. Derolez, *The Library*, pp. 206 ff.

dimensions, while the manuscript, as always with Marcatellis, is very large-sized, having a height of nearly 40 cms.

The frontispiece in the printed edition, with an allegoric representation of the three-headed Philosophy (*rationalis, naturalis, moralis*), the seven Arts, the four Church-Fathers, Aristotle and Seneca has been closely copied in the manuscript (Pls. 3-4). In the same way, the numerous small text-illustrations have been copied without alteration. In some cases, however, the workshop master has ordered an entirely new picture for Marcatellis, thus departing from the printed image; this we see in the illustration at the head of the Book dedicated to Geometry, where instead of copying the woodcut the painter has made a new composition in the symmetrical style often to be seen in Marcatellis manuscripts (Pls. 5-6).[49] In contrast to the general rule, in the manuscript under discussion the strange tendency is obvious to increase luxury as work advanced: the second half of the book contains numerous additional illustrations, which do not occur in the printed model: large full-page miniatures like the picture of theology (again in the symmetrical professor-and-students scheme), or smaller scientific illustrations.

It would not have been difficult to discuss many more examples of the practice of copying and adapting printed books for the library of Raphael de Marcatellis. Perhaps attention may be drawn on the ending-leaf of Marcatellis's manuscript copy of Trithemius's *De scriptoribus ecclesiasticis*.[50] Of course this bio-bibliographical survey of Christian world literature, although of considerable length, was too short, even when written in gigantic gothic script, to fill a volume on its own; so the *Philobiblon* of Richard de Bury and two treatises by St John Chrysostom were added to it. In this way the manuscript depends on four incunabula, issued respectively in Cologne, Basle, Alost and again Cologne. Copying has been carried out most accurately, as is seen in a close confrontation of the Trithemius text in the manuscript and in its model, the Amerbach edition, Basle 1494 (Pls. 7-8).[51] Both include the Latin poem written by Sebastian Brant in praise of Trithemius's bibliographical work.

But it is time to draw some conclusions. It must be clear now, that copying printed books was not only an out-of-date and easy practise to make rapidly manuscripts for a few wealthy and maniacal bibliophiles. It was at the same time a means – the only means in fact – to possess a manuscript copy of texts not

---

[49] Examples in Derolez, *The Library*, pls. 15, 17, 19, 61, 80, 97,99.
[50] Ghent, University Library, MS 67; cf. Derolez, *The Library*, pp. 193 ff.
[51] BMC, vol. III, p. 755.

Plate 3. Gregorius Reisch, Margarita philosophica *(Freiburg im Breisgau, Johannes Schottus, 1503), f. 1r°.*

Plate 4. Ghent, University Library, MS 7, f. 1v°.

Plate 5. *Gregorius Reisch*, Margarita philosophica *(Freiburg im Breisgau, Johannes Schottus, 1503), f. 6v⁰*.

The copying of printed books for humanistic bibliophiles 157

Plate 6. Ghent, University Library, MS 7, f. 120 bis v°.

LIBER

Soliloquiorū hominis ad deū: li. j
De pfectu uirtutū: li. j
De abstinentia carniū: li. j
De usu floccorum: li. j
Epistolarū ad diuersos: li. j
Collationes uariæ: li. j
Carmina & rhythmi:
Et quædam alia breuia.

Dū olim diuinæ uocatiōis.
Egressus fossam cubiti.
Tuæ fratnitatis auctoritas.
Reuerēde pr̄ nuper a me.
Licet inter oēs q sinistre.
Licet nihil in me sit quod.

Claruit in præfato monasterio Spanhem: ante introductionē reformationis no/
uissimæ Burffeldensis: Anno domini Mill. CCCC.XLV.

Ntoninus: ordinis fratrū prædicatorū: archiep̄us Florētinus: natiōe Italus
uir in diuinis scripturis eruditissim⁹: & sæculariū litteraȝ nō ignarus: inge/
nio excellens: & clarus eloquio: in declamādis sermonib⁹ ad populū famo
sus & celebris opinionis: nec minus uita & cōuersatione q̄ scīetia reuerēdus. Scri/
psit multa & præclara uolumina: quib⁹ ad ædificationē militātis ecclesiæ magnifi/
ce laborauit. E quib⁹ extat opus magnū & celeberrimū: in quattuor nō paruis uo/
luminibus diuisum: quod prænotaṫ:

Summa casuū cōscientiæ: li. iiij
Chronica ingens & notabilis: li. iij
Instructoriū cōfessorū: li. j
De censura ecclesiastica: li. j
Sermones de tempore: li. j
Sermones de sanctis: li. j
Et quædam alia.

Q̃ magnificata sunt.
Loquar ppositiones ab in.
Defecerūt scrutantes.

Cōuertimini ad dominū.

Moritur post multos studij sacrati labores nō sine opinione sanctitatis: sub Frede
rico imperatore tertio: Anno domini Mill. CCCC.LIX. Indictiōe. vij. sexto no/
nas Maij. Sepultus apud sanctū Marcū sui ordinis couentū.

Eonardus de Vtino: ordinis fratrū prædicatorū: uir quidem in diuinis scri
pturis studiosus & eruditus: & sæcularis philosophiæ non ignarus: in de/
clamādis sermonib⁹ ad populū excellentis ingenij & præcelsæ opinionis:
Scripsit pro utilitate prædicantiū quædam præclara opuscula: quib⁹ memoria sui
nominis ad posteritatis noticia cum gloria trāsmisit. E quib⁹ ista ferunṫ:

Sermones de tempore: li. j
Sermones de sanctis: li. j
De legib⁹ p quadragesimā: li. j
Et quædam alia.

Diuinorū interpres myste.

Claruit sub Frederico imperatore tertio: Anno domini Mill. CCCC.XLV.

Obannes de Capistrano Aprucij oppido non longe ab Aquila urbe: ordi/
nis fratrū minorū sancti Bernardini Senensis olim discipulus: uir in diuinis
scripturis eruditus: & in iure canonico egregie doctus: ingenio excellens
& clarus eloquio: uita quoqȝ & religiosa cōuersatione deuotus: diuini uerbi prædi
cator celeberrimus: qui multos uerbo & exemplo ab iniquitate cōuertit. Scripsit
quædā nō paruæ utilitatis opuscula: de quib⁹ ad me pauca puenerunt:

De cupiditate: li. iij
Contra Hussitas: li. j
Sermones uarios: li. j
De passione domini: li. j
Epistolas nōnullas.
Et quædam alia.

Nolite uobis thesaurigare.

Claruit sub Frederico imperatore tertio: Anno domini Mill. CCCC.L. & nō sine
opinione sanctitatis.

Plate 7. Johannes Trithemius, De scriptoribus ecclesiasticis *(Basle, Johannes Amerbach, 1494), f. 113v°.*

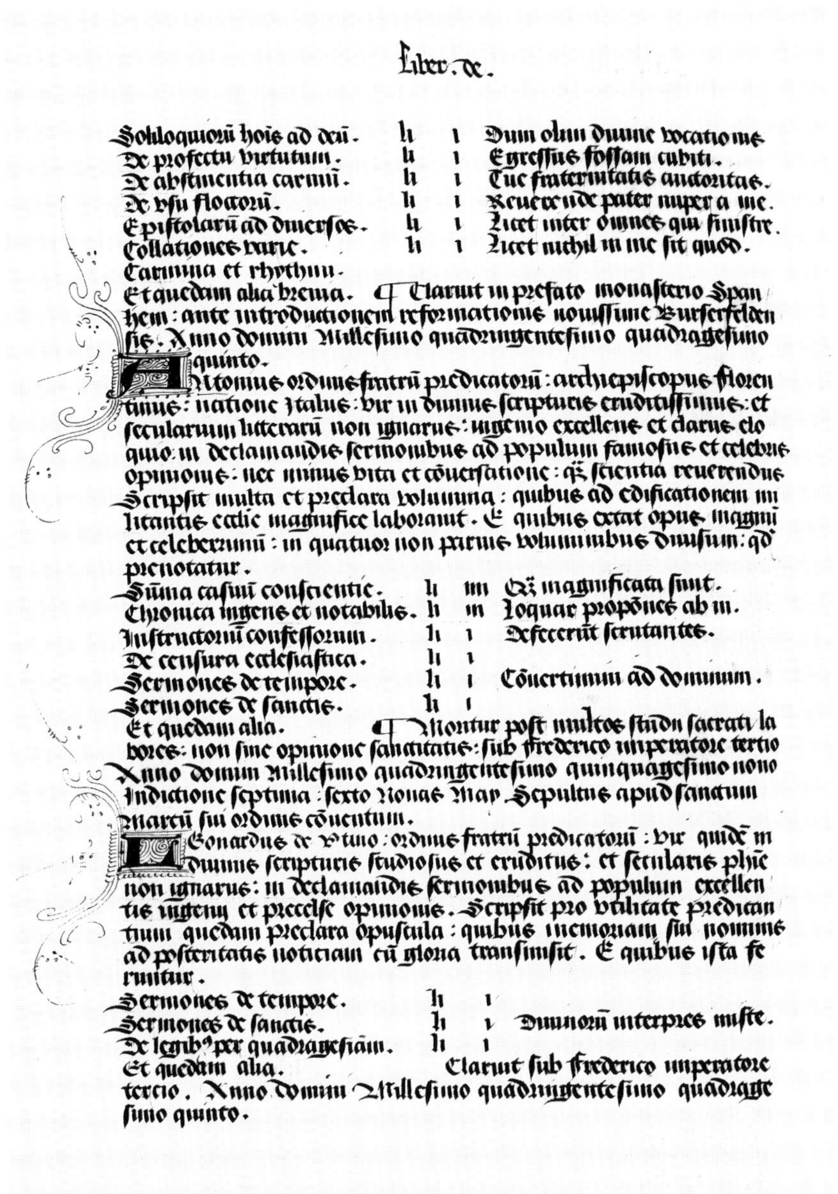

Plate 8. Ghent, University Library, MS 67, f. 178v°.

circulating in the bibliophile's own country. Indeed, the question why the collector did not buy the printed book instead of having it transcribed at high cost is not simply a matter of luxury. In the case of Marcatellis at least we see that more than half of all the incunabula which served as models for his manuscripts are not to be found in any present-day Belgian collection,[52] a fact which may not be without significance: most probably they were not actually on the book-market in Flanders, and Marcatellis had them borrowed from Italian friends.

Moreover, as we have seen, copying printed books was also the only way to obtain corpuses of texts on the same subject: so the Ghent abbot obtained a *corpus Platonicum*, a corpus of Alexander literature, two collections of *astrologica*, a corpus of Aristotle commentaries, of geographical treatises, of Greek historians etc.

In connection with this, transcribing printed editions should not necessarily be a dull and useless activity. Not only had the different books to be chosen and brought together which would supply the text for a single manuscript, but in some cases only specified separate texts from an incunabulum had to be copied, putting on one side the remaining texts.[53] And in many instances the text was afterwards corrected, which could result in very comprehensive additions and alterations. Finally it should be mentioned that not only some manuscripts are totally independent of printed sources, but that in some others the printed source has been merely the starting-point from which an entirely new work has originated. Such is the case with Marcatellis' gigantic anonymous Gospel commentary, written and illustrated starting from an early edition of Gerson's *Monotessaron*.[54]

---

[52] This appears from a control in Polain (Belgium).
[53] Derolez, *The Library*, p. 299.
[54] Ghent, University Library, MSS 17 (first redaction) and 11 (final redaction, in two volumes, dated 1504); cf. Derolez, *The Library*, pp. 218 ff. and 247 ff.

The parallel and fascinating contribution by Michael D. Reeve, *Manuscripts copied from printed books*, in *Manuscripts in the fifty years after the invention of printing. Some papers read at a colloquium at the Warburg Institute on 12-13 March 1982*, ed. by J.B. Trapp (London, 1983), pp. 12-20, was published after my paper had been prepared for the printer. It offers important documentary material in the field of classical Latin texts, mainly in Italian manuscripts, together with a witty commentary.

Discussion

A summary

The chairman of the general debate was Mr Torkil Olsen, National Librarian of Denmark, whose presidency over the afternoon's proceedings was greeted with special enthusiasm, Torkil Olsen being the founder of Odense University Library. Torkil Olsen invited the audience to ask questions about the respective papers according to the order in which they had been given.

J. Gerritsen opened the discussion by asking Joseph Scott to substantiate his theory that the original edition of the Nuremberg Chronicle numbered as many as fifteen hundred copies. The estimate, he agreed, was more or less correct (though a bit on the high side), but Gerritsen called for 'solid evidence'. Scott explained that his estimate *is* partly inferential. The solid evidence he could refer to is the existence of between eight and nine hundred copies of the Nuremberg Chronicle even today. Considering the inevitable reduction of the number of copies over a period of five hundred years, he inferred that with so many extant copies, the original edition size could hardly have been much smaller than fifteen hundred.

Ursula Altmann, commenting on edition sizes in the fifteenth century generally, remarked that books in the vernacular were usually printed in only two or three hundred copies. However, Latin works, notably law books, would be printed in considerable numbers, a large edition consisting of about two thousand copies and, in one known instance, running as high as four thousand copies.

Ursula Altmann's paper had spurred Svend Gissel from the Royal Library of Copenhagen to the following complementary remarks. We reproduce these at full length, since they not only supply further details from the Danish scene, but also plead for consideration of a subject which, although it had not been taken up in the Symposium, should not, of course, be ignored:

During the lectures of today and yesterday we have been introduced to important aspects of the development from script to book, especially in the fields of religious and humanistic literature, and also of the history of libraries.

I should like here to outline shortly some of the main conditions of this development, these being

1. the technical invention of printing,
2. the ideological background,
3. the economic background, and
4. the channels of market communication.

As a historian Rektor Trommer in his opening speech emphasized the importance of considering the 'whys' and 'ways' of communication as regards the history of the printing of each book. Of all the four conditions I mentioned I think that the case of the very first printer, Johann Gutenberg, offers very fine illustrations.

1. The general background of the invention of printing must have been the fact that the demand for reading material was growing so fast that it could no longer be met by the scribes. The demand was no longer measured in hundreds, but in thousands.

2. There was a compulsory and large market in the church service books of all the bishoprics in the Western world – and also, by the way, in school books.

3. In the individual church provinces, in its huge capital, and in its own markets, the church had a guarantee (4) that the expenses would not be made in vain. Furthermore, some editions, especially those of the missals, were so expensive that they crossed the frontiers between church provinces with some local additions.

I have undertaken a small investigation in an area belonging to the bishopric of Odense, namely the island of Falstria, with 27 parish churches. We have from the year 1597 inventories from each of these churches – with registers of church silver, church bells, church books and so on.

Concerning the books, only two manuscripts were left. Most of the churches had three printed books or more: Bibles, prayer-books, graduals, passionals, manuals, and so on. Most important is the evidence of the Bibles. Most of the churches had the new Danish Bible from 1589; some of them, also the old Bible of 1550. This Bible – that of King Christian III – was printed in three thousand copies, and two thousand of them went to Danish and Norwegian churches, each of which was calculated to acquire a copy. This example shows something of the importance of a compulsory market.

By German scholars, the Latin Bible is estimated to have been printed in some hundred thousand copies, and the same goes for the most famous collection of legends, by Jacobus de Voragine.

While the ecclesiastical handbooks derive from the great centres of the church from the time of the Counter-Reformation (above all from Rome, which printed the Vulgate and the Roman Missal), the humanistic literature represented a freer or capitalistic market and was centred above all in the great city states, Venice, Nuremberg, and others. Also in this field we may calculate with great numbers of copies. The law books constitute a special problem, with at least some kind of a secured market.

It is to be stressed, however, that printed and imported literature was not allowed to be antagonistic toward official religion and politics. An example of this is the fate of the books of religious dissenters in the sixteenth century. We have also in Denmark examples of this from the days of Absolutism in the eighteenth and early nineteenth centuries. A lot of poems were circulating that were not likely to pass the censorship and thus were never printed. These poems were morally and politically subversive. They only exist in copies made by hand and are now being registered.

In my opinion the case of Johann Gutenberg himself is very illustrative of this whole development. German scholars have shown very great attention to the problems of Johann Gutenberg; but I feel, that they should still not be ignored in a general context, such as ours.

The development 'From Script to Book' cannot, at least in my opinion, be studied without paying attention to Gutenberg. This is an idea for the next symposium on the subject.

In response to the paper on the book-copying performed by fifteenth-century humanistic bibliophiles, Thelma Jexlev agreed with Albert Derolez that the distinction between manuscript and printed book is a modern one, and that few medieval Scandinavians would have distinguished between the two types of book. Derolez remarked that *when* a distinction between manuscripts and printed books is occasionally made in library inventories, this seems to reflect a difference in value rather then any difference in content.

Derolez went on to inquire into the reason why certain types of manuscript continued to be made long after the invention of printing: "There must have been various reasons why a person wrote his manuscripts even after the invention of printing. Certainly one is that the text is not available in print, and when you want to have the text, you have to copy it yourself. There also seems, among certain people, to have existed a need to write manuscripts for a different reason – a slightly 'humanistic' reason, we might call it. We know, in Flanders, in Bruges, of very important persons, who wrote in their large manuscripts. We possess the inventory of one of the famous men of his time, Anselmo Adorno in Bruges, a knight and ambassador to the King of Scotland. In this inventory, a very small one, there is a couple of texts copied in his hand. These are Classical texts, which he could probably buy at the time, nevertheless, he has copied them himself. So I think there must be something of a humanistic idea, of the feeling that, like men of Antiquity, 'you must have done things yourself' – a man must be able to do every kind of work with his own hands. So that may have been another reason for copying manuscripts."

Erik Petersen followed up on Derolez's remark by pointing to the highly personal book a writer might compile, since he could select material of special interest to himself from a wide range of sources and thus "design his own book". In many ways, argued Erik Petersen, this type of manuscript might be compared to the present day sheaves of Xerox copies amassed by students. He felt that the medieval miscellany, like its modern off-spring, would tend to render the printed book superfluous. Derolez mentioned that for a period the library manuscript did, indeed, constitute a competition to the printed book, but that it lost its competitive strength in the second half of the fifteenth century, when only elitarian collections continued to be made. In this connection Derolez added, as an amusing corrollary, that the renown of late Flemish illumination rests upon one such elitarian type of manuscript, namely the book of hours. The books of hours occupied virtually every eminent illuminator in Flanders, while other kinds of illustration were in the hands of second-rate artists.

Joseph Scott expressed surprise at this last comment and pointed out that surely first-rate work can also be found in other illustrations besides those of the books of hours, for example in Flemish copies of *De Consolatione Philosophiae*. Derolez restated his view and questioned the quality of even the illuminations mentioned by Scott.

Apart from discussing the possible medieval criteria for distinguishing between handwritten and printed books, Derolez tried to indicate the bases on which people would distinguish between paper and parchment books. For example a certain preference by institution libraries, monastic libraries, and church libraries for vellum instead of paper was probably due to the durability of parchment compared to paper. But occasionally also differences of content can be established: thus vernacular literature is predominantly found in paper manuscripts, which seems to point to "a tradition which links language and the material of the book".

Norman Blake's paper on Caxton as printer and publisher caused Torben Anders Vestergaard to raise a general question about the relationship between commercial interests and book printing. How often would printers undertake the risky business of being their own publishers instead of merely printing what others commissioned them to publish?

Blake answered that both printing and publishing are commercial ventures, since both publisher and printer have to make financial investments, and run financial risks, in connection with their activities. The publisher may have to wait ten years to see his investment in two or three hundred printed copies return to him. The printer, although he may expect his product to be paid rather sooner and so seems to be selling his services rather than taking a personal risk, has *his* investment in the press, in the paper, and in the employment of people who have to be kept constantly occupied.

The commercial aspect of printing proves relevant to the discussion about edition sizes which had been raised earlier in the debate. The great expenses connected with publishing and the difficulty of assessing the market probably influenced the size of Caxton's editions: these seem generally to have been "on the side of caution rather than expansiveness", small rather than large, each edition probably consisting of no more than two or three hundred copies, according to Blake's estimate. This estimate gains support from the fact that several of Caxton's books were reprinted once or twice in the course of his career, sometimes within six or twelve months of the original edition.

Concerning the relationship between printer and publisher, Blake pointed out that today we tend to think of printing in terms of three people, the printer, the publisher, and the bookseller; but as far as the fifteenth century is concerned, such a distinction cannot be maintained. Clearly Caxton represents all three functions: he prints, he publishes, he sells. Sometimes he would act as a printer to other people, and sometimes he would act as his own publisher. He must also have had a hand in the distribution of his product: the facts that Caxton settled at Westminster, close to court, judiciary, and civil service, and that he appealed to his local market through advertisements, seem to suggest that "distribution was local rather than diverse". On the other hand, the trade of printed books must have been very well-developed, if we judge by the speed with which Caxton got hold of continental books and remember, too, that there is evidence (though not unambiguous) that within ten years of their publication, some of Caxton's books were available in Scotland.

Derolez agreed with Blake that Caxton "was first of all a businessman" and saw in that fact his advantage over a number of colleagues with artistic ambitions, who tried to apply the standards of manuscript copying to their printing activities. We know of several producers of luxury manuscripts who on taking up printing, would try to produce luxury printed books and got ruined. Their failure and Caxton's success combine to confirm Derolez' "impression that there is a contradiction between manuscript making and the making of printed books". This impression he also supported on bibliographical evidence: in fifteenth century Italy, the great centres of manuscript copying were Florence, Milan, Naples and Rome, whereas the city of Venice produced very few manuscripts. "So the link between commerce and printed book was very strong, while the link between manuscript and commerce was a weak one".

In response to Helmar Härtel's paper on the development of Nether Saxon libraries in the fifteenth century, Tore Nyberg inquired about the commercial distribution of manuscripts produced in German monastery scriptoria.

Härtel explained that while the Brethren of the Common Life did copy manuscripts and sell them as a means of financing religious life, the monasteries would copy mainly to meet their own needs. This was certainly the case with the Bursfelder congregation, which mainly produced devotional literature, i.e. literature intended for monastic use. No texts were copied which would appeal specifically to secular tastes. Occasionally, when a brother convert entered the monastery, he would bring with him a number of books compiled during the period before his entrance; but after entering the monastery, he himself would begin to compose devotional works.

Tore Nyberg asked if it was, indeed, true that at some stage the scriptoria had ceased to function altogether? Härtel answered that he was inclined to think this was the case, although decisive proof of his view is impossible to obtain. He pointed to the incompatibility between the demanding and expensive activity of manuscript production and the monastic decay of the period under discussion. He could also refer specifically to the example of Clus, where, after the reform, there was such a shortage of written material that manuscripts had to be purchased from outside to form the basis of new collections.

Derolez indicated that we find the same picture all over Western Europe. Although most monasteries would originally have their own scriptoria, manuscript copying fell into neglect in the course of the thirteenth century, when in general both the education of monks and the copying of manuscripts passed to the universities. Belgian and Dutch manuscripts from the thirteenth and fourteenth centuries, for example, are very rare. Only with the Benedictine reform movement is monastic manuscript production resumed.

Härtel agreed, but called attention to the Franciscan friars, who employed copying extensively in their educational practice. In one manuscript, for instance, he observed how a young friar had first copied a certain text and had then, thirty pages later, composed his first treatise on the basis of that text. In this progression from copying to commenting Härtel saw a telling example of the Franciscan emphasis on the role of manuscript copying in the learning process.

The final lecture, about the first printed book in Danish, by Torben Nielsen, prompted Thelma Jexlev to enquire if a certain Thomas Bogtrykker (i.e. Thomas Printer) mentioned in an undated census from roughly 1510 could have been a collaborator of Gotfred of Ghemen? Torben Nielsen answered that Thomas Printer may very well have been an associate of Gotfred, but that it is not necessary to postulate the assistance of a collaborator to account for Gotfred's achievement.

Torkil Olsen closed the discussion about individual lectures by inviting general comments. Erik Petersen proffered the rather disturbing opinion that the whole symposium had been a 'misnomer', since to distinguish between 'script' and 'book' in the manner implied by the title is a mistake. He felt that the symposium ought to be rounded off with a last-minute attempt to devise a better title and called upon suggestions from the members of the audience.

Joseph Scott admitted that in preparing his lecture he had promptly forgotten the actual title of the symposium and proceeded on the assumption that the conference was named 'From Script to Print'. The word 'book' was, indeed, unfortunate, since both manuscript and printed work are books. This produced a learned profusion of kind attempts to salvage the actual title of the symposium from the anathema hurled upon it by Erik Petersen. But the most memorable defence did, 'despite its kind intention', condone Mr Petersen's criticism. Mr Derolez indicated that among the large number of colloquies, symposia, and conferences which the fifth centennial of the printed book would provoke, this one in Odense would be the most memorable; since its title was not, it was understood, correct, but for that reason the easier to recollect among other titles!

The Missale Nidrosiense 1519: an appendix

by LILLI GJERLØW

Two more copies of the Nidaros Missal of 1519 have been traced. Thanks to the kind collaboration of Professor Niels Krogh Rasmussen of the University of Notre Dame, Indiana, I had extracts of the relevant catalogues.

One is registered in Seymour de Ricci, *Livres de Liturgie imprimés aux XVe et XVIe siècles faisant partie de la Bibliothèque de son Altesse Royale le Duc Robert de Parme* (Paris/Milan, 1932), no. 73, pp. 36 sq. In the summary description of the book the number of leaves are wrongly given as 312 instead of 303. The text is complete except for f. C.vij. = pp. 601-602, for which facsimiles of the leaf have been supplied. "Le dernier f., qui est sans doute blanc, manque". The title-page is reproduced; beneath the title "Sevaldus Thoma 1626" is written in a humanist hand. That year Queen Christina of Sweden was born; her arms are stamped on the back of the book, so later in the century it must have formed part of her library. Its present whereabouts are unknown.

The other one is catalogued in Enrico Stevenson Giuniore, *Inventario dei libri stampati Palatino-Vaticani edito per ordine di S.S. Leone P.M.*, vol. 1, parte 2 (Nieuwkoop: B. de Graff, 1966), pp. 220-221, no. 2427 (= Pal. II. 419).

The text is complete, ending with Poul Reff's colophon, f. C.ix. verso (=p. 606). However, it is followed by a leaf with writings from the early sixteenth century. Could this be the missing end-leaf, untraced in all the copies known to Lauritz Nielsen (see LN, no. 182)? No signature is mentioned by Stevenson.

The writings on this leaf is a *Missa pro tribulatione* with the introit *Omnia que fecisti nobis domine,* probably the mass of Sunday 20 after Trinity of the Nidaros Missal (g.xvi = p. 335), with the same introit, the collect *Omnipotens et misericors deus uniuersa nobis aduersantia,* etc., and with the offertory *Super flumina babilonis.*

The book is bound in brown calf leather. For a description, see Ilse Schunke, *Die Einbände der Palatina in der Vatikanischen Bibliothek*, 2, in *Studi e Testi*, 217 (Città del Vaticano, 1962), p. 121, Pal. II.419 = Stevenson 2427. At the top of the back cover is the stamp of O(tto). H(einrich). C(hurfürst)., at the bottom his slogan M(it). D(er).

Z(eit)., that is the Elector Palatine who ruled only from 1556 to 1559, but a life-long collector and the real creator of the Palatine Library. It was bound by one of his famous artisans, Peter Betz, after 1556.

So far the naked facts. However, there could be no doubt that the Palatine Missal once belonged to Olav Engelbrektsson, the last archbishop of Nidaros who, in the turbulent 1530es, made a last desperate stand against the oncoming Protestantism.

The exiled King Kristian II's ill-fated expedition to Norway in 1531 ended with his imprisonment for life (1532). However, his father-in-law, the Emperor Charles V, the guardian of Kristian II's children, considered them the legal heirs to the kingdom of Denmark-Norway. In 1535 Kristian II's elder daughter, Dorothea, was married to the Count, later the Elector Palatine, Friedrich II. Negotiations on their behalf were afoot between the Emperor and Archbishop Olav. In 1536 the Emperor sent a small naval force to Nidaros, but the Archbishop waited in vain for further action on his part. With the triumph of Protestantism in Denmark, his position became untenable. On Easter Day 1537 he embarked upon one of the Emperor's men-of-war and fled the country, a man of sorrow, who had good reasons to enter the mass *pro tribulatione* on the last leaf of his missal. He died in Lierre, Brabant, early in 1538.

With the cessation of hostilities, negotiations between the Palatinate and the Danish Crown resulted in an agreement concerning the archives of Kristian II, and, with them, those of Archbishop Olav. In the 1540es they were transferred to the Palatine Library in Heidelberg.

The fate of the Palatine Library is well known. In the first phase of the Thirty Years War, the Elector Palatine Friedrich V, the "Winterking", was defeated by Duke Maximilian I of Bayern who conquered Heidelberg. He offered the Palatine Library, manuscripts and books, to the Pope in gratitude for his support during the war. In 1623 they were transferred to the Vatican Library, since then the home of Olav Engelbrektsson's Nidaros Missal.

One thing remains a puzzle. Why did the Elector Palatine Otto Heinrich provide the misal with a new binding? Could Archbishop Olav have brought with him an unbound copy? Or, had the binding been damaged during its peregrinations? Purely aesthetic reasons may also have induced Otto Heinrich to have the original binding replaced by one of his own craftsmen.

December 1986

Members and associate members of the Symposium

Jens Peter Ægidius
Lone Albrecht
Ursula Altmann
Flemming G. Andersen
Lise Præstgaard Andersen
Merete Geert Andersen
Karen Ascani
Christian Axel-Nilsson
Annelise Bach
Jørgen Chr. Bang
Hans Basbøll
Lisbeth Baumgarten
Connie Beck
Lise Bek
Else Bekker-Nielsen
Hans Bekker-Nielsen
Helene Bekker-Nielsen
Karen Bekker-Nielsen
The Berserk Society
Norman F. Blake
Ådel G. Blom
Marianne Børch
Anny Bøttger
Graham Caie
Birte Carlé
Michael Chesnutt
Karsten Christensen
Jákup Christiansen
Margaret Cormack
Jennifer Cummings

Niels Danielsen
Albert Derolez
Betty Djurhuus
Napoleon Djurhuus
Dorrit Einersen
Ann Ellefsen
Hans J. Frederiksen
Suzanne Geall
J. Gerritsen
Svend Gissel
Lilli Gjerløw
Olaf Grunert
Angela Guski
Andreas Haarder
Britt Haarløv
Niels Haastrup
Helmar Härtel
Jan Ragnar Hagland
Eyvind Fjeld Halvorsen
Birgit Hansen
Erik W. Hansen
Per Harbo
Kate Harris
Guðrún P. Helgadóttir
Þorbjörg Helgadóttir
Svend Hendrup
Gustav Henningsen
Lilliane Højgaard
Dietrich Hofmann
Judith House

Members and associate members of the Symposium

Shaun F. D. Hughes
Gerda C. Huisman
Jacob Isager
Jens Juhl Jensen
Jytte Jensen
Kurt Jensen
Povl Johs. Jensen
Søren Skovgaard Jensen
Thelma Jexlev
Jørgen Højgaard Jørgensen
Stefán Karlsson
Jonna Kjær
Hans Anton Koefoed
Kirsten Koefoed
Else Marie Kofod
Hans Krog
Lis Helmer Larsen
Lorents Larsen
Poul Steen Larsen
Karin Lidell
Louise Lillie
John Lind
Flemming Lundgreen-Nielsen
Julia McGrew
Jørn Moestrup
Ervin Nielsen
Hans Frede Nielsen
Torben Nielsen
Morten Nøjgaard
Søren Noe-Nygaard
Tore Nyberg
Esther Nyholm
Oloph Odenius
Torkil Olsen
Thorkil Damsgaard Olsen
Ivar Orgland
Gitte Overgaard
Birte Ovesen

Niels Oxenvad
Hermann Pálsson
Carl Th. Pedersen
Frederik Pedersen
Rita Pedersen
Viggo Hjørnager Pedersen
Erik Petersen
Armando Petrucci
Roger Pinon
Iørn Piø
Mette Pors
Grete Schmidt Poulsen
Hans Otto Poulsen
Alex A.A. Quaade
Julie Randlev
Tove Rasmussen, Kbh. F
Tove Rasmussen, Kbh. S
Gunnar Ries
Anne Riising
Bent Ringsted
Jørgen Ringsted
Margit Lave Rønsholdt
Bent Rohde
Jens Peter Schjødt
Jørn Schøsler
Reinhold Schröder
Ulrik Schrøder
Joseph W. Scott
Birgitte Seider
T. A. Shippey
Bengt Algot Sørensen
Preben Meulengracht Sørensen
Stofnun Árna Magnússonar á Íslandi
Arnfinnur Thomassen
Birte Tobiasen
Aage Trommer
Else Varnild
Elisabeth Vestergaard

Torben Anders Vestergaard
Hans-Uwe Vollertsen
Mette Wad
Gerd Wolfgang Weber
Erik Koed Westergaard
Ole Widding
Vibeke Winge
Mogens K. With
Lars Wollin
W. C.M. Wüstefeld